The Unlikely Tr
The Complete
By Deborah L

Part One

The bizarre journey of a podgy middle aged diabetic

To Robert and Martha,

Whilst training is important, family is everything.

May you always have the courage to follow your dreams

Prologue 1

At 41, borderline obese, diabetic (with previous heart problems) I didn't exactly have "triathlons" as a potential hobby. To be honest, it wasn't something that I ever thought I'd see myself doing either.

In fact, it wasn't even something that had ever crossed my mind or been on my radar. If you'd approached me a decade ago and told me that I would have competed (I use that term loosely) in triathlons, I'd have said you were barking mad. However, in starting this book, I began to reflect upon what has brought me to this point. I hope to take you through the highs and lows of what has made me the person I have become today. A typical 40-something lady - only one that has had a midlife crisis which has gone a bit far.

I'm not going to lie to you, this book is short, very short, a novelette. However, it is also very cheap. I reckon in the last week or so you've probably spent many times more than this on a takeaway coffee or sandwich. This book will last longer than that...just.

Being short and cheap has a few advantages. Firstly, you've only got to set aside an hour or so to read it. And being cheap, if you get to the last page and you think the ending is rubbish you haven't wasted too much of your time or money on reading it. I would like to think I could guarantee you won't feel cheated out of the cash you'd splurged on buying it.

You may be reading this on a "Look Inside" feature, I often do that too. Has the title, cover and opening few lines grabbed me enough to take the plunge and buy it?

A few of you may be thinking "but I'm not into sport" that's OK, neither was I not so long back.
You may think "I'm not diabetic" and that is fine too, my diabetes is a sub story, if you like. However, if you want to relate to a 40 something woman that had a crazy idea and was hell-bent on achieving it, then read ahead.

Whilst this may be a kind of bizarre autobiography of one facet of my life, I want it to be more than that. I promise, dear reader, that I will be honest, which in parts may be amusing, in parts may be upsetting.

I also have to apologise (well I don't, but I'm going to) about the number of Lauras in my book. Sadly, when you are writing a true story, with real people, you are stuck with their real names. I like the name Laura mind, if it was fiction, I may have called a character Laura anyhow. However, this is not fiction, this book is 100% fact, warts and all, everything you are about to read is what happened in my journey in becoming The Unlikely Triathlete.

But enough of this small talk, I want to transport you to early morning, Sunday 5th July 2015.

Chapter 1

The alarm on my Fitbit began vibrating at 4.30am, I didn't need it to, I was already awake. I felt in equal parts excited and terrified. The day was here, the day I would be competing in my first triathlon. I'd already been on Facebook for around half hour reading the comments from my friends wishing me luck for today. I'd also been reading the kind remarks from the followers that I had picked up on my "The Unlikely Triathlete" Facebook page. My stomach was in knots, I had a whole botanic garden of butterflies fluttering around in my stomach. I knew I needed to get my arse out of bed and into the shower.

I turned on the en-suite light, the noise of the extractor fan sounded louder than usual, in that bizarre way that the volume always seems to be noisier in your house when it is an hour for quietness. I turned on the shower and sat on the toilet to have my first morning wee whilst waiting for the water to heat up. I hear an indignant meow as Sabrina, my gorgeous black cat, walked into the bathroom and began rubbing herself against my leg. She loves a fuss at shower time, but at this ungodly hour she is a little less enthusiastic than usual. This probably isn't helped by the fact that my morning wee has "developed" somewhat as my nerves make their way through my digestive system. I think it's probably for the best, as at least I've gone to the toilet before I've raced.

I finish what I'm doing, put down the toilet lid and make a mental note to flush when I get out of the shower. I step under the lovely flowing hot water, taking care not to get my hair wet, I was not planning to wash my hair this morning, not enough time, and I knew I'd be needing another shower later. However, at that point a large spindly spider decided to land on my bare breasts. I let out a little scream, mostly through shock as I quite like spiders. In my effort to safely remove him from the shower, and away from Sabrina, my hair gets soaked. I try and decide if this is some karmic message, but can't fathom what a falling spider and wet hair would be, so I shrug it off and continue my washing, being very careful not to remove the marker pen numbers which had been written on my arm and leg the day before (with hindsight, I needn't have worried, it took days to scrub that pen off).

My shower finished and toilet flushed, I make my way downstairs to have some breakfast. Being diabetic, I knew I needed to have a good breakfast despite my nerves making me feel more nauseous than hungry. I put two slices of homemade granary bread under the grill and pop a mug half full with milk into the microwave. I continue making my latté, making strong espresso in my coffee machine, all whilst scoffing an overripe banana. The toast burns slightly, but as time is of the essence, I eat it anyway having first covered it in cashew nut butter. This, dear reader, has now become my race breakfast of choice. Banana, strong latte and cashew nut butter on granary toast.

I sit in silence on the sofa in the living room, eating my breakfast and start mentally going through what I needed to do before I leave. Must remember to feed the cats. Sabrina hadn't followed me downstairs, I guessed she was curled up with Harry cat who was on the bed when I got up. Sophie, the youngest of our three cats was sat next to me on the sofa, purring. I hear movement upstairs, Phil my long-suffering husband has got up. I had planned on letting him have another half an hour's sleep as let's face it, what husband wants to get up at that kind of time on a Sunday? I'm guessing my commotion had woken him, he just hadn't been ready to let on that he was awake.

The rest of the morning before I arrive at the venue is a bit of a blur. I vaguely remember checking that I had put everything into the van. I'd written a checklist to ensure that I hadn't forgotten anything. I can't even remember if it was Phil or I who drove the half an hour to Pencoed Leisure Centre, the location where I would do something new.

What I do clearly remember is being stood outside the van in the rugby club car park next door to the leisure centre. I had my nice new road bike, my bag ready for the transition area, and my stuff to shower afterwards. I turned and looked at Phil, he snapped a picture of me and said "May the Gods of the Gnome Candles be with you". I laughed and said "thanks".

You are probably thinking what a strange thing to say. However, a few days before when I was having one of my pre-race nervous meltdown rants that the poor fella had been forced to endure, I said "I just pray for no mechanicals" meaning I hoped nothing went wrong with the bike on the bike stage. Phil, only half listening, had thought I'd said "I just pray for Gnome Candles". And so the phrase was born!

I walk into the distance, struggling to direct my bike.

Image 1 - The actual photo mentioned above

Chapter 2

"Are you awake, Debs?" Phil whispers in my ear. I am, but I'm not sure I am ready to get up. Too much good food and wine the night before makes me reluctant to move from my slumber. It is the 28th July 2012 and we are awaking in the Celtic Manor resort in Newport.

I reluctantly agree to get up, a decision which if I hadn't made, may have sent my life in a quite different direction. It was the day after the London 2012 Olympic Games Opening Ceremony. An event, which whilst we watched a bit of in our hotel room after our slap up meal, had largely passed us by.

However, we get up, get ready and go for breakfast. We notice a number of people wearing GB kits which we thought was pretty cool, although we felt slightly sorry for them knowing that they must have missed the ceremony in London the night before.

We finished our breakfast and headed back to the lift. We were following an attractive young woman wearing a GB kit. We see a little girl start to get very excited as the athlete approached. The little girl stops her, delight evident as she hands over her autograph book and a pen. The athlete smiles at the little girl's grandfather who was just as enthused as his younger family member, whilst wishing her good luck. We get into the lift, and are joined by the athlete, I decide to strike up a conversation with her to find out what event she was doing. She is as friendly and as chatty to us as she was to the little girl and grandfather. She speaks with pride as she tells us she is doing the "Team Pursuit". We smiled and nodded politely, neither of us having a clue what that was or who she was. We reach our floor and leave the lift, we wish her luck. With the doors closed, Phil says "Do you know what the Team Pursuit is Debs?" I shrug my shoulders, clueless. We were going to learn, and fast.

"Inspire a generation" - that was the slogan of the London 2012 Olympics. The meaning, to inspire a future generation of athletes. However, this slogan ended up having a rather remarkable effect at inspiring Phil and I, hardly the target audience!

We researched team pursuit and discovered it was a track cycling event, we also discovered that the girl we met was Joanna Rowsell, a medal hopeful and a rising star. We decided we would watch the track cycling, and watch we did. We were in awe of the amazing skill and talent and we suddenly became huge track cycling fans overnight. We followed Team GB Cycling with enthusiasm, passion and commitment. We were hooked.

Shortly after the Olympics, Phil made a suggestion that we hire some bikes and give cycling a go for ourselves. I had not been on a bike for 24 years, Phil for over a decade, but having a childlike nature and a sense of adventure, it seemed like a really good idea. We hired the bikes on a sunny day and had a blast. It's true the saying "It's like riding a bike" even after my near quarter of a century break I could still remember. What I had forgotten was what incredible fun it was.

We immediately decided that we were going to buy bikes of our own, and we did. Cycling became a new love of ours.

I'd had a rough few years leading to this point, and whilst I don't want to bore you with all the ins and outs like an old lady who sits next to you in the doctor's waiting room, it is an important reason why meeting Joanna Rowsell was a catalyst in me starting exercise to improve my health, so you need to know.

A few years before, I had swine flu. It was during the time of the big pandemic where you couldn't read a newspaper or turn on the news without hearing about it. Most people ended up with illness for a few days, others were not so lucky. I was one of the unlucky ones. The swine flu virus decided to make my heart race, which ended me in hospital with an enlarged heart. It was a truly terrifying time for Phil and I, with our fears amplified due to the fact that both my parents had died in their 40's with heart problems. I was petrified I was going to die too. It was also at this time that I developed diabetes, although it would be a few years before I would finally get my diagnosis. I had a few challenging years health-wise, where the slightest cold would set my heart racing and I felt constantly unwell. Which I now know was due to the undiagnosed diabetes.

Looking back, meeting Jo was a pivotal time in my life, had I not have met her, I'm honestly not sure if I would have started cycling, which ultimately became the starting point of me taking my health into my own hands the way I have.

Image 2 - Meeting Joanna Rowsell-Shand (now married) again at the Revolution Series track championship in August. Thanks Jo for letting me use the picture, you are my hero

Chapter 3

It hadn't been a particularly unusual commute to work on the bike. Cycling to work had become rather a guilty pleasure. It gave me an air of satisfaction knowing that I wasn't sat in traffic jams and was burning fat off my body rather than valuable fossil fuels. It was something Phil and I did whenever we had the chance (being lucky enough to work a matter of metres from each other with our different offices).

If I'm honest, we have taken a fair weather approach.... If it's raining in the morning we car share, if it's not we cycle...simple! We have become slaves to the Met Office forecasts, analysing "precipitation probabilities" like a gambler studying form on the horse racing, is it worth the bet or isn't it?

I don't mind if it's hammering down when I leave the office, but there is nothing worse than cycling to work in the rain without the prospect of a warming bath at the other end. This particular day, the weather was kind, albeit cold, and I was sat at my desk eating my low sugar granola and berries and drinking a flask of latté whilst catching up on my emails. I stumbled upon a staff forum page with an advert asking if staff were interested in a beginner triathlon. I don't know what possessed me to open the post, it wasn't really "my thing" but curiosity made me read.

The post was from a lady, in another office who I had never met, and she was signing up for this beginner triathlon and was trying to get others to join in. I read with interest. A 400m swim, in a swimming pool. A 17km cycle. All finished with a 3km run. I found myself thinking "I reckon I could do that".

I met Phil for lunch that day, as we walked around Swansea City centre doing our errands and picking up shopping I mooted the idea to him.

"What would you think if I did a triathlon?"

He looked at me quizzically, a bemused look I have often seen during our marriage when I have caught him off-guard with an off-the-wall suggestion.

"A triathlon?" He replied.

"Yes."

"But you can't run."

He had an excellent point, whilst I could swim (with a frankly appalling level of skill) and I enjoyed cycling, I couldn't run across a road without hyperventilating.

"I could learn." I replied.

He shook his head, I knew he thought this was a moment of madness, and I wouldn't be surprised if he believed I'd forget the idea, that I'd see sense.

However, this thought kept developing like a really annoying itch. The more I mentally scratched it, the more it took hold. As the days passed I was gradually talking myself into it, thinking "doing a triathlon would be really cool". By that by that stage, February 2015, my cycling had become a comfortable habit, more a mode of sustainable transport than any real heavy duty exercise. My diabetes, whilst well controlled, was a concern, I was having 6 monthly heart protection hospital appointments and had come to a conclusion that I had reached a stale-mate. I was fat, borderline obese even, and despite my regular cycling and healthy eating my weight had plateaued at a pathetic level that made me a "statistic".

Even though swine flu and genetics were the main drivers behind my diabetes (my Mum and Grandfather both being diabetic before they died), a frustrating little devil perched on my shoulder kept gnawing away at me saying I was diabetic because I was fat. I didn't like this devil! I'd worked hard, kept my blood sugars at a decent level, was well medicated and exercised more than the government recommended 150 minutes a week. Yet my weight was static and I felt like a pig.

"Do the triathlon" I kept telling myself. My logic was, maybe a new focus would give me a renewed energy, a new level of fitness, a new challenge to motivate myself and maybe shift some much needed pounds. I thought, and I pondered, and I thought some more.

A few days later, I sat watching YouTube. Dame Sarah Storey was attempting the hour record. I'd watched her achievements at London and found her to be an amazing woman. What she had achieved as an athlete despite her disability was something that I would challenge anyone not to be inspired by. I watched her intently, I could see the pain in her face as she just kept pedalling and I was motivated. If she can do this, I can do a triathlon. Dame Sarah may not have broken the world record that day, but she did make me think that as long as you have given it your all, you can do no more.

I could do something amazing. I could give it my all, I signed up to that first triathlon, the one mentioned in the work post there and then.
Decision made, no turning back.

Chapter 4

You've taken the plunge, you've gone online, you have entered the event. This is amazing, it's that important first step. Then the fear cuts in. I'm doing this, I am actually going to do this. Holy shit, I need to learn to run, get back in a swimming pool and train for this bad boy.

I am ashamed to say (looking back) that I went into a 'rabbit in the headlights' mode and didn't really do that much for the first couple of weeks. However, this was in part due to a recurrence of an elbow injury. Ah, the elbow injury. Gaining that injury was the day I graduated from casual bike commuter to hardcore cyclist. Dear reader, this is a story I need to tell you.

It was a Wednesday, it was late October, the clocks had just gone back and the evenings were getting darker quicker. The kind of night where it was a total toss-up as to whether you'd get home before it started getting too dusk-like. That time of year when you arrive at the cycle rack and think "Do I or don't I?"

when deciding whether to put the lights on when cycling home. This particular day, for a reason that escapes me, I'd left work earlier than Phil. We'd pre-agreed this and decided that we would meet back at the van.

At this point, I should point out why we were cycling to the van and not to home. We live at the top of a 2 mile hill, a HUGE hill, the kind of hill that you see even the most hardened cyclists on their fancy carbon fibre road bikes struggling up. I was not, in any way, shape or form, prepared to tackle this hill after an 8 hour shift in the office. So instead, we cut our 10.5 mile each way commute into a 7 mile each way commute by parking at the start of the cycle route.

So, anyhow, this October Wednesday. I leave the office, I get to the cycle rack, I decided "Yes" to the light question and I make my way, happily plodding along on my cheap and cheerful Giant hybrid. I think the decision to meet at the van was a good one, Phil was a much faster cyclist than me and plodding along at my sedentary pace was really starting to piss him off. By meeting at the van, he'd be able to don his virtual go faster stripes and not be held back by the wife.

The first half a mile is a cycle/bus path on the road, it's fine. Sometimes busses and taxis get a little arsy with you as they think it's their stretch of road, but the little picture of a cycle on the signs gives me enough security that I think to myself that if they don't like it, well they can just sod off. Then the cycle path starts, a glorious shared route with pedestrians taking you out of the city centre. It pauses for a brief while, where you are sharing the road (although this has now been resolved with a new shiny path, yay) before rejoining the path back to the van, with just a few roads to cross en-route.

It was on this little road section which was sandwiched between path and path that "the incident" happened. The road is quiet, the back of an industrial estate and a quiet residential street. I was happily cycling on the industrial estate section, approaching a corner. I could sense a car coming up behind me. No biggy, I was confident on the roads. Then a lorry came around the corner on the opposite side of the road.

What happened next, dear reader, will probably shock you as much as it shocked me at the time.

The car, which at that point was starting to pull along side me, decided to veer left when it saw the oncoming lorry on the opposite side of the road. Everything started to go slow motion, the car had decided to veer left, veer left INTO ME! The car, a school of motoring car, made contact, my elbow was whacked by the wing mirror.

Now I'm no expert on driving tuition, so stop me if my assumption on this is a little "off" but that wing mirror moved and the collision with my unsuspecting right elbow made quite the noise. You'd have expected that the instructor would have stopped, checked what had happened, realised that the cyclist was now very stationary in the gutter, they'd surely stop to check they were ok, right? What did they do? Here is what they did, they drove on, like nothing had happened.

I'm there, in the gutter, thinking to myself "What the fuck has just happened?" I get up, shocked, but with a weird air of calm. I think my head was psychologically protecting me to not totally grasp what happened and ultimately not go into meltdown that I'd been hit by a motorist, a learner driver.

I would like to have been a fly on the wall in that school of motoring car. What on earth is this instructor teaching the next generation of drivers "Ah don't worry, it was only a cyclist, it wasn't as if you hit a dog or anything."

In my shock, I neither got the number plate, make of car or even the school of motoring the car it belonged to. When questioned later I could only respond with the very unhelpful "I don't know, it was a cream colour."

So, back to the gutter, I get back on my bike and think to myself "I've got to get back to the van" and so I cycle. With every peddle stroke I feel pain, and after about a mile I start to sob. Not because of the pain, but because my brain has finally processed that I'd been hit by a car. I reach the van, I open the back of the van, but instead of loading my bike in, I leave it strewn across the road and sit on the back of the van crying my eyes out. When Phil arrived, only minutes later, but what felt like an eternity, I composed myself and told him about my most eventful commute to date.

So, that's the elbow injury, and due to me being an idiot and whacking it again with some stage lights (don't ask) at the time I signed up for triathlon, my training was already behind schedule.

Chapter 5

My Dad, God rest his soul, was a gadget freak. Whenever the latest thing came out, he had to have it. My Dad was the first person I knew to have "the Internet" (which became very frustrating when I used to try and phone home and the line was always engaged, ah the good old days of dial-up) and the first person to get a DVD player with Dolby Surround Sound. I think I have inherited some of these genetics.

I'd been on the look out for "wearable technology" for a while, the new craze that had started where people had fitness gadgets intrigued me. However, being my Dad's daughter, I didn't want a basic step counter. I wanted it all. I had set the criteria I wanted... Heart rate monitor (without a pesky chest strap), GPS and sleep recording. Having signed up for the Tri (get me using abbreviations like a pro), my search began again in earnest and I discovered that technology had caught up with my needs. The new "Fitbit Surge" was the answer to my prayers. I read reviews, I watched online tutorials and decided I wanted this, no scrap that, I NEEDED this for my training. So, an online reserve at Argos, and a Surge would be mine.

Ok, I guess that maybe going to a swimming pool, or putting on some trainers may have been a more appropriate committal to competing, however, I'm quite sure that Dad was watching me and saying "Get the gadget", and so I did.

Now anyone that is reading this who has a Fitbit will appreciate this one. The things are bloody addictive. You suddenly have a new obsession with steps, with floors, with calories in, calories out and woe betide when you start accumulating Fitbit friends as suddenly the race is on to be at the top of that step leader board. I can say, hand on heart, BEST PURCHASE EVER.

Having the GPS seemed like a pretty awesome idea, as I could look at where I'd ran and see how far I'd gone. One evening, I decided it was time to put it to the test and do my first training run.

I have never been a runner. The concept is a fairly simplistic one, like walking, only faster. I'd been walking since I was a toddler, adding extra pace can't be that much of a challenge? I looked through my wardrobe, I had some scruffy tracksuit bottoms, the kind you'd never be seen dead in outside the house. You know the type, face it ladies, we all have these items in our closets, like skeletons! You happily wear them around the house to do the cleaning, but if someone knocked the door you'd be gutted! These were the only things that I felt were suitable to cover the lower part of my body for running. I grabbed an old tshirt and some trainers that were covered in dust at the back of the wardrobe, hidden, embarrassed to be there, like the porn magazine of apparel.

I changed, step one done. I opened the front door, step two right there. I set my fancy watch and told it I was running, half expecting it to go "Really Debs? Really?" and off I went down my little cul de sac hoping that I wouldn't see anyone I knew. I found that I was starting to enjoy putting one foot in front of the other in a slightly speedier manner than I was used to, this lasted probably around 200 metres at best when the realisation hit me. I was wearing my "fat" jogging bottoms, my "pre cycling" jogging bottoms, the ones that were now too big for me and were currently heading south of my hips!! AHHHHHH!!! Panic set in, my trousers were falling down, I tried holding them up at the sides, I probably looked like a circus clown. I admitted defeat, turned around and slowly walked home deflated.

"You weren't long." Phil said.

I explained what happened.

"Why didn't you wear cycling leggings, you moron, they are Lycra."

Now you suggest it dear husband, now!

Chapter 6

There comes a point when you've been Googling triathlon training plans for such a length of time that you really should stop procrastinating and actually start training. In two final flourishes of my delay tactics I did two things. The first was going to a popular sports retailer to buy some new swimming costumes and new trainers (the old ones really weren't up to the job). The second was to design a triathlon training plan to stick on my fridge.

The training plan I was actually quite proud of, it counted down the weeks with pictures for me to tick... A swim picture, a cycle picture, a run picture, a couch picture to make sure I had a rest day and in the last 8 weeks I'd put in "brick" training. This was a whole new concept for me. Basically, a brick session is where you go straight from one event to the next, so swim to cycle or cycle to run. The idea was that I would be ticking something every day.

To provide me with extra motivation, I decided I'd be more invested in my training if I was doing the event for a cause. In chapter one I mentioned my three lovely cats, these cats had all come from a local rescue centre, a centre which is entirely reliant on charitable donations. So I set up a charity donation page to raise funds for them. (I set a target of £200, I am proud to say I ended up raising £428).

During my research phase I'd come across the couch to 5k programme, and following my failed first running attempt I decided following this plan would be a great idea. I downloaded it onto my phone. I bought an arm holder for my phone (this triathlon malarkey was starting to become expensive) so I could listen to the lovely Laura "voice of couch to 5k" her dulcet tones encouraging me over whatever music I decided to play. I often thought that Laura had no idea whether I was running or not. I imagined foxing her, she'd tell me I only had another 60 seconds to run, when in reality I'd have my feet up on the sofa, a large glass of wine in hand. This mental image got me through a number of the harder runs.

The first run, whilst a greater success on the clothing front; cycling leggings, tshirt and new running shoes, it was a harsh reality check that my running fitness was non existent. I needed to run for 60 seconds, walk for 90 seconds and repeat. I thought those 60 seconds would kill me! Good gosh it was hard, but I kept with the programme. After a few weeks, I found my fitness was better but my legs hurt a fair bit. A learning curve that the muscles I needed for running were different to the ones I'd built through my cycling. But I knew I just needed to keep going.

I hadn't finished the couch to 5k programme when Darren, a friend I'd had since school, suggested that I enter my first 5k race. He assured me that people of all abilities would be entering and that it would be a good experience. I agreed, and besides, I'd decided that if I could run 5k, I would definitely manage the 3k I needed for my triathlon. The race was arranged by a local running club and was being held down the seafront on a Wednesday evening. I decided "what the hell" and I entered.

Race day arrived at an alarming speed. When I registered for the race and got my timing chip my nerves really hit me. I was going to enter a real life race. The reality of what I had let myself in for suddenly became a stark reality. I was about to run, with a whole bunch of other people. I'd only managed 4k in training, I'd be running further than I ever had before, in public. I apologised in advance to my friend, I was going to be dreadful, I was going to be last. His wife, Laura, assured me that she was picking up the back of the race, so she would be last and that my time didn't matter, finishing did and whatever my time I'd have run the same distance as everyone else.

My heart was racing as I was stood at the back of the group on the start line, when the gun went off my head was awash with thoughts about how completely insane I was. But one foot in front of the other I began to run. Laura, stayed with me, it wasn't long before I was clearly in last place. A few young lads were stood on some grass at the side of the route, they were laughing at me. For many women this would have been upsetting, for me it actually spurred me on. They weren't running a 5k, they were stood mocking people who were trying to improve themselves, at least I had entered, I didn't see them in Lycra putting in an effort.

I part ran, part walked, with Laura alongside me providing me with even more motivation than I was used to from "app Laura". She was very encouraging, as were the many people who were clapping and cheering at the side, telling me I was doing brilliantly. I wasn't doing brilliantly, comparatively I was doing appallingly, but I was doing my best.

When the finish line was in sight, Laura said, "I have to be last, off you go, sprint to the finish". I wouldn't call it sprinting, but I did keep up a moderate jog to the finish line to rapturous applause from the spectators. I was knackered but I'd achieved it. That was the first time I really believed that the triathlon was in my grasp. My time? A pathetically slow 45 minutes and 1 second, last by a considerable margin, but I had just ran 5k, the furthest I had ever run, the time was irrelevant, the achievement was everything.

Debs Triathlon Training Plan

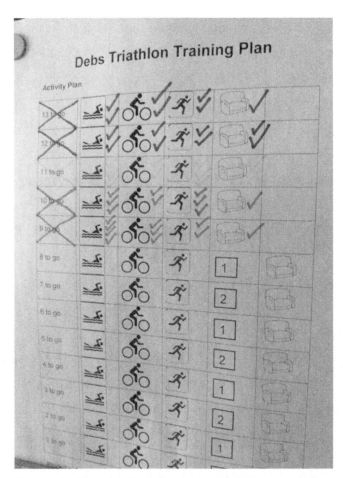

Image 3 - My training plan, part filled in, sat on my fridge

Chapter 7

People often ask me what I need to do as a diabetic athlete. Firstly, I should add I do not class myself as an athlete, a fitness fanatic, possibly, an athlete, hardly.

My type of diabetes is an unusual one, Type 1.5, an autoimmune version which had been brought on by the swine flu. It has many similarities to Type 2 in that I am not insulin dependant (well not yet anyhow) and my condition can be managed by oral medication, diet and exercise. However, I am firmly of the belief that with all types of diabetes you need to get under the bonnet about what affects you.

I'm getting on my soapbox now, but having seen my mother lose her life in her mid 40's due to heart problems relating to her diabetes, I find it hard to grasp why the NHS isn't doing everything it can to support newly diagnosed people. When I had my diagnosis I asked for a test meter and blood testing strips. These are not given out routinely to non insulin dependant diabetics. I have had a battle on my hands, since diagnosis, to get a pack of 50 test strips added to my bi-monthly prescription. 50 strips, every 2 months, only 50, less than 1 a day! Any additional ones I have to purchase myself.

Call me stupid, but surely the only way a diabetic is going to know how their blood sugars are doing is by testing them? Diabetic complications, as we hear every bloody day in the press and frankly I'm sick of it, are bankrupting the NHS. Why? Because uncontrolled high blood sugars result in very expensive complications.... Heart problems, kidney problems, blindness, amputations. Surely providing people with cheap test strips will allow people to be informed, realise what spikes their blood sugars, realise when the disease is progressing so they can get help sooner. Apparently not, but then what do I know, I'm just a diabetic that wants to stay alive, limbs intact.

So, getting off my soapbox and onto a typical day feeding myself for my exercise and life. What I eat tends to vary depending on whether it's a weekday or the weekend and in true women's magazine style like they do with all the celebrities, I'll outline a "typical day". Sadly, you won't get any pictures of me tucking into an apple, staged against a pure white background, I'm not a cliché!

Weekday breakfast

Low sugar granola, berries, bit of single cream to wet it. Two large skinny lattés.

Lunch

Tends to be a salad with a homemade salad dressing. My ultimate favourite being a goat's cheese, caramelised walnut and beetroot salad.

Dinner

Some meat or fish (bought at the farmers market or fishmongers) with plenty of vegetables from our allotment. On occasion we will have pasta or brown basmati rice but not every day. I will cook with butter and cream with wild abandon and damn it I love a nice glass of wine to wash it all down. I am passionate about the provenance of my food and cook everything from scratch. When we are relying on food to fuel our bodies, surely the best, unprocessed nutrition with the least amount of chemicals is going to be the best.

Snacks

I may have some nuts, a banana, or sometimes even a biscuit if I'm hungry, this usually happens in work when I've cycled. My body lets me know when it needs more fuel. I will drink at least two litres of sparkling water a day.

Weekends don't tend to be massively different, although breakfast may be a bacon sandwich, egg on toast or sometimes even a cooked breakfast. Lunch tends to be a more haphazard affair depending on what I have to do, so salads rarely make an appearance at the weekend. Often it's some multi grain crackers and some nice blue cheese.

What some celebrity nutritionist person would tell you is how I could cut calories and what is good or bad about what I have eaten. Honestly, I couldn't give two hoots what anyone thinks. My experience of "eating to my meter readings" has taught me that a low carbohydrate, high fat approach makes me lose weight, keeps my blood sugars constant and keeps me feeling full.

These days, I've only got to look at white bread or white rice and my blood sugars rocket. I'm not saying my approach would work for everyone, but it has worked for me.

About 8 weeks before my triathlon, something quite amazing happened. For a few days, I found myself getting dizzy, a classic sign of low blood sugars or "hypos" as us diabetics like to call them. This one particular day, I was cycling alone. Phil was away with work and so I was left to commute with just my thoughts as company. By that stage, most of my waking thoughts were triathlon related and on this particular commute I was having debates with myself on whether I should buy a road bike to race instead of using my trusty hybrid.

I was around two miles from the van, when suddenly everything went a bit blurry and I thought I was going to faint. I stopped, took a long drink, and steadied myself. I actually felt a little bit scared, I was losing my balance on the bike and worse still I didn't have anything sweet with me to bring my blood sugars back up. I knew I had to keep going, but that cycle was the first time I was ever really grateful that Phil had made me buy a medical alert bracelet.

Thankfully I got back to the van in one piece, and instantly grabbed the emergency pear drops that we keep in the van as quick fix hypo remedies. I sat in the van for a while until I no longer felt shaky and drove home.

The following day I managed to get a last minute appointment with my GP. I explained my training, I explained that I'd been getting low blood sugars and then he said "I think we need to halve your medication". I was a little taken aback if I'm honest. My experiences with my Mum and grandfather and everything I had been told from diagnosis was that diabetes was a progressive disease and that medication would gradually need increasing with time, but here was my GP telling me my medication could reduce! My diet and exercise were having such a positive effect on my diabetes and my health that my medication was getting HALVED! The unheard of. I'd done it, I'd achieved the holy grail of diabetes management.

Chapter 8

Sometimes life can be a funny old thing. I am a member of a forum for bass guitarists. Here we talk about strings, amplification, what type of bass will get the best tone and we also talk about life and random rubbish in an Off Topic arena. Wanting to soak up any tips like a sponge, I started a "Let's Talk about Triathlons" topic to see if anyone else had ever done one and if anyone had any pointers.

You can imagine my surprise when one member, who literally lives 20 miles away from me, sent me a private message to tell me he used to compete for GB!! Kert has become my mentor in many ways, he answers my stupid questions with patience, he gives me pointers and advice and he is always honest, reigning me in when I get too exuberant.

About two months before the triathlon, I'd said that I'd found a local Tri group on Facebook and had been chatting to a few people. He told me to get down there and join in.

It took a couple of weeks to build up the courage, but one Wednesday evening I headed down to the running track to meet up with people and give it a go. Kert had said to me that triathletes are a welcoming bunch, and support people of all abilities as they want to grow the sport. He wasn't wrong, I was welcomed with open arms by Celtic Tri. The running track session affectionately known by the members as "House of Pain" is designed to improve speed, not exactly my forte! However, I joined in and did my best.

I got talking to a few of the members and a few of the coaches. One coach told me I couldn't have picked a better night as he pointed out the members who had raced for the country, who'd done Ironman, who were regular medal winners at age group racing and there was me, the fat 41 year old woman doing 400 metre laps slower than the rest who were doing 800 metres! Did they laugh at me? Did they blank me? No! In fact, the very opposite, they patted me on the back and told me good effort, they praised me for having a go, they motivated me. I decided there and then I was joining up.

Mike, one of the coaches, also told me that they did swimming sessions and that there was a fabulous session on a Sunday afternoon and that I should come along.

I haven't spoken about my swimming much yet. I am the kind of swimmer that can just keep going, I can swim for hours. This sounds great, doesn't it? Until you hear the sting in the tail. I was very very slow and I had a blinding fear of sticking my head under water. You are probably thinking "And yet this lunatic has signed up for a triathlon?", yes, yes indeed I had.

The first swimming session I attended, the coach, Phillipa, lulled me into a false sense of security, she let me do my thing. The following week I was not going to be as lucky.

I got into the pool, and was about to do a few warm up lengths in my marvelous "Debs stroke" (which ultimately is doggy paddle but as that sounds ridiculously embarrassing, I have renamed it!). I'd got to the end of my second length, when one of the coaches, Rob, leaned down at the side of the pool.

"Why aren't you sticking your head under water, Debs?" he asked, casually.

"Because I can't." I replied.

"Yes, you can."

"No, I can't, I'm too afraid."

"What are you afraid of?" he continued pressing the issue, relaxed but firm.

"I'm afraid of water going up my nose and swallowing water." I replied.

"No, you are not," he continued "You are afraid of drowning, right?"

I nodded, head down, thinking what a right tit I must look.

"I'm here, there is a lifeguard just there, do you really think either one of us is going to let you drown before 4 o'clock?"

I shook my head, and so it started.

Rob was finally going to get me to overcome my fear, get my head under water, and turn me into a proper swimmer. That Sunday afternoon he spent the whole session with me, letting the other swimmers get on with their drills. He had the patience of a saint but also the authority of a drill sergeant. By the end of the session I would be able to put my head under water with ease and he achieved his goal. He messaged me after I'd got home, he told me I had "Lady Balls", something he's said to me a few times since. I've taken it as a compliment.

Rob has worked hard with me, as have the other coaches. There have been times I have loved them, times when I could have cheerfully strangled them, but they have made me push my boundaries and made me find courage in me that I never knew I had.

For that, I will be eternally grateful, and my swimming, whilst still has a long way to go, is getting there. I actually enjoy having my head under water now, but let's not get too ahead of ourselves in my tale.

Chapter 9

And we are back to Sunday 5th July 2015, I've said my goodbyes to Phil, who is heading out to a vantage point on the cycle route so he can get some photos of me, and I have awkwardly steered my bike and my belongings to the transition area. My heart is beating twenty to the dozen and I must look like a Roman Christian who had stepped into the lion's den at the prospect that the day of the triathlon had come.

One of the marshals starts looking at me, I look lost, like a child that has lost their parent in a department store and just doesn't know what to do. My virgin triathlon status is screaming from my demeanor and he steps up to assist. He helps me put my bike on the rack and set up my transition area. He's kind, he's encouraging and he tells me to smile, it's going to be OK.

My bike and clothes left, I decide it's time that I go to the swimming pool changing rooms and get into my bather. I'm about to walk into the reception area when I hear a shout.

"Debs!"

I turn and look, only to be met with Laura, a new friend I had made at Celtic Tri. I look at her in shock, its 6.15am and there is one of my new friends from my triathlon club, she had come to support me.

I wanted to cry, I couldn't believe that someone would have been that crazy to get up and watch someone who was virtually a stranger.

"I just wanted to be here to support you for your first triathlon." she said as we hugged.

A minute or two later, I saw Christine and Sarah walk towards me, two more of my triathlon club friends. I felt loved, I felt humbled, I felt special. Three friends I'd known for only weeks had got up at an ungodly time, had given up their Sunday morning to watch me, to be there to give me moral support. I think that was when I first really realised that when I joined Celtic Tri I hadn't joined a club, I had joined a family.

Image 4 - Left to right: Christine, Laura, Me and Sarah

Chapter 10

Long gone are the days when Sunday is a day of rest, a day for lie ins and pyjama days. More often than not, my alarm goes off at 7am and I head to some training session I have planned.

Picture the scene, the local swimming pool opens at 8am. I know I have to do a "brick" training session. I'd been putting it off for too long but knew I needed to have the experience. I had driven to the swimming pool in the van, my new shiny road bike in the back (I did talk myself into it, and am glad I did as it is awesome!) and I was about to embark on the unknown.

I walked into the changing room, wearing my bather, cycling leggings, a t-shirt and my trainers, carrying a towel and my car keys.

I put the keys and my outer clothes in a locker and take my towel poolside.

I swim, Debs stroke, for 400 metres, 16 lengths, the same distance as I would need to do on my Tri. I get out of the pool, grab my towel and head back to the changing room. I wipe down my arms and legs and start pulling my cycling leggings over my wet bather. A woman looks at me quizzically, I continue to get dressed, she continues to watch me with the confusion obvious in her face.

"Love," she says, her Welshness and nosiness radiating through like a beacon, "You've forgotten to take your bather off."

I laugh, "I'm practicing for a triathlon." I reply.

"Are you nuts or what?"

You've got to love the honesty of strangers!

Time waits for no man, and in a real life, tri time would be ticking in Transition, so I run out of the swimming pool, throw my towel into the back of the van and get my bike out.

The first mile of that cycle was rather disconcerting. That feeling of being dripping wet whilst on a bike is an unusual one. I wouldn't say its unpleasant as such, but it certainly feels a bit weird. However, once I'd been on the bike for a while I'd forgotten I was wet and got on with the cycle.

Cycling is increasingly turning into an extreme sport and my first brick session was no different. The route I had chosen had one narrow section where it is impossible for drivers to overtake safely. Not wanting to take any chances, you do become a lot more cautious when you've been hit, I took primary position. This means cycling in the centre of the lane. I was aware of the car behind me, but I was cycling at a fairly respectable pace, my cycling speeds much improved on the dedicated road bike. However, when I reached the wider road section and I pulled back over to the left, the blue Ford Mondeo driver decided to yell from his window "Get off the fucking road!" Delightful.

I wish for a day when everyone can just share the road in peace. I'd probably added 10 maybe 15 seconds onto this driver's journey, so he hurls abuse.

If I had a pound for every driver that I have heard say "We pay road tax, cyclists don't." then I'd probably have enough money to upgrade to a carbon fibre frame! And to all of you that may share this view, right now, I would like to say this. "It's not road tax anymore, the tax you pay is based on emissions, my bike doesn't damage the environment, doesn't damage roads, oh and I do pay tax for my vehicle as I am also a driver." so put that in your pipe and smoke it!

Chapter 11

I like to make jokes when I'm nervous. Call it a defence mechanism rather than a wish to be a stand-up comic. With my Celtic Tri friends having left me for the observation area I was again alone. I knew I needed to get changed into my bather and get ready to start my race.

We'd been told to gather 15 minutes before our swim start for our briefing. My swim start, the first "wave" was at 6.45, so dressed in my bather at 6.30 I joined the other competitors for the briefing. One lady was in a skimpy bikini, I found this an odd choice, but who am I to judge. I was wearing a boy leg bather, others were in traditional bathers or trisuits. What we did have in common was our timing chips wrapped around our left ankles.

"Anyone else feel like a tagged criminal?" I jest, looking down at my tag.

Some smiled, one let out a little laugh, a few looked at me like I'd pissed in their cornflakes. Tough crowd.

The briefing was just that, brief. "Don't run poolside, run when you get outside. You'll be told when there are two laps to go. Have fun."

We get into our lanes, two people per lane. I smile at the girl in the lane with me, she scowled, and instantly took her place on the outside of the lane, meaning I'd be swimming against the wall. It didn't bother me where I'd be swimming, I was in the pool.

Laura, who is a swim instructor and who knew some of the staff, was poolside. She was making her best endeavours to keep me calm, keep me focused. Up in the spectator area, Christine and Sarah were shouting "Go on Debs!" I was waiting anxiously for the gun to go off.

Bang! that was it, I lurch myself forward, pushing my Debs stroke for all I was worth, I was racing in a triathlon.

My lane buddy must have thought she was in the Olympics, she hurtled forward with her front crawl, splashing away to her hearts content. By the second length I'd discovered she had no idea how to keep in a straight line, and no concept of personal space as I was squashed further and further into the wall. As I swam, I could hear the cheers from my friends and I lost count of the number of lengths I had done. When the lane counter told me two laps to go, I could have sworn that I still had four more to do. But she was the one with the clipboard and I wasn't going to argue.

Swim finished, I walked to the door and then ran towards transition thinking to myself what a dreadful sight I must be. I see my friends, they are cheering, it's spurs me on. Sarah has her iPhone pointed towards me, I just know it's in camera mode. I scream at her "If that photo ends up on Facebook I'll kill you!"

One event down, two to go. My triathlon was in full flow.

Chapter 12

Facebook, it can be an odd beast, it can bring out the best and worst in people. You learn things about people that surprise you. It can make you laugh, it can make you cry, it can keep you connected to friends and family all over the world. On balance, I like it.

Whilst I was motivated to keep doing my training, I had an urge to do something else. On the "Let's Talk about Triathlons" thread I had started on the bass forum I had been posting about what training I'd been doing and how I was finding things. Reading it, I could also see the little improvements I was making week on week. Kert said to me "You'll be glad you did this, as you'll be able to look back and see how far you've come." He was right. It was then I was struck with the idea to start a Facebook page. The idea of blogging about my daily routines was appealing. I had been posting some things on my personal page, but was beginning to get fed up with people moaning at me that I was making them feel lazy. And so "The Unlikely Triathlete" was born.

I invited my friends to like it, promising that I would, in the main, be keeping my exercise away from my personal page. I also invited people from different groups to join, after the page was in full swing and I'd signed up, I invited my friends in Celtic Tri. I slowly, and rather surprisingly, started gathering followers. Most days I would count down the number of days I had left until the triathlon and what I had done. I'd share my thoughts and feelings and give shout outs to the people who had helped me.

I set up the page in late April, so still several months to go until my triathlon and only a month into my training regime. My charity page was also linked to my page so people could donate if they wanted to.

One day, shortly after I'd set up the page, I was sat in a conference at work. It was a typical conference really, some sessions inspiring, others that made you want to pull out your eyeballs with a spoon (just me? Oh ok then). It was during one of the inspiring sessions that I had a lightbulb moment. The session was about using videos to promote a message, I foolishly decided I wanted to make a video to try and raise more sponsorship for the animal rescue. I sent Phil a text message there and then from the conference chair to share my cunning plan. I did this on purpose. My husband is the most incredible, loving and wonderful person I have met, however, he is also a stroppy sod who doesn't react well to having things sprung on him. Having messaged him my initial idea it won't come as a surprise when we discuss it over tea.

The rest of the conference I didn't really concentrate on the sessions, instead I was mentally directing my "advert" it would have bold music, big titles, the cats, the purpose and me swimming, cycling and running. It was going to be epic.

I arrived home and cooked tea, it was a prawn and kale risotto, not sure why that stays in my mind but it does. I opened a bottle of white wine and Phil and I discussed the idea. He had also had a few ideas on what could be done. I giggled like a teenager as I realised that Phil was going along with this, he would be my cameraman, my director, my editor, he was my awesome, gorgeous, amazing husband.

We went to Afan Argoed the following Saturday morning, Phil armed with a camera. Afan Argoed is a gorgeous place to cycle, set in the beautiful Afan Valley it has everything a cyclist could wish for from family friendly cycle paths to hardcore mountain bike trails. Phil filmed me as I cycled past him, we found an interesting rock which I stood on top of and looked moody, I put my shoes on, my helmet on, I ran. We had some interesting looks that day I can tell you. He came home and started editing. We had a problem though, swimming footage!

I have an early morning swim pass to the local pool, the next morning I was there I enquired.

"Would my husband be able to come in and film me swimming please?" I asked, politely.

"Excuse me?" Was the reply.

"Can my husband film me swimming? Only me, it's for a promotional video I am putting together."

"Oh I don't know about that, we don't even allow photography."

"It would be in an early morning session when there are only adults." I added, appreciating the 'no photography when there are children around' driver which was probably behind the blanket no photography rule.

"I honestly don't know, I could ask the manager and get back to you. What's your number?"

They didn't get back to me, but that was OK. As luck would have it we were going to be on holiday in the Forest of Dean a week or so later. He filmed me there instead.

On our return from holiday, the editing finished, I published the video on my Unlikely Triathlete Facebook page and YouTube. Did it make a difference to what I raised? Probably not, but it was great fun to do.

Chapter 13

People call transition the fourth discipline of triathlon. It is a discipline that will take a bit of mastering, I think. I finished my run from the swimming pool to my transition area and I start wiping down my legs to pull on my cycling shorts. Christine stands as close as she can to the area, snapping me like the paparazzi, I love her for it but vow that those pictures will never be seen. Clothes on, I put my helmet on, sunglasses, cycling gloves and remove my bike from the rack.

Stage two, 17 kilometres ahead of me. I run my bike to the mount line, the point where you leave transition and officially start the cycle and I'm off.

I was familiar with the route having practiced it a few times and in all weathers. I'd vowed that I was not going to make the same mistake I had made on one of my training runs and take the wrong turn at a roundabout. Today the weather was cloudy but good. The marshals stood by the exit of the car park onto the road, they were stopping traffic for cyclists, I felt like a bit of a fraud, I mean, I wasn't a real racer!

I found I was breathing heavier than usual. The eclectic mix of nerves, swimming and getting dressed with an audience had taken its toll a bit. I pushed myself down a gear on the bike to give myself a bit of a break. There were marshals at every roundabout, pointing you in the right direction and cheering you on. I reached the first roundabout where Phil would be poised to get my photo.

"Alright love?" I shouted at him.

"Shut up and cycle." he grinned back at me, to the amusement of a marshal.

A few cyclists overtook me, but that's OK, I was happy to be out on the road giving it all I had. The course has a few inclines which drains your legs a bit, but recovery was to be had in the downhills. Undulating is the popular term for this terrain it would appear.

I reached the halfway point, a roundabout, I went around and then stopped. "Why?" I hear you ask. Well, you've probably gathered that my skill set in sport is very limited and whilst I had enjoyed cycling for a few years, I hadn't actually learned to drink and cycle. Needing a drink, I needed to stop.

"Are you OK?" another racer enquired on approaching me.

"Yes, just having a quick drink." I replied.

My pause was brief, 20 seconds at most, but as I cycled behind the lady who enquired about my well being, I watched with envy as she removed her bottle from the cage, pedalling confidently, took a swig and put it back. One day Debs, one day.

I was enjoying the cycle, even the long incline and I seemed to be flying up it faster than I had in my practice runs. Maybe it was familiarity, maybe it was adrenaline, I don't know.

I reached the next point where I knew Phil would be (he'd planned his spots and was whizzing around in the van trying to beat me to the next vantage point), he was there, camera ready.

A crowd of people were at this corner. One woman shouted at me "You were an inspiration in the pool." I shouted back "thanks" thinking she'd obviously got the wrong person.

I was wrong, as Phil later relayed the story to me, after I'd gone past she said to Phil, thinking he was an official photographer "That woman is an inspiration. She swam doggie paddle and she was still out of the pool faster than four other people." Phil tells me, he proudly replied "That's my wife!"

I continued my cycle, starting to feel quite proud of myself that I was over half way through and I was (gnome candles permitting!) going to finish.

Nobody had overtaken me for a while and I was totally in my groove, at one with my bicycle. In my head I was singing songs, Queen with Bicycle race was one that kept coming to mind.

I reached the last point where I would see Phil (the boy did good with his timings and plans, fair play) and I shouted to him to bring a few things from the van to the finish line. Gosh, I'm bossy even when I'm racing.

I get to the last roundabout, remember to take the correct turning (although it would have been difficult not to with a marshal directing on it) and I take the last turning into transition. I dismount at the dismount line and run my bike back into transition.

I hear Christine, Sarah and Laura, they are screaming my name, they are applauding, they are telling me to get my arse into gear and get running.

Two down, one to go.

Image 5 - Taken on the cycle route

Chapter 14

I was enjoying ticking my training plan. It gave me a weird sense of satisfaction. Each tick was a milestone, each day was progress, every week that passed I was putting in the hard work making sure I was as prepared as I could be.

I have to admit that keeping to a training schedule when you work full time is not easy. However, I had managed to incorporate it into my busy life. I'd favour an early morning run or swim rather than have it looming over me all day in work. I accepted the 5.30am alarm calls with good grace. I did this because I could see the difference it was making to me. From the day I signed up to the day of the triathlon I had lost nearly 2 stone in weight, 10kg, 22lbs! I felt amazing, I had more energy, I was fitter, I was happier, I was loving life. Stressful days could be eased away with a bike ride or a run.

It wasn't all plain sailing, however, life never is. One Saturday morning just over a month before my triathlon, I woke up with a weird pain down one side of my back. I woke Phil "Is there something on my back, am I bruised? It really hurts." he looked, an alarmed expression crossed his face and said "You are covered in spots, Deb."

Why do these things have to happen on a Saturday? I had Phil to photograph the spots and I sent the picture to some friends. A few confirmed what I had feared. I had shingles. Being diabetic, I was advised to get straight to the out of hours GP for anti viral medication as this would help me get better sooner. Apparently, being diabetic, I was at more risk of complications.

The out of hours GP was lovely, confirmed the diagnosis, and prescribed the anti virals and said.

"In no uncertain terms are you to train. You must have complete rest for a week and you can't get in a swimming pool until the rash has gone."

Worst week ever!

Thankfully it was just a blip, I waited the week and went for a gentle cycle, it felt good so I started to train again, albeit gently. I did have to wait another week until I went back in the swimming pool.

Training, like everything in life, has its highs and lows. I promised at the start I would be honest, and so I will share a little story that should you ever ride a bike I urge you to follow my advice. The more I trained, the faster I got and the bigger distances I wanted to do. Suddenly the shoe was on the other foot and I had now become a faster cyclist than Phil. He got the bitter taste of his own medicine as he realised what it was like to not be able to keep up. However, I say polishing my halo, I appreciated how that situation makes you feel, so I hold back for him!

Anyhow, I digress. It was soon after I got my road bike. I had been cycling in sports pants under my cycle leggings, I'd gone for a longer ride, I think around 20 miles. About three quarters of the way through I had this terrible pain in, how should I put this, my "sensitive feminine area", I wasn't far from home but this pain kept developing, it hurt like hell. I arrived home, went to run a soothing bath and looked in horror at my blood-soaked knickers! The sports pants had somehow managed to rub two great big cuts into my lady parts!! So, my lesson to you all, if you cycle, go commando and get yourself some anti chaffing cream. It's OK, you're welcome!

Chapter 15

I hurtled out of transition, small running drink bottle in my hand, half filled with apple juice, half filled with water, just a little carbohydrate to keep my sugars up whilst I raced.

The run was out of the main area, into an adjoining field which sat along side the dual carriage way, two laps of the field and then back to the finish line. I knew, as I was being supported by my triathlon buddies, that I needed to keep running until I was out of sight.

I was very grateful that I had done some cycle to run brick training. When you go from cycling to running something strange happens, the muscles in your legs suddenly get a big shock that they have moved from one activity to another and they protest. I was unaware that limbs were capable of independent thought, but triathlon has taught me otherwise. Your legs, knee down, no longer feel like your own, they feel like lead weights that just don't want to move. You are forced to send messages from your brain to "shut up legs" and keep going.

However, as soon as I was out of view, I slowed to a walk. To me there is no shame in that, after all it was my first one, I'd only started running 3 months previously and my goal for the triathlon was a simple one, I wanted to finish. I continued the first lap, half walking, half running. Other racers would pass and tell me I was doing really well.

I think this was when I started to really feel emotional, I had become so "in the zone" in my training it was only now I was actually nearly at the end of the race that the enormity of it all finally hit me. I'd endured illness, health benefits, unfortunate feminine injuries. I'd began to overcome fears, I was fitter, I was happier, I was healthier. This race was just a short time relative to the effort I had put in to get me here, but I had achieved something. I was doing something incredible.

I finished the first lap. A marshal was there to put a mark on your hand to show you'd completed a lap. I realised I still had my cycling gloves on, he put a mark on my arm instead.

The second lap felt harder than the first, I kept plodding part-walking, part-running and then a realisation hit me. I was going to be back in view of the public soon. Call it stubborness, call it pride, maybe even a smidgen of showing off but I wanted to keep up appearances and run for the spectators, for Phil, for my friends, so I walked the last third of the lap, keeping something in reserve.

I hit the main field, running again, I could see Phil at the finish line, I could see my friends and I ran. I was going to give my last section every ounce of energy left in my body. The atmosphere from the crowd, with the shouting from my friends flowed into me giving me the energy of life and love and support.

As I looked towards the finish line I was overcome with emotion, tears were rolling down my cheeks as I realised I had actually done it. I don't know what caused the tears to escape my body, part relief, part exhaustion, part pride, but escape they did. I couldn't hold it in, I threw my arms into the air as I crossed the finish line. I was a triathlete!

The fastest person that day completed the course in 49 minutes and 39 seconds. My time, a less impressive 1 hour 32 minutes 26 seconds, but it was my time, it was my best. I wasn't last, but I wasn't far off, but with every fibre of my being I felt like a winner.

Image 6 Crossing the finish line

Epilogue 1

So what was to be next for the Unlikely Triathlete. My Facebook post the very next day was the countdown to the next one. Well, you didn't really expect anything different, did you? Triathlon number two was set for Sunday 11th October. Maybe you will read about it, in the Unlikely Triathlete - Part Two - The return of the training plan.

Thanks and acknowledgements

To Phil - my love, my husband, my best friend, my official photographer

To my friends at Celtic Tri - you spur me on to be the best I can be

To Kert - who knew bassists could also be triathletes, hey?

To Rob - thanks for making me discover my "Lady Balls"

Finally, to all my friends and family. I love you all.

Part Two

Return of the Training plan

I would like to dedicate this book to anyone who bought Part One and decided to stick with me for Part Two. Thank you for making my many many hours at a keyboard worthwhile.

Prologue 2

They say that life begins at 40, maybe I'm a bit of a late starter, but my life changed dramatically at 41. This was when I decided to become a triathlete. My journey is documented in the first novelette of what is now becoming The Unlikely Triathlete series. With my first triathlon completed on Sunday 5th July 2015, I decided to keep going in my quest to give exercise my all, despite my lack of ability.

Some books are set up to be inspirational to someone starting out, yet you read and find out that some already skinny person who was already uber-fit, suddenly won some amazing race. Good on them I say. However, if you are hoping this book is the same, it's sadly not. I'll never win a gold medal, I'll never be on a podium, but do you know something? That is absolutely fine.

In the same style as the first book, this is a novelette. In other words, it's short. What this allows you though, is to set aside a short amount of time, have a cuppa or glass of wine (whatever floats your boat) and read away.

In this introduction I also feel the need to explain some triathlon distances as some are mentioned in the book:

Sprint – Swim tends to be 400-750 metres, cycle 15-25 kilometres, run tends to be anything between 3-6 kilometres.

Olympic distance – Swim 1500 metres, cycle 40 kilometres, run 10 kilometres

Half Ironman – Swim 1.2 miles, cycle 56 miles, run 13.1 miles (a half marathon)

Ironman – Swim 2.4 miles, cycle 112 miles, run 26.2 miles (in other words a marathon)

However, rest assured that I am firmly sat in the Sprint distance camp at the moment!

I hope you will enjoy my continued journey, I'm still rubbish, I haven't developed any amazing sporting ability overnight, but I'm still having a ball.

Chapter 18

Everyone should have a friend like Christine. She, in many ways, reminds me of a terrier. She is headstrong, she is fun loving and if you ask her if she wants to go for a run, she displays the excited exuberance of a pup with a lead, she is there. Also, if there is any mischief, she is usually at the centre of it.

She has a heart of gold, and a level of commitment which one could argue is obsessive, something that was evident on one particular Sunday morning.

We had agreed to meet down Aberafon seafront at 8.30am, this had become a regular occurrence, although usually Sarah would be in attendance too. Sarah was away this weekend, something I'm sure she was relieved about. It was absolutely bucketing down with rain.

There is rain, and there is rain, I half expected to look out at the sea and see an ark, Noah waving from the deck. It was torrential. Not only was this deluge of biblical proportions, it was also incredibly windy. In other words, hardly ideal conditions to run in.

However, whilst progressing towards my second scheduled triathlon, and following a far more structured training plan designed by the lovely Rob, I had a run I needed to do and Christine was daft enough to come with me.

We parked at our usual spot, I arrived first and waited in my car for her to arrive. Her car pulled next to mine shortly afterwards. She looked at me, smiled and raised an eyebrow as she looked at the weather. We both got out of our cars.

"So, how far do you need to run today Debs?" She asked.

"6k." I replied, sheepishly.

"Let's do this."

We have an agreement when we run, go at your own pace, there is no need run together, just do your thing and meet back at the coffee shop. This approach is something that I am grateful for. Both Christine and Sarah have done half marathons, they are both considerably faster than me. However, we start together and when we've all done the distance we have planned for the day we sit with a coffee and put the world to rights.

Christine and I start our run, I'd worked out my route to achieve the 6k, I was sure she was going to run further than that.

Within seconds, despite wearing a waterproof jacket, I was soaked to the skin. My feet squelched in my trainers. However, 6k I had planned and 6k I would do. I could see Christine ahead, she had reached the end of the promenade and had turned around to run in the opposite direction. As she reached me she said "The wind is even worse running in this direction." I reached the end of the promenade a few minutes later and turned around, Christine was speaking the truth.

Running into strong winds is hard work, but worse than that, it chills you to the bone. I dug deep and kept running, I was wet and I was freezing, hardly a good combination. Every puddle I ran through sent more and more water into my trainers and my feet were turning into blocks of ice. I saw Christine turn around at the other end of the promenade, I wondered how far she was planning to run today in these inclement conditions. As she passed me again she said "I'll see you in the coffee shop." I was guessing she wasn't planning too far.

When I reached the coffee shop, Christine was sat at a table looking as fresh as a daisy. She had a new dry hoodie on, why hadn't I thought of that? She already had a coffee in front of her, she motioned to the staff and within seconds a latte appeared in front of me.

I sat on the chair, and we chatted for a while. I become conscious that a pool of water was forming under my seat. Note to self, bring extra clothes next time!

"So Debs, have you signed up to do the Swansea 10k yet?" she enquired.

I nodded and smiled

"Good move." she grinned back at me.

She had been badgering me about it for a week or so, pushing me to push myself.

Yep, everyone needs a friend like Christine.

Chapter 19

I have seen a picture shared on Facebook a few times with the caption "Teach your children a love of bicycles and they will never have money for drugs". I may not be a child, but the concept also seemed to ring true for adults doing triathlons too. Not only do you need to love bikes, but there are two other sports to spend your hard-earned cash on. I have certainly seen my bank balance depleting at an alarming rate since I've taken up the sport! Not that I had planned to take up drugs you understand, however, reassuring nonetheless that I will never have money for them.

I guess being a triathlete could be fairly cheap, I mean, I could have completed my first triathlon on my original hybrid bike. I didn't NEED a road bike, I WANTED a road bike. However, I have taken the logic that I work hard, and you can't take it with you.

I am giggling as I type at the moment. Whilst writing this section, about my rather uncontrolled sporty shopping habit there was a knock at the front door. The postman, delivering some new cycling gloves I'd ordered. My name is Debs, and I am a sports shopaholic.

However, I do have an irritation about sportswear for women. Why does nearly everything have to include pink? I have never been a girly girl. I rarely wear make-up, I'd rather tie my hair back than make myself look presentable. I am happiest in jeans and a t-shirt, and whilst my wardrobe does include a few dresses, their trips from the hangers onto my body are infrequent, generally special occasions only when my usual outfits would look out of place. So, the colour pink and I are not a good fit. My sports wardrobe, however, has suddenly developed a splash of this colour, yuk!

I would say though, that as I am not a girlie girl and have the practical outlook of a Boy Scout, I can also rise above having to wear pink. Ultimately, it's just a colour, the practicality of the outfits is the most important thing. I review the ever expanding range of the colour in my cupboard... Pale pink, shocking pink, deep pink... My body wears it all, thankfully it is often paired with black, a colour which I feel much more at home in. My new gloves are black and raspberry, thanks retailer for trying to put a new spin on the word pink, doesn't change my feelings though.

Being unable to rein in my addiction, I had an excellent idea of my new "must have". Now that I was starting to take my running more seriously (well I had signed up for a 10k race). I was going to get a "gait analysis". I know many readers will understand the term, for my less sporty readers this is where some stranger will assess how you run, where your feet fall when you are doing it and make recommendations accordingly. I was starting to learn more lingo about different shoes, different styles. In honesty, there wasn't anything wrong with the trainers I had bought, granted I had bought the cheapest ones that had fitted me, but as I had in my head, graduated from the couch to 5k programme and was looking at longer distances, I felt I deserved to understand my feet better.

I had received my Celtic Tri newsletter. It was a joy to see it appear in my emails. I like these newsletters, not least because they include a whole range of places that give a club discount.
TechFeet was one of these places. I went online and booked an appointment for first thing on a Saturday morning, a Saturday I had scheduled for a rest day.

It was a fascinating visit, the able chap looked at my feet, I then had to run down a little stretch of mat which had an electronic pad, this pad would know exactly where my feet put pressure and would accurately assess my gait. The discovery was that I was a supinator, basically I favoured the outside of my feet. Most people I'd met were pronators, favouring the inside. Trust me to be different!

"Are you interested in looking at shoes today?" he asked me.

I nodded.

"Anything particular you would like to look at?" He continued.

"I'll look at anything as long as it isn't pink." I reply.

He disappears for a few minutes, returning with his women's shoes.

"There are only 3 pairs in your size which aren't really pink." he replies apologetically.

He shows me the first pair, "well these ones have a tiny bit of pink."

I try on all three, I test them out on a treadmill, I settle on the blue and orange pair.

I left the shop with a smile on my face, my credit card dented and a new pair of trainers complete with inserts to help my feet, oh and a few pairs of socks.

Chapter 20

Whilst Sunday mornings were spent running at the seaside, Sunday afternoons were spent in the swimming pool at the coached swimming sessions. A cohort of members were in regular attendance, many of us women and were affectionately nicknamed "The mermaids" by the coaches.

When you spend your Sunday afternoons with likeminded people, some strong friendships are forged. Between Sunday sessions we would support each other and keep up to date with each other's training on Facebook. However, this support was in "real time" in the pool.

Denise and Jo are two of these amazing likeminded people. These lovely ladies are both magnificent runners. Jo, also a talented cyclist, but our bond was sealed in lane one of the swimming pool, the easy lane. Admittedly, they are both better swimmers than me, despite the fact that I was starting to get more confident with my head underwater. However, we all know we have a way to go to improve and we all punch the water in anger when we are disappointed with our performances.

This particular Sunday, all three of us were obviously not feeling the love for drills. I have to admit I find drills quite an alien concept, using floats to improve your arms, fins to improve your feet. I prefer just swimming, but I trust the coaches and so I listen. However, Mike, the coach that was in charge on this particular Sunday, could see that we were all not as enthusiastic as usual. Denise was stressing about her breathing, Jo was stressing about her feet, I was just stressing generally. He sighed, admitting his defeat that he wasn't getting anywhere with us today and he took us up the deep end. It's ok readers, his motive wasn't to drown us like an evil monster about to drown kittens in a canal, he wanted to try something new with us, to do something he'd normally reserve for children. We would take a deep breath in, see how far we could sink, make us blow out all the air from our lungs and come back to the surface. A confidence exercise that our breathing was better than we thought.

Once Mike had been able to instil a bit more confidence in us all, he had us to all swim together back to the shallow end, we had to stick together, in a line. In honesty, that was the hardest thing I'd had to do in a pool for a long time. Trying to judge what your friends were doing, and staying in sync with them was a unique challenge. I can't see the three of us forming a synchronised swimming team any time soon.

Once back at the shallow end we had to, in turn, take a deep breath and see how far we could swim on one single breath. Another exercise normally reserved for the juniors, today adapted for grown women having a crisis of confidence. It was actually quite fun. I think we all surprised ourselves how far up the pool we went. Job done, Mike had brought us back, the mermaids were happy again.

Outside these coached sessions I also go to my local pool, sometimes I do drills, sometimes I just swim. Depends on what Coach Rob has scheduled into my training plan.

One Tuesday morning, I had drills allocated on my training plan, but on arrival at the pool I found the float cupboard locked. I wasn't too disappointed; I prefer just swimming anyway. I decided I would work my hardest at my front crawl. It was 6.15am, however, the pool was still filled with swimmers.

I've got to that stage now where I don't really fit into the pool politics. Half the pool is lanes, the other half left open. I'm too slow for the lanes, too fast for the open section. I tend to stay in the open section, unless I'm feeling particularly brave.

However, there is one massive downside to the open section, "the talkers", two women hell bent on treating the swimming pool like a coffee shop. Now I'm all for having a chat, but I'm not entirely sure that a swimming pool at pool "rush hour" is the best place to have a natter. Undeterred, this gruesome twosome do it every week. One swims breast stroke, one swims doggy paddle, they both swim slowly. They like to leave around 3 feet between them and have such inane conversations that I try and pull my swim hat further and further down my ears so I don't have to listen to them verbally spew out all manner of dull.

I've heard it all, woes about car insurance, woes about having to book a table for Sunday lunch a whole 15 minutes later than they wanted the table, woes about work colleagues. Kill me, kill me now.

You may think I sound cruel? Maybe I have activated my "bitch switch" when it comes to these pool irritators but thankfully everyone else moans about them too, the rest of us plodders stand united against the talkers.

Anyhow, this Tuesday morning, I had started a few lengths, I'd do about half a length proper front crawl, recover a bit with some Debs stroke and stick my head back under again. I'd reached the deep end and turned around watching "the talkers" walk down the side of the pool to the steps, they were predictably, talking. I sigh, resigning myself to the fact that I would need to start slaloming down the pool to avoid them. By the time I get to the shallow end they are already starting their assault to take up way too much space and bore us all to death. Today's topic, the apparently shockingly high cost of a Chinese takeaway.

I pause at the shallow end, joined by my dear friend. I don't know his name, he's a retired chap, he's also a diabetic, and if we are both stopped at the shallow end and having a breather at the same time, we have a brief chat. I like him, I like him a lot.

(Take note talkers, a brief chat, whilst stopped, at the shallow end. Try it sometime!)

"They are off again." he says rolling his eyes whilst looking at the talkers.

"Tell me about it." I reply, my eyes also rolling.

"Your swimming is coming on a treat, you are doing really well." he smiles at me.

"Thanks." I reply and hurl myself off the side of the pool. We never chat for long and have an understanding that when we are ready to swim, off we go.

I do a few more lengths without issue and then it happened. I was so in the zone with my breathing, bilaterally, every

third stroke, motoring up the pool like a pro that I wasn't
really paying attention.

Crash!

I'd collided head on with one of the talkers, who was
obviously so enraged about the expense of a Chicken Foo
Yung she hadn't seen me either.

I start to sink, I'm taking on water. I'm in the deep end. I
start to panic.

I make my way up to the surface, coughing and spluttering,
trying desperately to grab the side.

"Watch where you are fucking going". she yells at me.

Her friend scowls at me and I feel vindicated.

The swimming pool talkers are witches.

Chapter 21

Cycling speed is an interesting concept and so variable depending on where you are on the spectrum, beginner through to elite. I've watched in awe at the Velodrome as I've witnessed elite cyclists achieve speeds in excess of 40 miles an hour. I've watched road racing where women have cycled 80/90 miles and achieve average speeds more than 25mph. I dream of speeds like this, gosh I rarely get these speeds on downhills!

When I started cycling, my average speed was a pathetically slow 7mph. Over time, I managed to improve this to 10mph. The speed I was generally sat at when I decided to sign up to the triathlon, ok, I may have had the occasional run where I would reach the heady heights of 11, but fast I wasn't. I knew this speed wasn't good enough and so I worked hard, managing to push it to around 13mph when I had my road bike. OK, I appreciate that part of this speed was down to a lighter frame and thinner tyres, but part was also down to my slimmer figure and increased fitness.

In my first triathlon, my average speed was 13.4mph, I was proud of this. I did wonder if I had anything extra to give though. Rob was going to push this boundary. I suddenly started to see "Time trials" in my training plans.

I questioned Rob as to what he meant by this. He told me "push as fast as you can, total balls out riding. By balls out I mean lady balls which you have plenty." I loved Rob, he always knew the right thing to say to motivate me.

It was a Sunday morning and the conditions couldn't have been any more perfect for a Time Trial. Warm but not too hot. Dry and still, not the typical South Walian winds which had become a feature of my training. I'd chosen the road carefully, a new road on an industrial estate. Traffic was light, particularly on a Sunday. I hoped I'd be able to push on without having to worry about other road users. The stretch had a roundabout at either end, I'd calculated that 6 laps of this stretch would be exactly 10 miles.

Still lying in bed, I asked Phil "Do you want to come?"

He shook his head and threw his head back under the covers.

I didn't mind going alone, most of my training had been a solo affair.

I drove to the start of the road and found a suitable place to park the van. I was feeling ready for it, motivated, I would cycle my hardest.

I set out, having first set my watch to record it so I could feed my time back to Rob. I started pedalling, pushing myself up the gears. I felt like I was flying. Two laps completed, I stopped for a swig from my bidon (a bidon is just a posh word for a cycling water bottle), I really am going to have to learn to drink and cycle.

Lap three was slightly more eventful, I saw my second motorist of the day. A van driver towing a trailer. However, when he pulled back to the left after overtaking me, he seemed to have forgotten the extra load behind him, we narrowly missed a collision. I shout abuse. He didn't hear me. I keep pedalling.

Lap four I had company for a while. I was just over half way through the lap when a cyclist caught up with me. A man, probably roughly my age, who looked super fit, rather handsome, and had an enviable bike. He cycled alongside me for a little while. He complemented me on how well I was doing. I guessed he hadn't seen too many podgy middle-aged women going flat out. I let him do the talking, responding only with one-word answers, I was making a massive effort, I didn't have the ability to speak. My monosyllabic responses must have sent a signal that I wasn't in a chatty mood, and he went ahead, I took full advantage of staying in his slip stream for as long as I could. When he reached the roundabout, he turned around and blew me a kiss and off he cycled at considerable speed into the distance.

Lap five, despite the grin on my face at having been blown a kiss by a random handsome stranger, I was in pain. The lactic acid must have been building in my legs, my lungs felt they were going to explode. "Keep going Debs, keep going" I knew I'd been doing well until this point and had to continue giving my all. I sensed my speed had slowed somewhat, I grimaced and started to increase my cadence, pushing my legs harder and harder, faster and faster.

The pain had passed by lap six, my body must have known that the end was in sight. I wondered how much my muscles hated me right now. Only six months previously they had been working my body in blissful ignorance, clueless that I was about to turn into a fitness monster, that I was going to start pushing them to new limits and new demands. The virtual finish line had approached quite quickly, I'd reached the end of the lap, stopped my watch, and stayed stationary at the side of the road, hyperventilating. I decide to stay stopped for a minute or so, rehydrating my body and waiting for my breathing to return to normal.

Once I felt more human again, I slowly cycled back to the van and loaded my bike inside, and drove home. I was looking forward to see what my watch had sent to Strava when I arrived.

10 miles, 39 minutes and 42 seconds, an average speed of a whopping (well for me) 15.4mph. I'd achieved the time trial in under 40 minutes and had got a faster average speed than ever before, significantly so. GET IN!

Chapter 22

My muscles had started protesting. I couldn't blame them really. My calves were like bricks and my hamstrings tight. Walking down the stairs in the morning had become a painful affair. They were crying out for attention.

I had tried to be considerate towards them, I'd been making my own mineral bath salts for a while, a mix of various salts I had heard were beneficial to muscle recovery, but my body had decided this was no longer good enough. I mentioned this one day to Christine.

"You need a sports massage." she told me.

"I've never had a sports massage." I replied quizzically, intrigued by the concept.

"I'll give you Kevin's number," she told me, "he's kept me ticking over, he's brilliant."

I sent him a text message, introducing myself, telling him I was a friend of Christine's and could he fit me in.

I knew he was going to Christine's house to give her massages, I wanted to go to him, I wanted to know if this was a possibility.

Dear reader, our house is a tip. It's a lovely house, in a fabulous little cul de sac, but inside is a level of untidiness and clutter that could easily get us on one of those "extreme hoarder" shows that you hear about. Our living room table, designed to hold magazines or mugs of tea is piled high with stuff, random stuff, from cat toothpaste to sunglasses, empty boxes to old VHS videos (do we even still have a video player? Ah yes we do, that would appear to be on the bottom of the pile). The "buckaroo style" formation of the table has now got so high that we have to hold a remote control in the air to change channels on the TV. But it doesn't stop there, half the large sofa is also full with stuff, stuff that can't fit on the table. Our hallway is full of musical items and allotment clutter. Our stairs are home to boxes meaning we can only walk up one side. I think you can see the picture. Our house is a mess, a lived-in mess, a mess full of love, but a mess nonetheless. I will rarely let friends in the house, let alone strangers.

Thankfully Kevin replied with a yes, I could go to him. Phew!

I discovered that Kevin was quite a popular chap, his client list ranged from amateurs like myself to premiership footballers. The guy was reported, by many, to be the best around.

I arranged a session straight from work one day. I set my satnav and headed towards his house. When I arrived, he answered the door, he's smiley and friendly and put me at ease. He invited me into the living room where the massage table is set up. His house is immaculate, I've been to show homes with more clutter. Everything was spotlessly clean and there wasn't an item out of place. I thank my lucky stars that he didn't need to come to my house, the shock would probably have been too much for him.

He asked why I was there, I explained my protesting legs and he set to work.

I don't know if any of you have ever had a sports massage before? If you haven't and you are imagining a nice relaxing treatment that you may get in a Day Spa then think again. I'd have prayed for aromatherapy oils and soothing hands. Instead, I had elbows thrust into my muscles with enough force to make me wince. Over the course of the session I let out a few choice words, but it was nothing that Kevin hadn't heard before. He assured me that whilst I would probably be a bit sore the day after, that it would be worth it.

He was right, I had pain the day after, but ultimately it had freed up some knots and made my suffering limbs ready for the next onslaught. And so, whenever I feel my muscles start to protest, I give them something to protest about and I book a session with Kevin.

Chapter 23

Training to run a 10k race isn't only about improving your distances. It is also about improving your stamina and fitness. My training schedule in Rob's capable hands, I was following his plan religiously. I had always been a good girl at school, a bit of a girlie swot if you will, I always listened to the teachers. This desire to listen and pay attention had translated easily with me following my training plan and listening to Rob.

At the start of the week, I would look at what was scheduled. I'd move things around a little to fit in with my work commitments. Blimey, keeping up a training plan when you work full time isn't an easy feat. However, I would do my best endeavours to have completed everything by the end of the week.

One session on my plan this particular week filled me with cold dread. Hill sprints. I read what was required of me. I'd need to run for ten minutes to a hill, sprint up the hill for 15 seconds, walk back down, and repeat, ten times! Then conclude the session with a final ten-minute run.

I knew the perfect hill, it was steep. In fairness, I could have chosen pretty much anywhere in my locality. In my first instalment I said how I lived up a two mile hill.

However, the particular hill that I had chosen for this work out was fairly secluded and unlikely to draw attention to me whilst I repeatedly would be running up and walking down like a crazy person.

The session was scheduled for a day when I was due to have a late finish time in work. I knew this would need to be a morning run. On the D Day my alarm vibrated at 6am and I was straight up to do it.

As it worked out, the run to the hill was far less than 10 minutes, so I just ran back and forth on the flat until I'd hit the ten minutes. The hill I'd chosen was a concrete path nestled within a field. If I had chosen an afternoon to use this hill it would have been a hive of activity, with a children's play area forming part of this recreation area. I don't think that I've ever seen any young children play there. It was, however, a popular place for teenagers to hang out. I guessed at 6am I would be safe from the prying eyes and mocking comments of teenagers and I was right.

The first couple of sprints were actually easier than I thought, I gave myself a mental pat on the back for doing so well. However, by sprint number five it was starting to get really difficult. I carried on, however, on my walks back down I started taking my time a bit more, giving myself a longer recovery time in-between. Then on sprint number nine, it happened, from nowhere I felt the urge to wretch, it came as quite a surprise to me, from nowhere I just vomited. Thankfully, being in a field, it wasn't as horrendous as it could have potentially have been elsewhere. The grass happily accepting my surprising offering.

I stopped briefly, wondering to myself what had just happened, took a drink of water. Walked back down the hill and completed sprint ten anyway. I was not planning to fail. With the sprints completed, I slowly walked home, the ten-minute run was not going to happen, but at least I'd managed the sprints. I felt in equal parts a success and a failure.

Chapter 24

Sometimes the Met Office lies. Well, I don't think they do it intentionally, it's just that weather can be somewhat unpredictable. It was a Saturday morning, and the forecast the night before had promised glorious sunshine and a less than 5% chance of rain. Imagine my surprise when I woke up to see it was raining, heavily.

I had planned to do a cycle, and then after the cycle to go straight to the farmers market to collect our meat for the month. Phil had said before we went to sleep that he was going to do the cycle with me.

We woke up. The rain was thrashing against the bedroom window, Phil turned to me and said "You aren't really going to cycle in this are you?". He should have known me better. By that point in my life as a terrible triathlete, if it was on my plan, it was happening. I replied with "Well, I need to do it don't I!"

Phil got up too, he was coming to the farmers market anyway. However, his fair-weather attitude, some may say good sense, had resulted in him deciding to stay in the van whilst I cycled. I envied him if I was honest, he was sat with a flask of coffee, in the warm, listening to Radio Five. I on the other hand, was listening to the wind fly past my ears and the sounds of splashes as I cycled through rather hefty puddles.

I had come to the conclusion that, in a kind of self motivation mantra, it isn't the easy, good weather, sessions that make you a success. It is the hard, cold, wet days when it would be far too easy to stay in bed. Getting up and getting out was a sign of commitment, or insanity. No I'm going to stick with commitment.

It was one of my harder training sessions, and as I didn't have mudguards on my road bike, I had a lovely streak of mud all the way up my back. This was going to be embarrassing at the farmers market. I resembled a drowned rat, a muddy drowned rat. I was amazed Phil let me back in the van.

Let's just say that whilst picking up the meat, my appearance didn't go unnoticed. Some farmers thought it was great, others found it disturbing, they sold me meat nonetheless.

It was around this time that something else occurred in my cycling. My employers had opened up a "Cycle to work scheme". I looked in interest. Basically, I would have the opportunity to upgrade my commuting hybrid, paying monthly, interest free and tax free. To me, this seemed to be too big a bargain to pass up and I looked for what was the best hybrid I could get for a monthly cost that wouldn't dent my pay packet too much.

I am a big fan of Giant bikes, I think they are well made and are a brand I trust. My original hybrid was a Giant, as was my road bike, so my first port of call was to look at Giant. I found two potentials that looked like they wouldn't break the bank and I headed to my local Giant retailer to have a look. The first one appeared more mountain bike than a traditional hybrid, the tyres were huge! Having now got used to thinner tyres on my road bike, I decided that one wasn't for me. The second bike was a much better fit, a more traditional hybrid.

Our cycle to work scheme was run by a major retailer, anyone British should know it, if I say they are more famed for car parts than bikes and their sign is orange and black, I'd hope you'd know who I mean. This retailer doesn't stock Giant bikes, however, under the terms of the scheme they confirmed they would get any bike that you wanted.

It only took a couple of weeks for the bike to come. I headed to the store, excited, on the day it arrived. I'd asked for mud guards to be fitted, and the mechanic was very helpful, but due to not having a screw long enough for my bike frame, these mudguards were, in part, secured with cable ties. I think, with hindsight, that this should have been my first indication that maybe these people weren't quite as professional an outfit as one would hope.

My first week or so of riding the bike were a joy. Admittedly, I didn't complete a massive amount of mileage with my training rides still being completed on the road bike. Then the noise started. The chain ring set had three rings, the slow one, the middle one and the fast one. For every gear in the middle ring an awful noise could be heard. It disappeared in the slow ring and disappeared in the fast ring, but in the middle ring, the main ring, a weird, horrendous scratching noise was constant. I took it back to the retailer, they said they would sort it.

I collected the bike the next day, I was assured that the problem had been resolved. I am a trusting soul, so I loaded the bike in the van and believed them. The problem had not been fixed. My next commute to work, scratch, scratch, scratch.

I arrived to work and phoned as soon as I could. I spoke to the manager who told me to drop it in after work.

They kept my bike hostage for a few days, I phoned only to be told that there was no issue that they could see and I could come and get it.

When I got to the bike section, the guy I needed to see had not got in to work yet, but the chap on the bike section who I'd guess was late 20s/early 30s said he could help. I explained I was there to collect my bike, I was slightly agitated, knowing that they claimed there was not an issue.

The staff member got my bike, and then proceeded to tell me how the gears work.   I said to him "I know how the gears work." He then accused me of cross chaining (where you match gears inappropriately). "No I'm not." I replied, and said how the gearing where it was causing the most issues is an optimum ratio.

He then said something that I truly couldn't believe I was hearing "Well the gears are working perfectly on the stand, there is nothing wrong with the gears. It must be your weight on the bike."

Now admittedly, nobody is going to confuse me for a supermodel anytime soon, but I was now a size 14/16, two stone lighter than I'd been 6 months before. I was hardly ginormous.

That was when I got very very angry and said "Get me the store manager NOW!"

The store manager came over asked if everything was OK, I replied "No, your staff member is an insulting, patronising bastard."

I thankfully got the store manager to agree to come outside with me, frankly I think he was too scared of me not to. As I pedalled my bike around the car park he could instantly hear the problem and confirmed it was not right at all. I got through the full range of gears in my demonstration. I think I impressed the store manager, he actually commented on my speed. Showing my bike experience, and to prove I wasn't some naive beginner that he could walk all over, I told him "this is just my little commuting hybrid, as I don't want to mess up my racing road bike with mud guards and pannier racks." He promised to get it sorted.

Three mechanics and a lot of confusion later, they did find the problem. The idiots had left some plastic on the bike when they built it.

Photo: Getting wet doing the cycle mentioned in the start of the chapter.

Chapter 25

I guess when you train enough at some point you are going to get an injury. What nobody tells you is how utterly soul destroying getting an injury is. You are in a routine, you feel invincible, then suddenly ouch!

My injury happened after a long weekend away. Phil and I had been away watching the Revolution track cycling. It was the first track event of the season, and the inaugural event in the newly built Derby velodrome.

The velodrome itself was lovely, however, the seats were uncomfortable. I think the combination of uncomfortable seats and a long weekend where my only exercise was walking from the hotel to the event and back again had taken its toll and had been the catalyst for injury.

We arrived home on the Monday, we had the day off work and I was chomping at the bit to start training again. I had planned to do a 5k run. However, a kilometre in and I was in pain. My bum cheeks were sore and my shins were painful. I cut my run short and limped home.

I messaged Rob in a panic, what on earth was I going to do? He calmed me down, told me to not to run for a couple of days but that I could still do my planned cycle commute the following day.

A few days later, on Rob's advice I would try running again. He told me to run on grass, if that was possible (the surface, he hadn't suddenly recommended drug taking as an injury cure!).

There are some council owned playing fields near me. They are used for cricket in the summer and rugby and football in the winter. However, when the council decide to open them is a total mystery. I have tried emailing them for opening times, but sadly, no success. I'm guessing I'm not the only person who is frustrated by the lack of transparency as some kind person has created a path through the metal mesh fencing that people can use when the gates are locked. Is it trespassing? I don't know? But I pay my council tax, so I regularly break in to the fields using this alternative entrance.

I decide this is the best grass to do my run on, I walk for about a minute first just to warm my muscles up a bit and then I start to run. The pain in my shins, unbearable. I start to cry, not through the pain as I'm a tough sod, but rather part anger, part frustration. I was well and truly injured. I had to admit defeat and break back out of the playing fields.

Rob concluded that I had shin splints, they are quite common in new runners and people who have been increasing their distances. I was told in no uncertain terms, no running for at least a week! Thankfully, one saving grace of being a triathlete is that if you can't do one sport, you do still have another two. Rob confirmed I was fine to cycle and to swim. Just no excess walking and certainly no running.

After a week I had a message from Rob.

"Do you have a treadmill?"

The answer to this question wasn't that simplistic. Yes, I did have a treadmill, it was a 'spur of the moment' alcohol fuelled purchase that Phil had made several years earlier when he'd got on the weighing scales and didn't like the numbers! It had been used for a few weeks and then left to gather dust. So, we did, in the room we call "the study" have a treadmill. I've already told you about how incredibly untidy our house is, so it will come as no surprise to you that I couldn't get to the treadmill. It was covered in empty cardboard boxes that Phil was saving for some allotment purpose, and in front of it there were several boxes of stuff that had been dumped in there. So, I had a treadmill, yes. Whether it still worked and whether I could access it any time soon was still a total mystery.

I was nervous about mentioning it to Phil. The mere suggestion of needing to use it I knew was going to cause a rant of quite epic proportions as he would realise the work needed to reach this piece of unused gym equipment. I knew this would be compounded by the fact that we didn't know if unearthing it would be a futile exercise. It had been sat, unloved and unused, for many years. Would it work? Who knew?

We were sat having tea when I gently broached the subject.

"Darling." I say in my sweetest voice, him already eyeing me with suspicion as this was the tone of voice I always used when I wanted something "Do you think we'd be able to get to and use the treadmill."

He sighed "When do you want to use it by?"

"By the weekend?" I added, fully expecting what was about to happen. The nuclear bomb went off in the kitchen and Phil went into full rant mode about how I always do this, he never has any notice and boo hoo hoo he'd have to finally sort some boxes out.

Thankfully, whilst these rants are always explosive and fiery, they are also over quickly as he mentally works his way through a problem. Once he'd calmed down, he offered a solution on how we could sort things out. That weekend, the treadmill was unearthed, like an archaeological find, and deep joy it was working.

In the coming weeks, as my injury disappeared, I started running again. Rob wanted me to gently ease back by running indoors so if the injury re-appeared I could stop immediately and also he felt that a treadmill would be lower impact than the roads. During these early runs back I discovered something. I bloody hate treadmills! Give me the outdoors any day. Ok, I'm glad I've got it ready for use for the winter should it snow or be icy, but in the main I'll be sticking to nature's gym, the great outdoors.

Chapter 26

The next best thing to competing in a triathlon is supporting one. It was the August bank holiday weekend, and Llanelli would play host to two triathlons in one day... a women's only sprint triathlon and a mixed gender Olympic distance. Whilst there were members of the club competing in both, my attention was firmly placed on the sprint as a few of my friends were competing.

It was an early start, Christine, Sarah and I had decided to car share as we were all supporting. We met at a place where cars could be left and all jumped in Sarah's car. We were all looking forward to it.

For an August bank holiday, it was actually surprisingly chilly, I wished I had a jumper on under my hoodie.

We arrived at the harbour where the action was starting, and found a few other club members there supporting too. Coach Rob was there, and introduced the three of us to Sian. I had spoken online a couple of times to Sian, she was a woman with a clever wit and I knew instantly I'd like her in person.

We made our way over to the swim start area and were quickly joined by other the club members, also there to give support. Like in my own triathlon, I felt a pride at being part of such a caring club.

It was an important day, Laura (who had supported me in my first triathlon), Lynette and "the other" Christine (so named as I met her after terrier Christine) were all breaking their own triathlon virginities. I admired these girls, I thought they were amazing, mostly due to the fact that they were starting with the ultimate, an open water swim. I watched them, awestruck, as they stood at the start line in their wetsuits, about to hurl themselves into a harbour and swim around some boats.

I wasn't ready for open water, the idea of it terrified me, my club mates were fantastic for getting straight in and doing it.

Once my friends, and the other competitors, were in the water we shouted and cheered their names. We watched one by one as they got out of the water and ran to the bike transition, unzipping their wetsuits as they ran.

Whilst they were out on the bike stage it gave us supporters all chance to grab a warming coffee (gosh if we were cold, I shudder to think how cold the competitors were) and a chance to chat. I spoke a lot to Sian that day.

"What have you got planned, Debs?" Sian asked me.

"Swansea 10k is next, then the Amman Valley Sprint Tri." I reply "You?"

"I think I am signing up to Ironman Wales." her response astounded me.

A full ironman? A race where a marathon was just a third of what you needed to do, a feat of human endurance that would last the best part of a day. I decided she was insane, lovely, but insane.

She did, however, reassure me that a half marathon would be within my grasp. I made a decision I'd been toying with for a while. I was going to sign up to the Swansea half marathon the following year.

Chapter 27

I think that with every pair of running shoes, or in every running magazine or even as a "sticky" at the top of a running forum they should provide all runners with a health warning.

"Caution – when you start increasing your running distances you will, on occasion, get an overwhelming urge to poo!"

I really do think that every runner, once they go past 5k should be given this important piece of information.

The more you run, the more your digestion system works and this inevitably will make you want to poo.

Since my first realisation of this I have made it a public duty to inform other beginner runners.

It was a Sunday morning and I was alone. Christine was sunning herself somewhere hot, Sarah was in West Wales in a caravan. I was on my own down Aberafon beach. I had planned to run 8k. The 10k race was fast approaching and I was needing to increase my distances.

It was a cold morning, but it was dry and wasn't too windy for the seaside. I'd parked in my usual spot and had headed out alone. The first couple of kilometres were hard, they always were. It's like your body protests that you are running again, your muscles thinking "Why can't she just have a lie in and then have a fry up like normal people do on a Sunday?" but then they realise that your head is stronger than your body and they quit protesting when they realise you aren't stopping.

I had achieved the first 5k in a fairly respectable time and was feeling smug that I felt strong and only had 3k to go. However, at the 6k mark my stomach decided to protest. I suddenly had a shocking need to poo. Like really poo. Like the kind of stomach cramps you only get when you are going to get a dose of shits.

It wasn't even 8am yet, and I had left the house without going to the toilet. I'd had a latte and a banana before I'd left the house. Both food items that with hindsight generally make going to the toilet easier.

So there I was, early Sunday morning, I was at the seaside and I was desperate to go to the toilet. I stopped running immediately, I had no choice. I clenched my bum cheeks together and prayed I could make it to a toilet in time.

I got to the public toilets, they were locked! I actually physically slapped myself for being out so early in the morning. I continued, walking like a penguin to the coffee shop, it hadn't opened yet. I knocked on the door in the hope that they would take pity on me. The one staff member who was setting up ignored me. I knocked again, he looked up and mouthed "We're not open." Yeah thanks mate.

I had no choice, I had to walk back to the car. I almost fell into the car, as I tried to get in without separating my legs. Panic set in. I needed to use pedals. My feet would need to be apart by a good 12 inches. I started my drive home and prayed that I wouldn't crap myself on route.

It was, quite simply, the most unpleasant journey ever! Every bump in the road made me panic. I clenched my cheeks as hard as I could. How on earth would I explain it to Phil if I "had an accident". Thankfully, my running fairy godmother must have been smiling at me. I got home, shut myself straight in the bathroom, and thanked my lucky stars that I had had a very near miss!

Chapter 28

The day of the Swansea 10k had arrived. Even though I had been injured, I was over that now. And whilst I expected my time to be slower than I had originally aimed for, I knew that I was capable of completing it.

My longest training run in the build up had been 9k, I was hoping, and expecting, that the sense of occasion and the support from the crowds would see me through that unknown territory of the final kilometre.

Christine had messaged me early in the morning, she was competing in another race elsewhere. One of those obstacle type races. Her message read "Don't forget to have a poo before you leave the house." ha ha, thanks Chris!

I met Laura at the start line. I hadn't known that she was competing until the day before, she had kept her decision to enter quiet. I knew that she would do it though, and knowing that she was a faster runner than me, I also knew that she would do it in a faster time. I mentioned what Christine had said.

"Really?" she replied. I told her my training run story.

"I need a pee." she said and disappeared to the toilet. I do wonder if it was actually a pee that she went for!

She arrived back just before the race was due to start. We'd also seen "the other" Christine who was racing for a charity. She was wearing a charity t-shirt. Laura and I were both kitted out in our Celtic Tri running vests.

They lined the people up at the start line, it trailed back for what seemed like miles. You were put in pens according to your estimated finish time. I, predictably, was in the last pen, thankfully so was Laura. We knew that Jo was also running, although Jo was fast, she was in a pen far far away in the distance.

I saw Keith, a work colleague, in the same pen as me and we chatted.

"What time are you hoping to get, Debs?" he asked me.

"I'm hoping for 1 hour 30." I replied, adding "But I don't think I'm going to get it."

Then the gun went bang and we were off. Several thousand people all heading down the closed roads of Swansea Bay.

132

Rob had phoned me the day before to wish me luck and offer words of wisdom. He'd told me "Whatever you do, keep smiling."

Whilst running, I knew why, there were professional photographers everywhere and also people snapping pictures with their camera phones.

I was smiling, grinning even, enjoying every step as I was thinking to myself that only months before I could barely run for a minute and now I was competing in a 10k race. Ten whole glorious kilometres!

A couple of kilometres in and my grin stretched even wider. Donald a work colleague of mine was stood at the side of the road cheering! It was a wonderful moment seeing a friendly face, there to give moral support. I high fived him as I ran past.

Before I knew it I was approaching the 5k point. I noticed a few Celtic Tri members at that point. Armed, with camera phones. I did a rather pathetic goofy thumbs up as I ran past and grabbed my water bottle from a young lad who was handing them out to runners.

It was here I made a big mistake, I drank LOADS of water, gulped it down. It was a schoolgirl error but I was thirsty. A few hundred metres later I was hit with 'a stitch from hell' and forced to a walking pace. I'd read about gulping water and how it can give you stitches, but it was the first time it had ever happened to me, and bloody hell it hurt.

I walked for a little while, hoping the pain would pass quickly and that was when something amazing happened. People at the side of the road started shouting.

"Go on Celtic Tri" "Go Celtic girl, you can do it" "Come on Celtic Tri, you are over half way" "Well done Celtic Tri" "Keeping going Celtic Tri"

My club running vest had become a beacon for people to shout encouragement. I suddenly felt a great sense of pride that I was running for my club, and it pushed me to pick up my pace and start running again.

At around 8k, I saw Donald again. He told me how brilliantly I was doing as I slowly ran past.

The next kilometre was a challenge again, but the occasional shout out from supporters, mentioning the club in their cheers kept me going.

During the last kilometre, the unknown territory, I felt knackered but amazing. As I approached the finish line, at the side of the road were Darren and Laura, my friends that had encouraged me for my first 5k. They had also both competed and were wearing their finishers t-shirts and medals. I knew they would have finished ages before me, but they were there to encourage me across the finish line and yelled at me to pick up my pace for the final stretch.

"You are nearly there Debs, only 400 metres, get a bloody move on!"

I crossed the finish line, club Laura was stood there in her Celtic tri running top, having finished ahead of me and we hugged. We'd both done it.

My time 1 hour 28 minutes 51 seconds, I'd achieved my goal of under an hour and a half.

I picked up my bag from the marshals, in it was my medal. I decided I wanted to collect more "shiny things", they were nice. And with this thought in mind I went for a well-earned ice-cream.

Photo: With Laura after the Swansea Bay 10K

Chapter 29

It was the day after the Swansea 10k. I had been training really hard and I was tired. I'd also had a rather chaotically busy time in work. I was officially shattered and needed a holiday.

Thankfully, Phil and I had a week off, we were going to Manchester for the National Track Championships but had decided to make a week of it.

OK, I know that maybe some people wouldn't see Manchester as an ideal holiday destination, but we love watching cycling and Phil and I can generally entertain each other anywhere.

Rob had told me to have the week off, I deserved a rest week. But if I did want to do anything, that I could for fun, but no pressure, and no proper training.

I'd researched things that we could do in the surrounding areas and read up about cycling in the Peak District. So, we'd gone to Manchester in the van, with our hybrids slung in the back so if we wanted to cycle we could.

We had a few days of general sight seeing and then decided one morning, as it was a nice day, to head to

Bakewell. I had read about the Monsal Trail, an old disused railway line where you could cycle through five tunnels. It sounded pretty cool. I was also interested as they are trying to re-open a disused tunnel near us linking our Valley to the Rhondda. I'd even joined the Rhondda Tunnel Society to pledge my support.

The drive to Bakewell was windy and hilly and should have given us an indication of what we had ahead of us.

"Are we nearly there yet?" Phil asked, using his ironic childlike nature to voice his frustration that this was, in fact, much further from Manchester than we had originally thought.

We arrived and found a car park in the town centre. I said to Phil "I'm not doing anything until I've had a coffee." so we find a little coffee shop at the side of a river.

"Do you know how to get to this trail, Debs?" Phil asked

I wasn't entirely sure, I had an idea and knew it started near a disused railway station. I asked the man who served us in the coffee shop and he gave us directions. The directions made Phil look at me in a rather unpleasant way.

"You cross the bridge, go back through the car park" he starts with, all well with the directions so far "Then you turn right, go up the big hill, turn left up the other big hill."

Oops, big hill, other big hill. The look on Phil's face said it all.

"I thought you said the trail was flat." he angrily whispered when the waiter was out of ear shot.

"The trail is." I added, unhelpfully "I guess we just have to get to the trail first."

With caffeine inside us, we head back to the van and unload the bikes. Phil is in a temper, he's quietly seething thinking that I had purposefully deceived him. I can promise, dear reader, I hadn't. However, I guess the clue is in the name of the area, the Peak District, Peak. Lots and lots of Peaks!

We set off on the bikes. We are about half way up the first hill, I am a good few metres ahead of Phil, powering away in my "granny gears" to make it as easy as possible. I hear a shout from behind me.

"This hill!" he shouts "I didn't sign up for fucking hills."

I choose to ignore him, yes this was hard on a hybrid. It would have been far easier on a road bike. However, we were doing it.

The second hill was harder than the first, but we found the start of the trail. We also found the car park for the start of the trail. Oops, we could have parked here and avoided the hills.

Phil stopped for a minute or two "We could have bloody parked here." he confirmed what we were both thinking "I hate you right now."

His mood barely improved on the cycle, so I decided to potter in my own little world ahead of him, enjoying the scenery. We passed some other cyclists, some dog walkers and we headed through the first cold damp tunnel.

I stopped at the other side and waited for Phil.

"We really should get a photo of us by the tunnel."

He agreed.

However, him being a semi professional photographer, he needed to get the shot just right. He spent ages setting up the camera. A couple on a tandem come shooting through the tunnel, they nearly hit Phil as he's trying to set up. He looks cross. He sets up the timer and a mountain biker offers to take our picture. Phil tries to explain, and realises this probably makes him look like a stroppy sod. We eventually, after a lot of faffing and swearing, get what turned out to be a rather lovely photograph.

We continue on the cycle.

"I'm hating this." Phil reminds me.

Yep, I know sweetheart, you have a face like a slapped arse, I know you aren't happy!

We reach the final tunnel, cycle through, make a little video for my nephew and niece and head back.
With about a mile to go, we stop at a gorgeous looking coffee shop and have some food. Phil, seeing the end is in sight, and having a rather delicious steak sandwich, cheers up again.

Thankfully, the days prior to this on holiday and the days afterwards he was my usual, gorgeous lovely husband.

Although I vow to him that if I cycle in the Peak District again, I'm taking my friends and not him.

Photo: The picture from Bakewell

Chapter 30

Strength training. Apparently, it's important. I felt like an apple when Rob announced he wanted to improve my "core strength". Having eaten many apples and pears in my life, I know that cores are meant to be discarded, ignored, forgotten about. I wish it was the same with my core.

"I really want you to stick with these." Rob says, as he adds another Pilates session into my plan.

Apparently, the art of Pilates is a great one for improving flexibility and core strength.

I put on YouTube and get the link that Rob has sent me. A 30 minute beginner session with a cheesy American body beautiful who I instantly decide I don't like.

She starts guiding me through all manner of exercises. They are hard. They are horrible.

It is also rather difficult to do pilates and yoga when you have three cats. The minute they see you get on the floor on a mat is their cue to rub up against you, to walk under your legs that are in the air. It is a hazard for both me and the cats.

One day, I was doing a session when Phil said "You don't look like she does on the telly.".

No I didn't, she is awesome and I am rubbish. I try and push my legs up higher and let out a huge fart. Phil is in stitches, I am not.

Hate core training. That is all!

Chapter 31

It had arrived, the day of the second triathlon. I was as excited as I was for my first one, but thankfully a lot less nervous. In a weird way, I felt less prepared because I wasn't scared. Which was a bizarre feeling as I knew that I had trained really well for it. Better in fact, as I was now following a proper schedule by a real-life coach.

I had a slightly later start time than the one in Pencoed, so this allowed me a slightly longer lie in. OK don't get me wrong, I was still up before 6am on a Sunday morning, which I am quite sure is a criminal offence for most people.

I had got my bag ready the night before, so I knew I was prepared.

So the morning routine, I got up, showered, had my pre-race breakfast of granary toast with cashew nut butter, a banana and a latté and I was ready. Phil was ready too. He was armed with his camera in the hope that he could get some good photos of me.

"You need to get photos of Lynette too." I told him, whilst waving several pictures of her in front of him.

I think the fact that Lynette was also racing was one of the reasons I felt less nervous. Having a fellow club member and friend racing meant I had company. OK we wouldn't be racing together, she was in a later "wave" time than me, so would be starting her swim in the pool later. However, knowing that I would see a friend before, possibly during and after made me more relaxed.

We set off to Ammanford, Phil driving. We knew we wouldn't be able to park at the venue, so Phil dropped me off outside and kicked me out with my bike and my gear before heading somewhere else to park. He also had his bike in the van as he had decided that would be the best way to photograph me on the cycle route by cycling to two sections of it.

This triathlon whilst had the same swim and cycle distances, it had a longer run. Pencoed had been 3k, Ammanford information said the run was 5k.

I walked up the hill to the leisure centre, and was greeted by Lynette and her husband, an ironman, Steve. Lynette was getting her transition area ready and told me to set up next to her. She was positively beaming as she set up her brand-new bike onto the stand. It was a gorgeous bike too, it made my bike feel like the poor relation.

I put my stickers on the bike and helmet as hadn't done that the night before and we headed inside the building.

In the last triathlon I had done, our race numbers were written on us in marker pen. This triathlon, we had race tattoos. Temporary tattoos you needed to place on your arm. I'd never used these before and I was flapping whilst Lynette talked me through how to do it. It was actually really easy. Place tattoo on arm, get it soaking wet, peel off the backing paper. Job done.

We went back outside, by which point Phil had arrived. He had been looking at the finish line and didn't think he'd be able to photograph the finish. I assured him that this was OK. As long as I had some photos, I'd be happy. He wished me luck and it was time to get my normal clothes off and my bather on.

Chapter 32

Triathlon number two, sport number one. It was the swim leg, I got ready at the side of the pool. Due to earlier waves being faster than anticipated, I was actually going to be starting a bit earlier than expected.

I was given my timing chip and attached it to my left ankle.

I was shown the first lane, I'd be sharing it with an older gentleman. We smiled at each other as we got in the pool.

What I hadn't realised was that they were getting us to start in the deeper end. It wasn't a traditional deep end as it wasn't actually that deep. On tip toes, I could just about touch the bottom with my head above water.

"Do you want to go inside or outside?" I asked him.

"I don't mind." he said.

So we stayed where we were. I was on the inside and he was on the outside. I secured my hat and my goggles and waited for the countdown.

"5, 4, 3, 2, 1!"

I was off, triathlon number two in progress, my head under water, doing front crawl up the pool.... just over half way... then recovery with head out.

I turned at the top and did a bit more front crawl with my head under water again. I could see Steve sat in the viewing area, and I knew he would report back to Rob.

My lane buddy was doing breast stroke, so I didn't feel so bad about my half front crawl, half doggy paddle.

As the lengths disappeared, I found keeping doing front crawl had got too hard, it was slowing me down. So I made a necessary decision. The rest of the race was going to be doggy paddle. I was more comfortable with it, and I needed to feel comfortable with the race. Especially as I still had two other sports to follow.

Before I knew it, I was being told "two lengths to go" and my swim leg was over.

At least I had done some front crawl, it was progress from the first one.

Chapter 33

I started on the run from the swimming pool to the transition area. Well, I say ran, as everyone knows from the 1970s posters, you aren't allowed to run poolside. (I can also add that I neither dive bombed or partook in heavy petting whilst in the pool either). Once outside the building I did start to run. It is a weird feeling running in a wet bather, bare foot. Especially when you have an audience of people cheering at you.

I reached the transition area, and to my surprise I see Sian there, her face grinning as she shouts "Go on Deb."

"Blimey Sian, I wasn't expecting to see you." I said, forgetting for a minute that I was actually in the middle of a race and really should have been getting my arse into gear.

Seeing Sian meant a lot to me. I knew that she had just come off a night shift, however, instead of being sensible and going home to bed, she had driven 30 miles out of her way to support Lynette and I. Gosh, I loved my club and the people in it that I was honoured to call my friends.

I started wiping down my feet. Being in the front row of transition, I was aware that all the spectators (including my friends) had a rather uninspiring view of my fat backside in a swimming costume, whilst I bent over, picking things up. I tried to vary my body positioning.

It really was an appalling transition, I was so slow it was frankly painful. I tried to pull my cycle shorts on, however, they were struggling to be pulled up over my cold wet legs, the same with pulling my two in one top on. Being October, I had put a thermal top under my Celtic tri running vest, however, with hindsight I would have been quicker just putting on the two tops separately and not have tried to be clever. Then it was the worst bit, my calf guards. Since my injury, I had started wearing calf guards for longer runs. These were compression sleeves to protect my legs, as I attempted to pull one up my right leg it ripped, bloody fantastic! My left I took slower, then it was socks, shoes and my racing belt. Then onto helmet, gloves and cycling glasses and taking my bike off the rack (being very careful not to accidentally knock Lynette's shiny new bike). My transition time, a pathetically slow 4 minutes and 1 second, it had felt like even longer! It was a worse transition than my first one. I needed to put it behind me and get on with the cycle.

At the mount line, I jumped on my bike and started hurtling down the road. Then it hit me, I hadn't set my watch. I stop and put it to go. Why I don't know as I would have had my time from my timing chip anyhow! At the first major downhill leading onto the main road, I had a thumbs up from the marshal that there was no traffic and was able to continue at speed onto the main road. As I turned the corner, quicker than I was accustomed to, I lost my left foot off the pedal. I quickly lift it, in the hope that I didn't collide it with the pavement. I lose my balance a little, but manage to steady myself keeping me from falling off.

I start up the first hill pedaling hard, in front of me I can see a man on a hybrid with a rucksack on his back. I assume that he is someone on their way to work, their pace is slow and I start to worry about overtaking him. I mean I am in a race, and there is some unknown cyclist gently plodding up a hill whilst I am working my arse off. As I am about to reach him, he pulls over onto the pavement and then it hits me, this isn't some random work commuter, it's Phil, my husband and he has lost his first opportunity to photograph me.

"Hiya love." I say as I overtake him.

"How the hell did you get here so quick?" was his reply.

I didn't have time to reply to that, I was in a race and I was needing to get my speed up, and reach the top of this first little climb.

The cycle route is actually a very nice one, lots of little climbs, and lots of little downhills. Enough to recover. Having already ridden it twice in preparation I knew what to expect. Phil has accompanied me on these training rides, in fairness to him he had done for me exactly what he had done on the first triathlon. He'd downloaded the route maps, he'd then plotted it on Google earth, had driven me up and down the route and then had cycled with me. He was a total gem for this. I knew I didn't need to worry about the routes thanks to Phil's hard word, his love and his support.

So, I was racing the familiar route, I actually reached the roundabout at the turning point quicker than I expected. I stopped and had a drink, the motorbike marshal stopped to check I was OK. Not being able to drink and cycle was starting to get embarrassing now.

I head up the next hill, this one was a little tougher, however, I had already had benefits of cycling down the opposite side. I am part way up when another competitor, a young man, probably in his mid 20s overtook me, grinning, as he was obviously enjoying competing as much as I was.

These sprint triathlons are "non drafting" events, which means there has to be a decent distance between you, so you are told in the instructions that you can't slip stream other competitors. So, whilst I had to have a decent distance, he did however, give me someone in my sight to watch and try and catch.

We reached another downhill section and I was up into my highest gear, I had caught and overtaken the cyclist who had overtaken me. I had reached some cars, they were slowing down for a speed camera, I had to slow down too so not to go into the back of them. It was the first time in the race I had needed to use my brakes! The realisation hit me, if these cars were slowing down and I was slowing down I must be going faster than 30 miles per hour.... me going that speed!... I felt a little scared but mostly exhilarated, OK, OK, I felt a lot scared!

I reached the other roundabout on the route and there was Phil, he was going to get the photos this time. I grin at him but keep my speed as high as I could. I travel around the roundabout, barely slowing down, and take the final section of the main road before turning back to the leisure centre.

I'd finished it and had got back to transition to cheers from Steve and Sian. Two down, one to go!

Photo: on the cycle leg of the triathlon

Chapter 34

I put my bike back on the rack and take off my helmet, gloves and glasses. As I hadn't drunk much on the bike route, I take out my bidon and decide to take it on the run with me.

As I start to run, I hear Steve shout. "You need to move your race belt Deb!"

I hadn't used a race belt for my first triathlon. It's basically a belt which you attach your race number too. It has to be around the back for the cycle and around the front for the run.

I pull the belt around so my number is visible, change my watch from cycle to run as I was running and headed out on what was meant to be the 5K course.

The course initially takes you through some residential streets. People were stood on their doorsteps, clapping and cheering. I guess it was a little bit of excitement for a Sunday morning for these sleepy houses. Then the course headed onto a cycle path, off road, for the majority of the race.

I was struggling on the run from the outset, my calves felt really heavy. It felt worse than my first triathlon. My legs hurt, not injured hurt, I knew what that felt like, just a dull painful ache from feeling so heavy.

It was around a kilometre in, on the off road section, and towards the top of an uphill stretch when it happened. I knew I was going to be sick. Having had this experience in training, I knew what would happen. I vomited into a bramble bush, and slowed to a walk for a while, drinking my bidon to clear the taste. Thankfully, no other competitors were around at the time so like when it happened in training, I had no witnesses to my unfortunate incident.

I walked for too long really, a few competitors passed me heading back on their runs, many shouted words of encouragement as they passed. A few people overtook me. I temporarily felt sorry for myself. Then talked some sense into myself that this wasn't some training exercise, I was racing and needed to sort my act out. I forced myself to start running again, albeit slowly.

When I reached the turnaround point I looked at my watch 2.7km. 2.7k, not 2.5k!! This was NOT a 5k run, the swines!

As I was running back, we reached the point where Lynette was on her opening stretch of the run. We beamed at each other as we said hello. She was looking strong. I felt proud of her.

It wasn't long until I was back on the pavements, people cheered, but my legs had had enough. I had to slow to a walk again. I was walking down the road, my legs were hurting like hell, although I knew I didn't have far to go. It was then I saw Phil armed with his camera.

"What are you bloody walking for?" he shouted.

"I'm in agony love." I yelled back, feeling slightly indignant, as well, I hadn't seen him run in the last few years!

I knew I needed to keep up appearances for the camera, and so I ran, a bit. I wanted to save myself for the finish though, so once I was out of the camera lens range I walked up half the hill to the transition area and finish line. As soon as I saw people there supporting near the finish line I started to run. I could see the finish line, and my face was beaming. This triathlon had hurt, but I had done it. I had only gone and finished another triathlon, and a slightly longer one at that. As I crossed the line, my legs forgot they hurt and I felt victorious.

It was amazing to have crossed the line, I collected my finishers t-shirt, a bottle of water and a free banana and welsh cake, and went to see Steve and Sian who had been cheering.

I hugged them both and they told me I had done brilliantly.

Then Phil walked up, and after some confusion of where he was and wasn't allowed to go, he joined us. It was then he realized he could have photographed the finish.

I tell Steve that Lynette wouldn't be long and that she was looking strong on the run, you could see the pride in his face.

Shortly afterwards after we'd chatted, Lynette crossed the finish, she had done awesomely well.

I had aimed to have done this triathlon in 1 hour 45 minutes. My result was a little outside that at 1 hour 48 minutes and 22 seconds. But do you know something, that's OK. I did my best, I had tons of fun and I had completed another triathlon. I was now a semi-seasoned triathlete.

Photo: With Lynette at the finish

Epilogue 2

So, it was the end of the triathlon season. At the start of the triathlon season I had no idea that I would have become a triathlete, or a runner, or a proper swimmer. But I had done just that.

I needed to set my goals higher for the next triathlon season. With Christine's encouragement, I signed up for my first open water triathlon and thanks to Sian I signed up for a half marathon. All that stood in my way was 6 months worth of hard training in the closed season to get me ready. I'm sure you'll find out all about it, if you want to, in the Unlikely Triathlete Part Three!

Part Three
The Training Plan Strikes Back

Dedication 3

I am dedicating this book to Phil, when you get to the end I think you'll know why! My husband is the greatest.

Prologue 3

Blimey people, are you really still reading? Of course, you could have just stumbled upon this, the third part of my tale having not heard of this strange creature called The Unlikely Triathlete before. If you have you may want to read parts one and two first. It's not compulsory though. I do suspect that the majority of you have decided you want to continue to know more about my pathetic attempts at training and the sport of triathlon having read parts one and two.

It surprises me how people are interested in my endeavours. As the months roll on I find my Facebook page is getting more and more 'likes'. What first started as an outlet to not flood my personal timeline with exercise, followed by a few like minded friends, has now become a page where the followers come from all corners of the globe and are no longer my family and friends alone. Some are triathletes, some are runners, some are cyclists. It's actually quite humbling that people read and like my posts and my books.

I'd like to thank you for staying with me though. Knowing I have my alter ego to maintain is an excellent motivation to keep exercising. It struck me as interesting when I was saying this to Phil and he said "You are becoming more and more likely now Deb", I guess he was right. However, I will always remain The Unlikely Triathlete. I suppose there aren't that many female, over 40 diabetics competing, although I am happy to be proved wrong.

This book in the series is focusing on my first off season. Having completed my first triathlon season, and two triathlons at that, it was time to continue training and make plans for my second season as a triathlete. Before the season had finished, I had already booked my first open water triathlon and had booked a half marathon. Even though they were months and months away, having these booked and paid for was motivation to keep going and working hard. I needed this carrot dangling in front of me. I had a goal, I liked goals. I hoped that with a winter of hard training I'd be a better triathlete in my second season. I knew I'd never be elite; I'd never be good even, but as long as it was keeping me healthy and I was enjoying it then it was time and effort well spent.

With this in mind, I will start this sequel on Monday 12th October, the day after the Amman Valley triathlon.

Chapter 35

The day had caught up with me quickly. It was the day of my six-monthly heart protection clinic. After the swine flu had weakened my heart, with my family history of heart problems and with being a diabetic, these clinics had become a feature of my year. I didn't mind them, I actually found it reassuring that the hospital was taking an interest in my health.

I had a shower and got ready. I had tried to scrub the temporary race number tattoo off my arm with a flannel, it still sat prominently on my arm after my triathlon the day before. It wasn't budging, it would have to stay. I had breakfast and left for the hospital.

I had my blood test results with me in case they hadn't electronically fed through to the hospital. I had read them and they were good, in fact they were better than good, they were bloody marvelous. My blood sugar readings were sat in non diabetic territory they were managed so well, my cholesterol was normal, my other bloods, liver, kidney etc were also all normal. I went to appointment with a spring in my step.

I arrived at the front reception desk in the diabetic centre where the clinic was held. I told the receptionist that I was there for my appointment and took my seat. Like most visits to the heart protection clinic I was the youngest patient by a mile. Most of my waiting room companions were in their sixties or seventies. A few looked at me quizzically, obviously wondering what a comparatively young woman was doing at such a clinic.

The nurse called me first to take my blood pressure and weigh me. She weighed me and remarked, "Good grief you've lost some weight since you were last here!" Then she took my blood pressure, textbook normal, and the best reading I had seen for many a year. I was guided to the next stage waiting room to see the consultant.

It wasn't long before I was called in. As she walked me from the waiting area to the consulting room, I could see her looking at my arm. Ah yes, the race tattoo. When we got in the room, I broke the ice.

"I'm really sorry about the tattoo," I started. "I competed in a triathlon yesterday and it wouldn't wash off."

"You did a triathlon yesterday?" she asked, looking impressed.

"Yes." was my simple reply.

We sat down and we talked through my incredible set of results, we discussed my weight loss and my training. It was then she said the words I never thought I would hear a clinician say.

"You are amazing, keep doing what you are doing, we don't need to see you again, I'm discharging you back to your GP."

It had been over 6 years since I first had the blinding fear of my heart problems and now I was being discharged from the hospital and was officially fine!!
I fought back the tears of joy as I left the hospital.
My joy, however, was short lived. I couldn't shift the huge grin from my face the whole day, however, come the night time that all changed.
The day before, during the triathlon, Steve had made an off the cuff remark that he wasn't feeling very well and felt a bit sick. That night he came down with a sickness bug. The same day, other Celtic Tri friends who had seen Steve on Saturday had also come down with a sickness bug. As I headed to the toilet in rather a hurry, the realisation hit me, I too was coming down with the sickness bug. What a bug it was too, lasting from the Monday night until the Friday night. It did, however, give me chance to reflect and send lots of messages to Rob about my future plans as a triathlete.
"Have you thought of a Half Ironman?" Rob asked on one message.

The honest answer was I had thought about it. It was something that I potentially wanted to work towards, in a few years maybe if I was still enjoying competing in triathlons.

"I mean next year Deb." Rob had replied.

Now that I hadn't thought of, not at all. I was planning year two to be open water as my major achievement, more sprint triathlons and maybe, just maybe, an Olympic distance. A half Ironman, not so much.

We did agree, however, that I would stay on a challenging training plan, as I wanted to continue to push myself. I just needed to get well to start training again.

Chapter 36

It had been over a week since I had last done any exercise. I was starting to feel human again, all the unfortunate symptoms of the bug had subsided and I was back eating normal food instead of the bland things like toast or crackers that had featured so heavily whilst I was unwell. The fact that my nutrition had been poor for a week had taken its toll. My face had erupted in spots like I was a teenager again. I felt sluggish and bloated.

I had needed to take quite a few days off work sick. I hated taking time off. My previous illness when I had the swine flu and heart problems had resulted in me needing to take months off and even though I was healthy now, every day I needed to take made me feel like a liability to my employers. I know that everyone gets these viruses, I know that everyone gets colds, it is inevitable at some point, however, the fact that I am diabetic throws another spanner into the works in that I also have to try and walk a tightrope with my blood sugars too. Any illness can send them spiraling out of control. I hated that. So, I just wanted to get back to work as soon as possible.

On my first day back, a Monday morning, I had decided that I needed to do my run before work. I was expecting to be tired that day, it's weird how any time off makes you shattered on your first day back, whether you've been off through illness or holiday. I'd set my alarm for 6am thinking I could manage a quick 4k run before getting ready for work.

I was awake at 5.45, before my alarm. Phil, surprisingly, was also awake too. He got up, he'd decided he was going to cycle to work. This wasn't an option for me, I was working from a different office that was too far away. I got up too, thought I'd start my run a bit early.

I started to look for my running clothes, I honestly didn't know where they were. They weren't in the usual cupboard. I was guessing that they were at the bottom of the washing basket, I'd hardly done anything whilst I was unwell, certainly not any household chores like washing. I grab cycling leggings and a t-shirt instead. They'd have to do for today. However, it was cold October morning and all my running leggings were cropped so I convinced myself it was probably be for the best anyhow. I dress, and head downstairs.

Phil was making a coffee.

"Have you done lunches for today?" he asked.

I had bought salad leaves, there was ham in the fridge and there was still some salad dressing in the bottle that I'd made previously.

"I haven't assembled it." I reply "I'll sort it when I get back."
I grab my cycling jacket off the back of a chair in the kitchen and head towards the front door setting my watch to record my run. As I fly out of the front door, I yell to Phil.
"I haven't got my keys and I haven't got my phone." and I was off.
It was still really dark outside, even the street lights didn't seem to make a massive difference. I was a few streets away when I was struck with a thought, I didn't have a water bottle either. This was going to be interesting I had never been for a run without taking a drink with me.
The first kilometre I was flying, probably helped by the fact that it was mostly downhill. It was good to be back in the game. I realised how much I missed exercise when I wasn't able to do it.
The second kilometre I had slowed slightly, probably as this was also where I hit my first hill. I became conscious that up ahead that there were two men, dressed in black, walking slowly. I had become accustomed to seeing dog walkers on early morning runs, but the sight of two men walking alone struck me as a bit odd. As I approached them, I got thinking about the recent sexual assaults that had happened to female joggers a few miles away. OK, these attacks had been by a sole male perpetrator, but I suddenly felt vulnerable and regretted leaving my phone at home.

As it happens, I passed them, they wished me a good morning and I felt more relaxed. Why was my mind working overtime? These men were probably just on their way to work or something.

I turned at the end of the road and was faced with my nemesis, the big hill, the massive hill. It was a what goes up, must come down moment. I'd had the joy of the downhill at the start of my run, now it was time to climb the beast. I ran for a bit, but the absence of a drink, my mouth as dry as a desert, I slowed to a walk. I struggled even with the walk, my saliva felt thick in my mouth, it was disgusting. I turned back into the housing estate, a flat section again, and I picked up the pace to a brisk jog again. Even though I had become rational about the men I had seen earlier, I was still not 100% secure. As I ran through an alley that I regularly run through I felt vulnerable again, it was dark, no street light in this. I convinced myself that the worst that would happen would be that I would run through dog poo. As I reached the end, onto another street and the reappearance of street lights I see two shadows on the road, I turn quickly to see who behind me. There was nobody there, both shadows were mine, a trick of the street lighting.

I got angry with myself. "For fuck sake, Debs, you are not the kind of person to be afraid of your own shadow!"

I complete my 4k run, and reach my front door.

"How was your run, Debs?" Phil asked. Concerned that it was my first run after my illness.

"Fine." I lied.

I had come to a decision; I was a wuss running in the dark. I would need to re-consider my early morning runs. God forbid, I may need to change them to treadmill runs instead. A couple of months later, after realising I wasn't actually a wuss and having rediscovered my lady balls, I was to have another disconcerting morning run. This time I had an encounter with the law.

It was early, around 6.30am, it was pitch black and a fresh December morning. I was about 2 kilometres into my run when all of a sudden, a police car pulled up along side of me and stopped.

The officer wound down the window and said. "We have had reports of suspicious behaviour in the area."

Indignant, I responded, "I'm not suspicious. I am a triathlete and I am training."

They left and I continued my run, insulted.

It was only some hours later after I had taken to Facebook to voice my distain that Nikki, one of my club friends said: "They were probably wondering if you had seen anything suspicious, Debs, it's always runners that see burglaries and find dead bodies."

That was when it had dawned on me, I was running near where a few attempted burglaries had taken place, they were hoping I'd be a witness. I felt like a tit.

Chapter 37

He had been toying with the idea for a while. Watching my speed and the pleasure I was getting from my road bike, Phil had come to the realisation that he wanted one. It was an idea I wholeheartedly supported.

One morning we made a decision, we both had quiet days in work, so that lunchtime we would go to Giant and look at bikes.

I had one condition in my mind. Phil couldn't get a better spec bike than I had. Call me selfish, but buying my road bike was a big decision, and I was competing on mine. Phil wanted his to come on training rides with me, he had no intention of entering any races, and with that being the case, he wasn't going to get a better one than me.

We drove to Giant to look at options.

"I may get a carbon fibre bike." he joked in the car on the way.

"You're bloody not." I replied.

When we walked into the store, I saw one of the staff members, he knew me from when I had bought my bike and said hello. We explained that we were now looking at a road bike for Phil. It took under five minutes to find the perfect one. A men's version of my bike, same specifications and everything. He test rode it in the car park and we said we'd take it. I love making spur of the moment decisions.

The first ride we had together was a revelation. I had a twenty-mile ride on my training plan. We had decided to cycle a familiar route and also do a few laps of the road I had used to time trial. Phil took to the new bike with ease and for the first time in months we were keeping pace with each other. I'd push him and he'd push me, but we were on a level playing field. It made me far more positive about cycling together.

As we eased off a little at the end, Phil turned to me and grinned.

"This bike doesn't half get a decent speed up."

I nodded and grinned back. I sensed I was really going to start enjoying some training rides with my hubby and this made me very, very happy.

Cycling with Phil was a joy. We were enjoying our cycling commutes on our hybrids too. However, as they had opened a new campus for the University on our work commute route, the cycle paths were getting much busier than they had been before.

On one cycle home, I noted something. That cyclist wasn't wearing a helmet. He was the first student type cyclist we had passed that commute, so I decided I would count them. For no reason other than my own curiosity.

On cycles to work at 7am we wouldn't see any student aged cyclists, only commuters like ourselves. On our cycle home at 4pm we would see a lot.

Over the three mile stretch from the city centre to the campus, I counted 39 student cyclists. I had also counted how many were wearing helmets. Four of them, that's right, these may be academic scholars studying towards their futures, but only just over 10% of them had the good sense to wear a helmet. I'm sure their mothers would be appalled, shocked and horrified. I know I was.

Chapter 38

The day had arrived for my second 10k race, the eponymous Richard Burton 10k. A race held in the honour of the actor who was born in the Afan Valley village where the race was held.

It was a struggle to wake up. The night before, I had been performing as a bassist, I hadn't arrived home from my gig until gone 1am. I had then awoken with cramp in my calves at 4am.

I felt pitiful as I moaned to Phil.

"Why did I agree to run this today?" I moaned "I'm too old to be a rock star and a triathlete."

He laughed at me, but knew full well that I knew what I had done when I signed up to it.

I dragged myself out of bed and made my famous race breakfast and sat on the sofa with Sophie cat, lamenting my appalling sense of organisation that I had agreed to do the race.

I left the house a bit on the late side if I'm honest. So it came as no surprise to me that parking had become quite a serious issue in this sleepy village. Panic set in as I realised that I had to park about a kilometre away and walk to the registration. I was hoping that I wasn't cutting my time too short.

As it happened, I was in plenty of time. I registered, got my timing chip, t shirt and my race number. Having the t-shirt then concerned me. I was on my own, I didn't have anyone with me and my car was parked a kilometre away. There was no way I would have chance to take it back to the car and get back in time for the race to start.

"Do you have a bag drop or anywhere I could leave it?" I asked the girl.

"Sorry." she replied, whilst shaking her head.

What was I going to do with my t shirt?

I make my way to a table at the side of the room to sort out my timing chip and my race number.

The timing chip was an ankle one like they use in triathlons, not the usual shoe lace one or plastic strip on the race number that I'd had in previous races.

A fellow competitor asked me for help as I was attaching my ankle chip.

"Do you know how these things work?" he asked me, adding "I've never used these in a race before."

"Yes." I replied, "We use these all the time in triathlon. Do you want me to give you a hand?"

He nodded and I took his strap and wrapped it appropriately around his ankle.

"We look like a bunch of tagged criminals." I added as I stood back up.

He burst out laughing, "That's brilliant!" he says through the laughter. Finally, I get the right response to that joke!

179

With my chip around my ankle and my race number attached to my running vest with safety pins I was ready to head outside and hopefully find a few of my club friends. Considering it was a November morning it was actually surprisingly hot and I didn't feel cold at all in my running vest. I walked near the start and found a group of Celtic Tri members. I wave as I approach them.

I walked up to Sian first, as she greets me, I say.

"I haven't got a clue what I'm going to do with this t-shirt." "Leave it with my husband." she very helpfully replied. So that is what I did. I told her that I'd get it back from her at some other time so that she didn't have to wait for me to finish. Sian was fast, I was slow, and knowing she had been working nights I didn't want her to hang around to wait to give me my t-shirt.

We spoke to other members, Tracey, one of the coaches was racing with some friends that she was training to run the London Marathon for charity. Other experienced and the more elite members were also there, we chatted away. Even though some of these members were Ironman achievers (male and female) and could achieve amazing things in the sport, they were still super encouraging towards me.

"I'm going to be last." I said to Tracey.

"It doesn't matter if you are." she replied, adding "At least you are doing it."

I truly believed I would be last. My 10k personal best was just under an hour and a half. Looking at the last two years' results, the last finishers finished a good 5 minutes ahead of my PB. However, I was positive about this. I didn't mind if I was last. This was about me doing it, about me getting another t-shirt for my collection and getting another "shiny thing" when I crossed the finish line, it was all about the medal. And, of course, if you are last you are getting the best value for money on your entry fee!

The gun went off, and off we all went. I watched as my Celtic Tri friends got further and further away from me in the distance. By about 2km in, I turned and looked behind me, nobody had overtaken me for a while, so I wanted to check what I was already suspecting, I was last. I grinned to myself, my predication was correct.

One very interesting thing about being last, is that there is always someone behind you. The sweep, clearing up the back and ensuring safety. The sweep in this event was a man on a bicycle.

"I'm sorry you need to cycle so slowly." I said as he was cycling along side me, slower than snails pace.

He grinned at me, "That's ok." he said.

He would stop for a while and chat to marshals, then cycle and catch me back up. I felt like I was being stalked as I kept sensing his approach behind me.

As I continued to run, some local residents were outside their houses cheering.

"I'm last and I don't care." I shouted to many of them as I slowly ran past.

And I really didn't mind at all, I was actually really enjoying the race. I imagined what it would be like nearer the front of the race whilst people were running at the same fast pace, running together. My run was a solo attempt, I could see a few runners in the distance, but there was nobody with me. It was like a formal training run, on my own, doing my own run at my pace.

My watch vibrated to let me know I had hit another kilometre milestone, 4km. I looked down at my watch and realised my pace was looking really decent for me. By this point, I had already run up a few inclines, I knew that I would have more downhills in the latter half of the race. I felt strong and proud even though I was slow.

A few minutes later I passed a house, it had bunting, loud music playing and a few generations of a family cheering very enthusiastically. A lady who looked around my age shouted to me.

"You are looking really strong and really fresh."

She was right, I felt strong and I felt like I had a lot to give. I was running my race intelligently. Not feeling intimidated by faster people, running at a comfortable, achievable pace for me.

The section to the 5 kilometre mark was a very steep hill. I knew it well as it was the hill that led to a car park at the start of a cycling trail that was a frequent route for Phil and I. I walked up the hill, there was no shame in that. As I walked, I caught up with the woman that was the last competitor ahead of me. She was stopped.

"Are you OK?" I asked.

"Yes, just my knees." she replied. I was actually surprised how old she was up close, she was incredible.

I reached the water station and after learning my lesson not to gulp water from the Swansea 10k, I instead had the marshal to top up my own water bottles which I had in a running belt. I'd be able to take my time and drink when I needed it.

I ran across the famous viaduct and saw a Celtic Tri member taking photos at the end.

He cheered, "Come on Debs, you are doing brilliantly."

At the 6km mark I looked at my watch again, I realised I was heading for a personal best. I only had 4km left and my splits were far better than my first 10k in Swansea. I had also finished the hills, it was flat and downhill for the rest of the way. I couldn't stop grinning.

The older lady caught me up again.

"Is this your first 10k?" She asked me.

"No, my second." I replied "and I'm heading for a PB."

"Well done." she said "It's not about times for me anymore, just finishing."

We ran together and chatted for a while. I told her about my diabetes and previous heart problems. She told me that she was 77 now, but had been a serious competitive runner in her youth but had never lost her love of running. At 7k she said.

"I'm going to ease up now, but you keep going."

I could see she was struggling running on the downhills but admired her for continuing to run, at her age, with her dodgy knees.

I was catching up to another runner, she was wearing a Swansea 10k t-shirt and she now had a target on her back. I was feeling strong, I was going to catch her and overtake her. It was my mission.

We played a cat and mouse game for about a kilometre, I'd overtake her, she'd overtake me, I'd overtake her again, she'd overtake me again. However, I could see her pace slowing and mine was increasing knowing I didn't have long left. I overtook her for the last time, and on glancing back occasionally I could see her dropping further and further behind me.

It was the final kilometre, I'd lost my bicycle stalker now having two women behind me. I looked at my watch again and started to cry a little, I was definitely going to get a personal best. I was definitely going to do it.

As I approached the finish line, I could see Sian, Tracey and David from the Tri club all along the finishing straight cheering me. I felt so much pride as I crossed the line and got my medal.

I walked back outside and collected my t-shirt from Sian. "Thanks for waiting." I said to her, knowing that she really needed to be in bed.

I walked back to the car with a spring in my step. I'd just had a PB. I didn't know the exact time but it was a few minutes better than my previous 10k race in Swansea. I saw a few club members on the walk back, and when each of them asked how I'd done. They were really pleased and supportive when I told them I had a PB.

When they published the results later in the day, my time was 1 hour 22 minutes and 53 seconds. I had shaved a massive 5 minutes and 58 seconds off my PB. Delighted is an understatement to how I felt!

Chapter 39

Cycling outside is awesome. The sensation of the wind in your face and the sense of freedom is one of the greatest joys I know. I love cycling, of the three sports it is my biggest passion and love (partly due to the fact I can share it with Phil too).

However, there are times when cycling isn't practical. When it's too wet, when it's too windy and when there is too much ice and snow.

At these times, cyclists have a few choices to make. Some don't cycle at all, some use a spinning bike, some have a turbo and some have rollers.

I first considered an indoor trainer a couple of years before I started my life as a triathlete. I liked the idea of a turbo, but it was a big decision to make. Luckily a friend in work had a turbo that they were able to lend me, so one Christmas I was lent a turbo. I discovered something. I hated it! I didn't like the static feel to it, it was harder to rotate the pedals. I decided a turbo was not for me. I was glad to return it.

"We could try rollers?" Phil had usefully suggested.

We went to two bike shops, neither would let you try rollers in the shop. Also, I didn't have a friend who could lend me a set.

"Shall we just buy them?" Phil had asked.

It wasn't a cheap investment. We read up a lot of the pros and cons of them.

Pros

Use your own bike on them.

No need to have an extra back wheel to clip in.

Cons

Bloody hard to balance on the things. They are considered by many to be a death-trap.

On reading tips online, they suggested cycling on them in a doorway, that way you could stop yourself from falling by hitting the doorway instead. We decided we had the ideal doorway between the living room and kitchen and we bought a set.

For anyone not familiar with rollers, basically it is a frame, at the back of the frame are two large cylinder rollers, your back wheel sits between these and it is what makes you static, and not hurtle across the room into furniture. On the front is one large cylinder roller that your front wheel sits on. The front roller and a back roller are joined together with a giant elastic band.

I will never forget my first time on them. I hadn't been that unbalanced since my stabilisers were removed when I was a child. I collided with some considerable force with both sides of the doorway, ended up bruised and could only tolerate ten minutes at a time it was so knackering. So hardly surprising that they didn't have a great deal of use until the start of the "off" season.

"Have you got a turbo?" Rob asked on one email.

"No, but I do have rollers." I had replied.

With the bad weather starting, these rollers would become my friend. I was scheduled to do three cycling sessions a week. If the weather was too bad to commute by bike or go on a long social weekend ride then the rollers provided an ideal alternative.

I am getting much better on them now. Granted my balancing isn't fantastic, but the reliance on the doorway is becoming less and less and I can now manage an hour on them. It is still a very hard workout though.

Chapter 40

It had got to the point where I had been running consistently. I was slow but I could keep going. I'd finished two 10k races and was running around three times a week. I remember one day looking at my training plan for the week ahead, and seeing three runs scheduled in my plan, one 3k run and two 5k runs and I found myself thinking "Oh, only short runs this week".

I caught myself, stopped myself, and came to a realisation. I was a proper committed runner now. I think anyone who views running 5k as a short run must surely be a committed runner. I thought back to my early runs, my early couch to 5k days when I felt that 2k was a distance that was a monumental challenge. However, suddenly, and without any real notice, 5k had amazingly become a short run. I almost had to pinch myself. How did this woman, who 6 months previously couldn't run to the end of the street, now view 5k as being short?

It did make me think, 10k was achievable but challenging. However, I had signed up to complete a half marathon. Would I ever get to the point where I would think of 10k as being a short run?

All these thoughts gave me a moment of clarity. I was turning myself, slowly but surely, into something roughly resembling an athlete. Granted, by taking up the sport in my forties I was never going to achieve any form of athletic greatness, but I had turned myself into a fitter, and dare I say it, happier version of my former self. I loved exercise, I loved the endorphins it gave me, and if I'm honest, I loved that I could eat a bit more nice calorific food, like cheese, safe in the knowledge that I was burning it all off.

When I started to run and hit the 5k mark people would say "Do a parkrun."

A parkrun for anyone that doesn't know is a 5k race that takes place up and down the country at 9am on a Saturday. However, at the time when I needed one the most, the nearest one to me was quite a distance away. It was disappointing, I'd have quite liked to have done one.

After a while, when I was running more and running longer distances, I discovered it was happening, Swansea would be doing a parkrun down the seafront. I was excited at the concept and registered on the website.

The first event came around quite quickly, I had arranged to go with Christine, Sarah and a lady I hadn't met before called Sue. We all piled into one car and headed to Swansea. It was a rather wet day, not uncommon in South Wales but we were all excited about the arrival of the park run.

We parked up a short walk away, and debated on whether or not we needed coats.

We walked across the road and it was very windy. We gathered inside the coffee shop that was going to be the regular host for the event, we huddled together in the cold whilst waiting for the start.

It was actually a nice run once it started, although my jacket was soon removed as I got warmer as I ran.

Mother Nature had decided to be kind to us, and the rain stayed away the whole run.

Whilst my running distances had improved, my speeds had not, I came last out of the four of us. However, Christine had been slower than usual. As we sat drinking a post race coffee, she told us that her foot had really been hurting for a while. We were to discover a couple of weeks later that it was in fact a stress fracture and she needed to take some time out from running. I knew how awful this was going to be for her.

I was unable to do the park run the week after, however, the week after that I was in. A few club members had agreed to go. However, when I woke up it was absolutely bucketing down.

I traveled alone to the venue, Christine wasn't running due to her injury and Sarah had a children's party to attend. When I arrived, I looked for my club mates, but could only find Jo.

In many respects it was lovely that it was just the two of us, it was great to have a catch up with Jo. As we looked at the torrential rain, we gave ourselves kudos for being the only ones hard enough (or stupid enough) to run in that weather. It was freezing, made worse by the sea breeze. When the race started, Jo ran with me for a while, but I was soon telling her to go ahead. By this point hailstones had started to fall. They stung as they hit my skin, and even my eye balls, ouch! This was not a great day for a run. The puddles were deep and my feet were soaking.

I realised I was towards the back of the race (story of my life!) as the walkers that had been at the first parkrun were not in attendance at this one. I watched as the faster runners passed me on the return along the opposite side of the path. I was envious that they would soon be able to get into the dry.

As Jo passed me on the return, we gave each other a soggy high five.

I ran with a woman and her daughter, who must have been about 11 years old, for a while. At around the 3.5k mark, the daughter had obviously become fed up with both running and the weather. Her Mum bribed her with pancakes when she finished.

I said, "Can I have pancakes too?"

The Mum laughed and we chatted. She asked whether I did anything else apart from running. I told her about triathlons. She said she wouldn't mind giving it a go but she was worried about being rubbish.

"I'm rubbish." I told her proudly "It doesn't stop me."

I'm rather embarrassed to say that on this run, the first book in my tale had been released and I told her she should read it to see that she could do triathlons and that she should check out Celtic Tri.

The daughter gave up running, and I continued. As I reached the seafront on the last little stretch, the wind almost blew me to the finish, Jo was there with her husband and son, they were shouting at me to do a sprint finish. Which I did, and managed to knock 3 seconds off my PB. OK, three seconds isn't much but a PB is a PB!

Parkruns were great, and my training plan permitting, I was hoping to do more. What a lovely way to start a weekend. They have now started one in the woodland park behind my house. Parkruns, they are a bit like buses, you wait ages for one and then two come at once.

Chapter 41

Rob had encouraged me to add cycle trips to the club Facebook page. He thought it would be good to have some company from fellow club members. I had done it a few times with no success, however, one Sunday in the pool I got talking to Jo and she agreed to come cycling with me the following Sunday morning.

I posted up on the page that Jo and I were planning a 25-30 mile cycle around the Gower coastline and would anyone want to come.

As the day approached, Anna (who had signed up for an Ironman and was swimming with us) and Adele (who had completed Ironman competitions) also said they would like to come. With Phil wanting a nice ride on his road bike too, the five of us gathered at the seafront ready for our ride. The weather forecast had said it was going to be dry but cloudy, however, less than a mile in and it was raining that fine awful rain that makes you feel really wet. Personally, I didn't mind. The weather had been so bad I had completed far too many rides on my rollers and far too few outdoors, so I was just glad to be outdoors.

Amazingly, this was the first time I had ever cycled with someone other than Phil. I had never found myself cycling in a peloton before. It was a little disconcerting; I was used to Phil's cycling style alongside me. I was amazed how closely to me Adele was cycling. It was a very valuable lesson for me and I enjoyed having a chat with her and finding out more about her. Whilst I had interacted with her online, I had never met her in person. She gave me confidence that, one day, doing a half Ironman would be well within my grasp.

Phil seemed to be really enjoying being out on a ride with four women, he was like Charlie with his angels. He cycled with everyone and chatted to everyone.

I was enjoying the route that Jo had picked. A mixture of cycle paths and roads. I was conscious that the pace was slower than I had anticipated, I didn't know if it was due to us all being too polite to say "Get a move on" but this ride was about being social and having fun, and so the speed didn't really matter. It was actually great to be out in a group.

We had cycled around 15/16 miles when we were on a single-track road. Jo had warned us that there was limited traffic and if a Range Rover came hurtling towards us, then get out of the way, as he never gave any consideration to his two wheeled road companions.

A mile or so down the road, Jo was up ahead and I heard her shout "cattle grid". I have always had a bit of a fear of cattle grids. I had been over a few on my hybrid and found them a challenge, balancing was a real issue on them. I had, however, never been over one on a road bike and I had never been over one in the rain. I panicked. Totally panicked. Panicked with huge and shocking consequences.

My first mistake was I hit the breaks.... Wrong!

My second mistake was I put my foot down.... Wrong!

My third mistake was being unable to keep my balance as I slowly slid over it... Wrong!

I totally lost control of my bike, I had somehow become completely powerless.

Everything became slow motion as I knew that I was going to fall off. I looked, helplessly, as I could see myself heading for the ditch to my right. I shouted to my friends, rather unhelpfully.

"And I'm off." as I started my decent off the bike into the ditch.

I repeated over and over in my head "Please don't let me land in the water, please don't let me land in the water." but inevitably, that was exactly what happened. I landed into approximately two foot of muddy, freezing cold water.

I lay there, feet in the air, resigned to the fact that from my knees to half way up my back I was submerged.

"Oh shit, Oh shit." I hear Jo yell.

I see Phil jump off his bike and run towards me, Adele is also at my side within the seconds.

"Are you OK?" she asks.

"Is my bike OK?" I reply, being a total and utter cliché, it was unintentional, it was just genuinely my first thought when I realised I had no pain.

I seemed to be in the ditch for an eternity, but in reality I'm quite sure it could have been no more than a minute. Adele tries to yank me out. I am too wedged and too heavy. Phil grabs my other arm and between the two of them I am pulled out of the water, I am soaked and I am totally covered in mud.

"Come on then, let's go." I say.

"Are you sure you are OK?" Adele asks, the concern evident in her face.

"I'm fine, let's go."

We debate for a minute or so.

Did I want to knock the ride on the head? No!

Did I want to find a shop to get dry and warm up in? No!

Did I just want to continue and forget what had just happened? Hell yeah!

I'm not going to lie, I was wet, even wetter than everyone else despite the rain. My feet had taken on board a lot of water, and every time I needed to put my foot down it squelched.

I was uncomfortable, granted, but I just wanted to continue my cycle with my husband and friends.

Adele cycled alongside me, she was obviously still concerned about my well being. Worried I'd get too cold. However, I just chatted as if nothing had happened.

"You've got balls of steel." she said to me.

Anna said, "You have so much mental strength.", that or I'm just mental I think.

And then Jo came out with the best line so far.

"Deb, you may not want to know this, but I have a camera on the back of my bike, we may have just filmed that." AWESOME! I so hoped it had been filmed. I had started giggling to myself seeing the funny side to my stupidity, the thought that we may all actually be able to watch it was brilliant.

"I so hope you've caught it." I said to Jo.

The rest of the cycle was less eventful, I struggled with a hill and ended up walking it when I lost my gear (I'm blaming mud on the ring), I had to walk down a steep hill when I got too scared about the gradient and the ability to brake (Ok, I admit it, I was a little shaken up by my fall). And when my friends announced that they couldn't feel their feet anymore, I was actually reassured. I didn't want to tell them I'd lost the feeling in my feet as I had presumed it was a "wet ditch" related sensation.

We arrived back at the meeting point, said our goodbyes and headed off to our respective homes.

Chapter 42

Phil drove the van home. He had a tarpaulin in the van which he draped over the seat so I wouldn't get it dirty and wet.

He laughed at my muddy ponytail and ears.

I shivered, uncontrollably, I needed to be home and I needed a hot bath.

However, I also laughed. In fact, I couldn't stop laughing. I laughed so much at my ridiculous level of stupidity that I actually gave myself hiccups. Phil laughed and told me, tongue in cheek, that I had brought shame on our family. Whilst he drove, I posted on Facebook on my phone. A thank you to my friends for a lovely, but eventful, cycle. Phil and I both agreed that, ditch excluded, we had both had a lovely time. We had enjoyed the company and we had enjoyed the route.

The longer the journey seemed, the colder I felt. As soon as I got home, I ran upstairs and started running the bath. I instantly took off my wet clothes. My shoes were heavy with water. At this point, I realised how muddy everything was. I was caked in mud. I've seen people do cyclocross who have been less muddy. I start laughing again, stood naked at the top of the stairs and I start to hiccup again.

With my bath running, I sit on the end of the bed and look at Facebook. Jo's husband Mark had just posted to say how he had just watched the video footage and he couldn't stop laughing. Yay, it had come out. I messaged him "Please send it over when you can."

The club site becomes a hive of activity, people asking "What happened?" "Is everyone OK?" "Eventful?", my cycle mates added "The ditch was deep.", "Class act Debs, definitely hardcore." adding to the mystery of what had happened on this fateful Sunday morning jolly on the bikes. My bath run, I get in. I'd purposely made it hotter than usual. The feeling still hadn't come back to my toes. I lay there and as I scrubbed myself with a flannel the water became blacker and blacker. I had never seen such dirty water in a bath. I realised I was just sitting in my self-made bog and really I needed to get out.

I wrapped myself in a towel, I was still shivering, I added a dressing down over the towel, I was still shivering. I went downstairs and sat in front of the coal fire that Phil had lit to warm me up and I slowly started to defrost.

By this time the video had come through, I watched it and the tears rolled down my cheeks as I laughed like never before, I really was a tit of epic proportions.

Phil watched it, he's in total hysterics.

I message Jo. "Can I share this video?" I ask, thinking I wanted her permission as it had come off her camera. She replied "yep of course."

And so it was shared, on my club Facebook page, on my Unlikely Triathlete page and on a Facebook group I had recently found called Pathetic Triathletes, as, let's face it, that was totally pathetic.

In total my video got around 200 likes on Facebook, so good to have given a load of people a good laugh.

I still went swim training in the afternoon, although as I walked into the changing room instead of being greeted with speech, I was greeted with laughs. It made me happy making people smile and if you can't laugh at yourself then your life must be pretty rubbish. I wore my error with pride.

Chapter 43

Ho Ho Ho!

Not being a social athlete in previous years, I had never realised that social sporting events were held during the Yuletide season. The first one was the local Santa Dash 5k held at the seafront.

The day before the race the Met Office announced a severe weather warning for gale force winds. I suspected that the race may have been cancelled.

I woke up and checked Facebook, there was no mention of a cancellation, so I guessed it was going ahead. I watched as the trees behind my house were swaying chaotically in the wind and started to feel a little apprehensive.

"You aren't really going to run in this?" Phil asked me.

He knew it was a stupid question. I knew I would be seeing a lot of my club friends and the concept of running 5k dressed as Santa was an idea that intrigued me.

I left early to ensure I could get a parking space. As I sat in the car, I felt the movement of my car being pushed by the gale force winds. I couldn't believe that this large metal box was being forcibly moved by the elements. What on earth was going to happen to me?

Then I saw something rather amusing. Have you ever seen a seagull fly backwards before? No, neither had I. However, this poor seagull was flapping his wings with all his might and was being pushed backwards with the winds. I felt sorry for the little fellow, who quickly realised he was literally getting nowhere and brought himself to land. I started thinking about what the conditions would be like and was astounded that the event was going ahead.

After a while sat in the car, I made the short walk to the pub that hosted the registration. I registered, collected my Santa suit and looked around for my club mates. I spotted David and headed towards him. His wife Clare was with him, I had been speaking to Clare on Facebook the night before. Whilst we hadn't met in person, we were virtual friends and this was her first 5k.

"You feeling OK today?" I asked her, as she had been nervous the day before. She nodded.

Steve, Lynette, their son Owain and a few other people were also there. Owain had competed in the children's race and was showing me his t-shirt that he had received. I started to put my Santa suit on over my running clothes. I realised it was actually rather warm and asked Steve if I could leave my running jacket with him as he wasn't running.

I was genuinely shocked that they were allowing the race to proceed.

With only minutes to go, we walked to the start line, the winds were incredible and the sand blew in our faces like a cold version of a Sahara sandstorm.

"We must be bloody mad." I said to Lynette, who was walking sideways to try and avoid a face full of sand. At the start line, with so many people crammed in, there was some respite from the winds. It was a spectacular sight seeing so many people all dressed in Santa outfits. The run itself hurt; the sand being blown into your skin was painful. I soon deployed my Santa hat in a new purpose, a shield to protect my eyes from the sand. It worked, and when I reached the finish line I was proud to have completed my first ever 5k Christmas race in under 40 minutes.

The following day I had signed up for a charity Christmas jumper cycle. I didn't have a Christmas jumper, but luckily Christine (the other Christine) had one that she could lend me. This event was terrifying to me. Firstly, the winds were still pretty dreadful (although not gale force) and secondly this was a group of around 40 people cycling together. This was peloton city!!

The first 5 miles I really struggled with the peloton, people passing me on the left, people passing me on the right, people cycling too close to me, people braking ahead. I was tense and stiff on the bike and tried to keep my senses razor sharp. After a while though I relaxed and enjoyed the experience of having lots of different people to chat to. At the end of the 20 odd miles I decided I'd attend another group ride in the future.

The next Christmas related tale is not training related at all. It was Christmas Day. A quiet day just Phil, his Mum and I. Before his Mum arrived, Phil said something which both surprised and thrilled me.

"Deb, I'm going to do my first triathlon next year."

"Really?!?" I replied.

"Yes, I'm going to do Pencoed."

And that was that. My Christmas was made. All I needed to do was get him back in a swimming pool (after his 30-year absence) and get him started with running.

When my mother in law arrived in time for lunch, she gave me money to buy a wetsuit! This was indeed a very triathlon related Christmas.

Photo: At the Santa Dash

Photo: Christine and I at the Christmas jumper ride

Chapter 44

I think those of you that have read my previous books will appreciate that when you train whilst managing a chronic condition that there are issues attached.

A few weeks before Christmas I had been suffering with swollen ankles. A conversation with a GP I'd never spoken to before resulted in me being taken off a blood pressure medication as an experiment as swollen ankles were a common side effect. I thought nothing of it.

It was the day after Boxing Day, Phil and I decided to go for a nice long cycle to clear the cobwebs and to burn off some of the mince pies we'd been eating. We set out to do around 25 miles.

Our planned route was from Briton Ferry to the Mumbles sea front and back again. We parked the van in Briton Ferry and headed out. As we reached Swansea and the start of the coastal path it became apparent that the planned route could not be achieved. Over the festive period, sand had blown all over the paths into little sand dunes rendering the path unsafe for cycling. We contemplated the road as an alternative, but even that was sandier than it should have been. We made the sensible judgment call to turn around and resigned ourselves to the fact it would be a shorter run.

I can't say I was overly disappointed by this. I had been suffering with headaches for a few days, a fact that I had put down to the fact that I had been drinking a bit too much wine.

We were cycling home, we'd gone up a third of a mile incline which led to Briton Ferry bridge, the start of which continues this gradual climb. We'd just hit the top of it when I had the worst pain I have ever experienced. It was a headache so severe that it felt like someone had just hit me full force in the back of the head with a baseball bat. I stopped my bike, got off and collapsed on the floor. The pain intensified as it moved up the back of my head, over the top and to my forehead. My whole head now in total agony.

"Are you OK?" Phil asked.

Long story very short, I rested until the Dr's reopened. When I saw the GP, I discovered that my blood pressure had sky rocketed. I also discovered that I should have had a different tablet prescribed and shouldn't have been taken off the tablet I was on without replacing it. It was a scary and interesting lesson, and knocked my confidence a bit. I may feel invincible when I train, but ultimately, I am a woman with health issues and I need to be careful.

Chapter 45

Phil was a week or so into his training plan. His running was surprising me (he could already run 3k virtually as fast as I could) but his swimming was proving harder. In his youth, Phil had been a very talented swimmer and swam for a local club. There was a time when he could swim a mile with relative ease and he could sprint against the best of them. However, as he got into his teenage years, he lost the love of swimming and quit.

In the 30 years that followed, Phil barely got into a swimming pool. He had got in on a handful of occasions only. Even on holidays to apartment complexes with nice warm swimming pools he would never get in whilst I swam. He had been to the pool on his own, armed with my spare pair of goggles. He had come home deflated that his breathing was to pot and he couldn't even manage two lengths.

"Come to swim training with me." was my reply.

And so he did. He struggled the first week, not really knowing what to expect. But on week two he went armed with his completed membership form and annual fee and a smile on his face.

Both being in lane one (the easy lane) we would bug each other and make fun of each other and have banter.

"Are you two having a domestic?" Tracey the coach asked. We laughed.

"Are you always like this?"

We nodded.

Although, we both worked hard in the pool. Phil started to relax and chat more to the coaches and other swimmers and I enjoyed my swim, mostly oblivious to the fact that he was there.

I was, however, very glad. The most important member of my family, my husband, had joined my new family of the triathlon club.

Phil insists that he is doing the one triathlon at Pencoed and that will be it. However, dear reader, that is how I first started and look at me now!

I don't believe for one second, he will only do the one. It was only a few months ago he cycled in jeans without any "added protection", however padded shorts were added to the wardrobe or his "cock and balls pants" as he affectionately refers to them.

"I'll never wear Lycra." he confirmed. However, this was also short lived, as he's now got running leggings.

"I'm wearing shorts to swim." was his initial assessment. However, in the post this morning arrived a pair of "budgie smugglers" skin tight shorts.

So, at the moment I'm taking things with a pinch of salt. He even bought us floats this week for the pool. Hooked? Phil? Never!!

Chapter 46

There are days where training has a comforting monotony about it, and days where it's really out of the ordinary.

I woke up one particular day thinking the only unusual thing would be swimming in a new pool. The Afan Lido had recently opened its doors, a state-of-the-art swimming pool run by Celtic Leisure, the same company that ran my local swimming baths.

In my local baths, I had an early morning swim card, this entitled me to ten early morning swims and could be topped up when they ran out. This system suited me, as I tended to go to the pool twice a week.

However, early morning swims had become frustrating. With my speed and skills improved, I was encouraged by my friend Norman (the man from my earlier book who's name I didn't know at the time) to move up from the big open section to the lanes as I was just too fast. So I did.

However, this was not as straightforward as it sounded. Firstly, there were only 3 lanes. The furthest was used for coaching up-and-coming youngsters, next was the faster lane, then the slower lane. I was in the slower lane. On quiet mornings this was fine. However, on busier mornings it became impossible to train. Living in this lane (and I mean living as he does four kilometres every day! Or 160 lengths!) was this older gentleman. He swims a mixture of strokes, one being backstroke, badly, with arms flailing like he's about to drown. With only one or two other swimmers in the lane this can be worked around. However, some mornings there have been 7 of us in the lane. Including the antithesis of slow old man, inconsiderate fast guy. The polar opposite, who will swim over you soon as look at you and will display such inconsiderate behaviour in the pool that you are left at the end of the pool thinking "what the fuck is happening here?".

This one particular morning was my proverbial straw that broke the camel's back. I had been clouted by slow guy's flailing arms twice, not an usual occurrence albeit frustrating. Then I saw fast guy get in. My heart sank. There were 5 of us in the lane, he would make 6. I continued on, watching as he'd pound up the lane, oblivious to the carnage he was causing. When the inevitable happened and he overtook slow guy swimming straight onto me, I tantrummed.

I got out of the pool in a temper and I complained. The rather unhelpful response was "If you don't like it then try the Afan Lido." I checked my early morning swim card would be valid, I was told that it would be. So this particular morning I did.

I arrived at the Lido, armed with my new floats that Phil had bought me, and walked up to reception, excited about trying this new facility.

"We don't accept early morning swim cards." I was told.

It was like a red rag to a bull. "I checked and was told you do!" I replied, angriliy.

"It was the original plan." the assistant replied "but they didn't set the computer up to accept them."

We chatted for a while whilst I voiced my frustrations. He'd previously worked in my usual pool so he could appreciate it. He let me in the pool regardless, nice chap.

The pool itself was lovely, I shared a lane with one other chap. We stuck to our own sides and I did my drills with ease. It was a pleasure.

I'm not entirely sure I like the new pool from a functional perspective. The changing rooms are unisex, the showers are communal so you can't have a proper shower and the lockers are weird. But for an easy swimming session it was golden.

This particular day of training was going to get even stranger. The day before I had a 40-minute slow paced run on my training plan, however, work had got in the way and I didn't manage it, so I had made the decision to "double up". I started my run, and it wasn't long until a little tortoiseshell cat joined me, meowing loudly. Being a big cat fan, I acknowledged her and gave her a little fuss. She kept running alongside me. Weird, I thought, but I kept going feeling sure that my little companion would turn back, but she didn't.

I decided to do a small loop, it's just under a kilometre, so I wouldn't be taking this little miss too far away from her home and territory, thinking she would drop me and return home. But she didn't, she just kept with me. When my pace slowed a little, she would go in front, turn around and meow at me as if to tell me to "Get a move on."

This feline motivator stayed with me for my whole run, even coming up to my front door with me. She waltzed in like she owned the place and finished off my own cats' food (much to their disgust). I was concerned about the little girl though, as I didn't know where she was from or where she lived.

I phoned the vet.

"Hello, I've been followed on a run by a cat, she's followed me home, can I bring her in to see if she's microchipped and where she lives?"

I was told by the vet receptionist to bring her down right away, but if she wasn't chipped they wouldn't be able to do anything to help me.

Thankfully, she was chipped and only lives around the corner from me, so I was able to return her home.

However, that is one workout I don't think I'll forget in a very long time.

Chapter 47

A watt bike centre, Cycle Specific, had opened up not to far away from our club's area. A few club members had gone for various fitness tests and training sessions and they started offering club sessions.

A watt bike, for anyone who doesn't know, is a state-of-the-art training bike which can measure your pedal efficiency, your cadence, your power output, basically can say how effective you are as a cyclist and how you could improve. I was intrigued to give this a go. I know that these bikes were used by the British Cycling team to improve power and performance and whilst I know I was firmly nowhere near this camp, curiosity had got the better of me.

So, one Saturday, I signed up to the Celtic Tri session at Cycle Specific.

I drove to the venue, playing disco music in the car to try and motivate me and make me feel lively. I was in equal parts excited and terrified.

When I arrived, I realised that I was the only person who didn't have clips on their shoes, I would need flat pedals, although I was strapped into them just like I see with the sprinters in the Velodrome.

We started a gentle pedal, just to get us ready before the proper warm up commenced.

I looked around at the other club members, they were the elite of the elite, there were more Ironman tattoos that you could shake a stick at. However, I decided "in for a penny, in for a pound" I was going to give it my hardest effort and do my best to keep up with the elite, if it killed me.

Dylan, our coach, started the proper warm up .

"As you are all hardened triathletes," he started, my ears pricking up with alarm bells, "I'm going to give you the same warm up as Team Sky and British Cycling."

Holy shit!! Talk about out of my comfort zone. Increase your cadence, increase your cadence, 3 mins at 110rpm. Harder, harder, harder, and this was just the warm up. A call was made for a 6 second sprint, how high can you go? I actually surprised myself getting to 180rpm and 400watts of power.

I thought back to a video I'd watched of German sprint cyclist, Robert Förstemann powering a toaster to make toast. He needed to maintain 700 watts of power to do this. I was suddenly overwhelmed by his incredible strength, having been a long-time fan of his thighs!

With the warm up finished it was onto the main session.

"How many of you have signed up to Ironman Wales?" Dylan asked.

Hands went up around the room, obviously not mine!

"I thought so," he replied "so I've recreated the course and the hills for the main session."

I could have cried there and then. I knew I was in for a pounding. However, pain is temporary, achievement is everything, I was going to keep pedaling and try my hardest.

In the main, I could cope and keep up. The one area where I did have an issue when when the resistance was highest and we were asked to do out of the saddle efforts. Whilst my elite club friends were powering out of their saddles like it was a walk in the park, I'd manage 5 to 10 seconds before I'd have to recover in the saddle again. But that was OK. A year ago, I would have collapsed after the warm up. I got to the end of the session and felt proud that I had done my best. On arrival home I did some research on statistics on power. It is all about power to weight ratio. On the whole I managed around 1.6, deeply pathetic and puts me firmly in a recreational cyclist camp. However, I did manage short bursts at 4.9, far more respectable. Until I read that Emma Pooley, awesome triathlete and cyclist, typically maintains a power to weight ratio estimated at 5.1 when she races! I've seen her race and she is awesome (and super light weight!). However, when you try something like a watt bike for yourself, it does even enhance your respect and appreciation for elite cyclists. For me, well it was a fun and hard work training session. I know my limitations, I'll never be elite, but at least I always do my best.

Chapter 48

Mike, one of the coaches, put on the club Facebook page that he was planning a regular Sunday morning ride for some of the slower club members. He's quite an amazing individual is Mike. Week after week he supports the running track, the junior swim sessions, the senior swim sessions and now was planning a regular cycle too. Mike is also a paratriathlete, he has a disability which makes his legs weaker. However, this does not stop Mike from doing everything he wants, despite his pain. He's currently training for another Ironman. I have no end of respect for Mike, he is living proof that disabilities didn't need to stop you.

Anyhow, this first Sunday ride came around. We met in the carpark of a bike shop at 9am. There were a few of us on the ride, some which were quicker but fancied coming along. I was on my hybrid as my road bike was in having work done.

Turns out my arms are too short for my body. I'd been struggling with my road bike for a while, cramping up when I'd been on it for too long, and I'd come to the realisation that I was more comfortable on my hybrid. After a conversation with a bike mechanic, whilst sat on my road bike, he could instantly see the problem. My arms were each 2 inches too short! A decision was made, I was getting my road bike converted to a flat bar to suit my tiny arms!

So, back to the Sunday morning bike ride. We'd cycled up a mile incline and back down the other side and had reached our first flat bit of road. The road was quite quiet, meaning Mike was able to pull up alongside me and chat. "Deb, you are going to hate me by the end of this ride." he said.

"Why?" I replied, inquisitively.

"Because I am going to do some bike skills with you."

The ride Mike had chosen was beautiful, part road, part cycle path flowing along the coast. As we started to reach the path, on the last stretch of quiet road, Mike sidled up to me again.

"Deb, I want you to take your left hand off the handlebars and put it on your left thigh."

I knew where this was going. He was going to get me to step out of my comfort zone.

"I can't." I replied.

"Yes, you can. Take you left hand off the handlebar and put it on your thigh. You are pedaling forward, you are OK. Do it."

I paused, momentarily, trying to pluck up the courage to do it. I did it, my balance felt slightly off but soon corrected itself and I returned my hand to the handlebar.

"Now the same with your right hand." Mike continued.

I found this harder than my left hand, but still did it.

"Now I want you to do the same again but keep your hand on your thigh for 5 pedal revolutions." he said, matter of fact, instantly upping the anti.

I managed the 5 of my left, only 3 on my right.

"Good." Mike continued, unwilling to stop this bike development. I wondered if these were the same exercises he did with the children when he developed those.

"Now I want you to put your left hand on your right hand."

I pedaled for a little while trying to pluck up the courage.

It was hard, but I managed it.

"Excellent, now right to left."

Again, I tried to build my confidence to do it.

As with the first exercise, I found it harder going from right to left.

"Now I want you to do this." Mike said, pulling slightly ahead of me. I watched as he put his left arm behind his back.

"There's no way I can do that." I replied, alarmed.

"Yes, you can." was Mike's simple motivational response.

"I can't Mike, I can't." Fear well and truly taking over me.

Mike gave me a look.

"Why can't you?"

"I'm too scared."

"You can do this."

I continued to cycle up the road, I focused on the road and tried to block out the thoughts that were flooding my head that I was most definitely going to fall off.

However, my left arm went behind my back and returned to the handlebars without incident. I knew what was coming next.

"Now your right hand."

Again, it took me several seconds to switch off the demons in my head that was telling me I couldn't do it. My arm went behind my back and returned to the handlebars.

"Brilliant." Mike beamed "Now keep practicing those things until we reach the cycle path, as that's where the next part cuts in."

We reached the start of the path a few minutes later. Mike explained to the group that he would be continuing to do bike skills with both myself and Sonia.

Sonia has recently joined the club, she's a great girl who actually found the club through messaging me on my Facebook page. She'd said she wanted to join a club but didn't think there was one in her area. That's when I found out she was living in Swansea and told her to come along to Celtic Tri, she was now hooked and we had become friends.

Mike had commented that he noticed that neither Sonia nor I were drinking whilst cycling. This was skills reserved for the cycle path, no traffic, safe environment to learn.

As Mike was saying this, Sonia who was stopped, stood over her bike, dropped her bottle in the sand, thus making it undrinkable from the bottle. I'm not entirely convinced this wasn't a deliberate move!

We set off down the path, Mike was soon next to me, talking me through the process of my leg position needed to reach for my bottle.

I was terrified, I was so far out of my comfort zone that my brain was screaming at me, adrenaline running through my veins, I was in definite flight mode. I didn't want to fight. However, as I listened to Mike, I thought about the other moments when I'd felt like this. I thought of Rob and how he got me to put my head under water for the first time. I came to a realisation, it was only my fear that was stopping me. I can now confidently swim with my head under water, I could do this too. I had lady balls, I was no shrinking violet, I was going to do this.

"Reach down and touch your bottle." Mike said.

I did.

"Great, now this time grab it and pull it out, you know where it is."

I did it.

"Hand it to me." Mike said, so I did.

"Well done Deb, that's the first step."

He handed me the bottle back.

"Now rest it on your knee, grab it at the top, and slot it back in."

I did it! This was easier than I thought.

"Now do it again and take a drink." Mike said.

I pedaled, I stopped my legs in the position Mike had talked me through, I grabbed the bottle, I rested it momentarily on my handlebars, I took a long sip, and I returned it.

Then I gave Mike a high five. I had done what I thought was unimaginable, I'd drunk whilst cycling.

"Keep practicing." Mike said as he cycled off grinning.

When we reached the turnaround point, I'd done it a few times and felt confident.

"Well done Deb." Jo had said, impressed as she had known of my fear. "Now cycle just behind me and I'll get a video of you doing it."

Jo was becoming my official videographer, and at least this one was better than me falling in a ditch. I did a confident thumbs up at the end, and realised I was quite content cycling with one hand off the handlebars. I was turning into a proper cyclist.

Just before we reached the road section, I cycled next to Mike and I thanked him. I was overwhelmed with his support and for everything the club had given me so far. I didn't hate Mike like he said I would at the start of the ride, in fact the complete opposite, I adored him!

As we were cycling down the road, I was able to use my new found skills in anger. I'd drunk when the road was quieter (didn't want too many cars around in case I did stuff up).

Then I was approaching a roundabout, Jo and a few others were quite a way ahead. Sonia and Mike were quite a way behind. I needed to turn right, I put my arm out and indicated. However, a rather obnoxious woman in a Silver Ford Focus would not allow me to pull across, she was intent that she was overtaking me, on top of the roundabout. Then she did exactly what I suspected she may do. She turned LEFT at the roundabout, crossing my path and I nearly went into her. However, with my new skills, after slamming on my brakes to avoid the near inevitable collision, I started doing V's in the air whilst hurling abuse, she beeped at me in anger. Of course, she owned the road and as a cyclist I had no right to be on the road.

However, I was not prepared to allow this one idiot to spoil my day, as I cycled back to the car park I was beaming. I could finally cycle and drink. I was finally becoming a proper cyclist.

Chapter 49

Phil and I were due a holiday! We had booked to go to London to the World Track Cycling Championships. We tagged on an extra couple of days just in London before the cycling.

On the Tuesday, we had headed into London for the day. We had taken our cycling helmets with us. A decision had been made that we were going to rent Boris bikes! OK, I know officially they are called Santander Cycles, but everyone knows them as Boris bikes. When Phil had first made the suggestion before we left South Wales, I insisted that we pack our helmets. I was not about to cycle around London without some head protection.

We left the Science Museum and found a rental place. Phil had rented them a few times previously when he'd done some work in London. I, on the other hand, was a Boris bike virgin. I found the whole rental process really easy. Shame riding the damn thing wasn't as simple! Firstly, it is built like a tank. I mean, I'm quite sure that mopeds are lighter than them. With such a heavy cumbersome bike which only has three gears, riding at any speed is a near impossibility. I did my best in Hyde Park to give it some welly. Top gear, as much of a cadence as I could muster. 14 miles per hour! Pathetic! An average speed of 7 miles an hour during our short rental term.

I can see that they have an excellent purpose, I love the idea of them and think more cities should follow suit. However, hand on heart from a personal perspective, I'm not a fan.

I was a fan of something else though. We had chosen a hotel in Stratford so we could walk to the Velodrome every day. This meant we were on the doorstep to all of Olympic Park. I knew I had to do something. I had to swim in the Aquatics Centre. I looked at their early morning swim times, and headed off from the hotel one morning to go for a swim. Phil had chosen not to come with me, choosing instead to walk to the Velodrome to see if he could see any cyclists and get their autographs.

I got into the pool, it was beautiful. Surprisingly, I had a lane to myself. I guess I must have missed the early morning swimmers who would swim before work, but got in before the non-working parents had got in after dropping children off at school. I had done quite a few lengths and was taking a quick rest at the side of the pool when I saw him. The Adonis. This was a truly perfect specimen of a man. He was tall, large muscular shoulders, perfect muscles in his chest, defined and manly, a six-pack stomach, arms with biceps which were big enough to be seen, but not too big. He had a tattoo around the top of his arm, the black ink only just showing though his dreamy chocolate coloured skin. This man was simply stunning.

228

I then recalled something that Phil had told me. He'd remarked a few weeks earlier that he found it disconcerting that he couldn't see my eyes when I had my goggles on due to the mirrored lenses. And it struck me, this guy wouldn't be able to see my eyes either! I instantly pushed off the side doing breast stroke. Forget training, I was going to have a long perv at the hunky man!

He walked up the side of the pool and got into the empty lane next to me.... Result! I waited to see him push off from the side. I was sure that his swimming would be as beautiful and he was. I was wrong. The Adonis pushed off, started a rather dreadful doggy paddle, got 10 metres up the pool and began coughing and spluttering as he ended up under the water. It was so what I was not expecting, however good on him anyhow. He was obviously learning to swim. I returned to my front crawl, thinking it wasn't really that long ago that I had been swimming doggy paddle. I did, however, continue to enjoy the close-up view of his perfect legs as I looked at them underwater!

The five days of track cycling were exciting, wonderful and exhausting. I really enjoy watching the track centre as well as the races. When I see the elite, on rollers, no hands, it really does make me see the difference between normal cyclists and these heroes. The heroes of the week were definitely Team GB who topped the medal table. I just hope they can do it again in Rio.

Photo: On a Boris Bike in London

Chapter 50

I could delay it no longer. The time had come. I had to do it. I needed to be ready. I was to become the owner of a wetsuit.

I had scheduled a Saturday morning as "D-day". Christine had decided she wanted a wetsuit too (having borrowed a wetsuit last year). I asked Phil if he wanted to come too.

"I'll come, but I'm not buying a wetsuit." was his reply.

So, we picked up Christine and headed to Sharks Swim Shop, run by the lovely and knowledgeable Leah. Her business is mostly online (so if you need anything swimming related, she's the business), however, she does see local people in her living room.

Her house was like a shop, racks of swim suits, wetsuits, shelves full of goggles and swim caps. It was like a sweet shop for anyone loving the water.

Leah started with Phil.

"You aren't shy are you Phil?" she asked and before you could say front crawl, he was stripped to his boxer shorts ready to try on wetsuits.

The first one Phil tried on, an entry level suit, looked perfect on him. He looked surprisingly handsome as he stood head to toe in rubber (no, I haven't developed a weird fetish!). The second suit he tried wasn't as successful. He'd managed to get both legs into it, but as he tried to pull it up his legs it just wasn't going.

"I can't get it up." he said, frustrated.

Christine and I burst out laughing as we found his statement amusing. We laughed, we laughed and we laughed some more. Leah began man handling my man into the suit, but it was obvious that he wasn't comfortable. As he peeled it off himself as quickly as he could he announced "I'm having the first one." I knew he'd get one! Christine went next.

"Oh God." she exclaimed on realising it was her turn. "Now you are all going to see my leopard print knickers!" Thankfully, Leah respected Christine's modesty more that poor Phil's and gave her a trisuit to put on over her underwear, guiding her to a private room to put the suit on. In total, Christine tried three and we all agreed that the one she had decided to buy was the best. Whilst it took a while to get on, she actually was able to take it off fairly quickly. As she said "Let's face it, you can take as long as you like putting one on, it's taking it off quickly in transition that matters."

It was then my turn. Leah also handed me a trisuit, but I was happy to put it on over my underwear in the living room. I mean, both my husband and my dear friend had both seen me naked!

Using Christine's transition logic, when I tried on a clearance wetsuit from last year's stock that Leah was prepared for me to have at a rock bottom price, when I took it off with relative ease I had decided that was my wetsuit. I was thinking finding one for me was going to be slightly trickier, Leah reckons I have thin legs and decent boobs. I don't think my legs are thin, and in honesty, I don't think my boobs are that decent anymore (they have shrunk since I've been training, although in fairness everything has shrunk!).

We added a few extras in neoprene caps, wetsuit socks and all left as happy campers with our new additions to training. Now all we needed was the sea to warm up a bit so we could get in open water.

Chapter 51

Time was whizzing by at an alarming rate. The "off" season was nearly over and I needed to make sure I had my mojo and my "on" switch.

My first race of the season was to be a duathlon. The Vale of Glamorgan duathlon. It was to be held at a race circuit, with the two runs taking place on the race track, and the cycle taking place on the surrounding roads.

I had asked Phil to work out the cycle route for me. In fairness to Phil, this GPS ability is an amazing talent of his. He works out the route, goes onto Google Earth for some visual reference points and then drives me around it before we cycle it together.

It was coming up to the Easter weekend and Good Friday looked like the ideal day to do a recce of the course. Knowing that it was also a Club Championship race I put on the club Facebook page "Want to make Good Friday a Great Friday? Then come and cycle the Vale of Glamorgan duathlon course."

It was only after I had posted this, and had a few eager beavers wanting to join in that Phil reminded me of something. We had a big social event on the Thursday night, we had a hotel booked overnight so we could have a few drinks. We would probably not be in any fit state to cycle.

So, the Thursday night arrived. Phil and I went for an early tea first to line our stomachs for "a couple" of drinks. We met up with the rest of the social gathering and had a lovely evening where the wine and the cocktails were flowing.... lots of wine and cocktails.... too many wines and cocktails. I am ashamed to admit I had 7 large glasses of wine, and Phil had 7 cocktails. Lucky seven it was not. I awoke in the hotel room the following morning with the hangover from hell and certainly in no fit state to drive to the cycle route, let alone actually cycle it. I had to take to the club Facebook page, admit my stupidity and bow out graciously. Later in the afternoon, following sobering up, Phil and I decided that we would give it a shot. We drove to the race track, and drove the route. A few sections were single lane traffic, which at 8am on a Sunday morning would probably be perfectly acceptable. However, on a bank holiday, on one of the nicest days of the year, and being a major route to the seaside, cycling it would have been a suicide mission. We drove home deflated. Partly, as I also came to a realisation on the number of nasty hills on the route. I contacted Sian and asked her if she fancied coming with us on the Monday instead. I really wanted to cycle the route before I raced. She said she'd love to come. However, our hopes were to be dashed again with the arrival of Storm Katie and her 70mph gusts of wind on the route. We went swimming instead. I was starting to think I would never cycle the route.

Chapter 52

I was still feeling disappointed that time was running out and I hadn't cycled the route. What I hadn't expected was that my feelings of nervousness and trepidation were about to turn to despair, when what should have been a happy email came into my inbox and crushed me like a bug.

The email was the race pack for the duathlon. I read and realised I was totally screwed. The pack informed competitors that they were expecting the last cyclist back at 9am approximately with the last finisher completing the course by 9.20am. I have always been fairly good at maths, I tend to get the numbers games at Countdown, so it only took me a few seconds to do MY maths.

The race was starting at 7.30am. The first run was 5.5k. My 5k PB stood at 37 minutes and that was flat out with no prospect of a cycle and a further run afterwards. Add in the extra half a kilometre and not pushing myself too fast, too soon, I estimated my 5.5k time would be around 45-50 minutes. Then transition and then the 26k bike ride. I had driven the course, I had seen the hills. Whilst I hadn't ridden it, I guessed it would take me somewhere between 1 hour 15 and 1 hour 25. Add my pathetic times together and the cycle back time was looking to be 9.30am at best, nearer 10am at worst.

My eyes started to well with tears as I continued reading. There was to be a junior event after the adult event, they were going to be dismantling the adults' transition area at 10am, with another 2.5k to run, which I guessed would take me somewhere between 20 and 25 minutes having already endured what I would have, I realised it was incredibly doubtful, in fact pretty much impossible that I would finish the race and retrieve my bike before 10am.

The final nail in my proverbial soul-destroying coffin was to come when I read the phrase "the bike route has two cattle grids!" I had driven the route, I didn't notice the cattle grids. I am terrified of cattle grids, even more so after my ditch incident a few months before.

That was it, I was a broken woman. I started to cry. I messaged Rob, Sian, Mike and Jo on Facebook and I continued to sob. In fact, I bawled my eyes out, for three whole hours.

I had worked so hard during the off season, and my hard work was to be rewarded by crossing the finish line in my first event of the season and suddenly it looked like I was going to be forced to withdraw from the event.

Thankfully, my coaches and friends were more emotionally stable than I was and all came out with the same useful suggestion to email the organisers. It had been advertised as a novice friendly event and those times certainly didn't seem particularly friendly to a novice. As I said to Jo during one emotional outburst.

"I am so upset by this, and it has crushed my confidence. I know I'm shit, but I do my best and if they think a novice can complete it in under two hours I may as well give up this triathlon lark now."

Thankfully Jo, being Jo, reminded me that I wasn't a quitter and she talked me off the ledge in my head.

I composed the email:

"Dear Steve,

I feel I have to contact you after receiving and reviewing the race pack.

I competed in my first ever event last year with you guys at the Pencoed novice triathlon. If you look at the results you can see I was one of the last competitors but had a wonderful time and I went on to compete a further triathlon later in the season. And increased my running by competing in a few 10k races.

Looking forward to this season, I saw the Vale of Glamorgan duathlon and that it was described as being suitable for novices as well as experienced athletes. I signed up over Christmas.

However, following reading the pack I am feeling both concerned and upset if I'm honest. The pack says last cyclist in at 9am approx, last finisher at 9.20 approx and that transition will be rearranged for the junior event at 10am.

Being realistic about my abilities I am not going to get anywhere near to those approx timings. My current 5k PB stands at 37 minutes, and that is flat out and only doing 5k. I would estimate my 5.5k time is going to be around 45/50 minutes. Then the cycle, I have driven the route and know there are a few nasty short climbs (although I didn't drive over two cattle grids, so I am concerned I may have got this wrong), I'm guessing that will take me 1hr 15 -1hr 25, so that would have me arriving back into transition sometime between 9.30 and 9.55, then allowing for leg fatigue I'd guess the final 2.5k would take me 20/30mins, so realistically, I would be looking for a 9.50 at best 10.25 at worst finishing time. (And that's not accounting for any potential mechanical on the bike route).

Naturally, as you can appreciate, I am anxious as to whether I should still proceed with the event. I know for a fact that I am going to be considerably slower than your estimates and had I have known that before I had signed up I wouldn't have entered.

So, I guess my question is simple. Would you suggest that I withdraw? Are my slow times going to be an issue? I look forward to hearing from you.

Many thanks and kind regards Deborah"

I waited nervously for a response. The following morning, I received a lovely email apologising for any distress and confirming that times would not be adhered to. Ultimately, they wanted people to enjoy the challenge and the day.

Panic over, it was game on, the duathlon was back on. All I needed to do was give the cycle route a go.

Chapter 53

Phil didn't seem to mind that I had set the alarm for 6.15am on a Sunday. He'd become more accustomed to early morning weekend alarm calls since he had started his own training journey.

Only the day before, we were leaving the house at 8am, to do the Swansea Bay parkrun. Well, I say to do the parkrun, I actually had to do an additional 3 kilometres before I started it. However, we did start the parkrun together. We didn't run the 5k together though, his first attempt and he got an impressive time of 31 mins 57 secs, nearly 6 mins faster than my 5k PB! However, I'm proud of him, I'm not jealous at all, he has longer legs! (My excuse and I'm sticking to it!)

Anyhow, the 6.15am alarm call was to try one final attempt to do the Vale of Glamorgan duathlon route before the race that was creeping up at an alarming rate.

We drove to the start and were surprisingly quiet for a journey together. Usually we natter non stop, but this morning we were both quiet. I think I was still reflecting on the fact that maybe I just wasn't good enough to compete. I also couldn't get my head around the fact that I couldn't remember any cattle grids.

I shook my head free of all negative thoughts as I jumped on my bike. Since having my bike converted to a flat bar road bike I was loving my riding more than ever. No longer did I cramp up and I found the whole positioning comfortable and had an increased sense of confidence with braking (something that I would need to have that confidence with later on).

We started the route. The first two and a half miles the road surface was appalling, there were pot holes in the potholes! Although the hills were actually a little easier than I anticipated. After this first section of narrow roads and single carriageways the route took us onto the A48. The A48 is a very busy road in the Vale and has a national speed limit attached. It's a fast road. The first section was slightly uphill and then we hit the long downhill section.

242

I found myself hurtling faster and faster down the hill. I have a speedometer on my bike, but I just couldn't bring myself to look at it. I was terrified, I readied myself for the brakes if I needed them, the bike rattled underneath me. I had rarely been this afraid in my life. I get scared going above 20mph, I could feel this was faster, much faster. On reviewing my Strava data when I got home, I saw my maximum speed, an astounding 32.7mph! However, what was far more interesting was that was also the moment where I had one of my highest heart rates, not through exertion, but through sheer terror!

The next 5 miles were quite pleasant, a mix of downhill and inclines, with the inclines easier to attack as you had the speed from the downhills like a Newton's cradle propelling you back up the other side. Then at 7 miles in, there it was, cattle grid number one. It approached quite quickly, as it was at the bottom of a downhill. Thankfully my eagle eyes had clocked it and I braked heavily. I stopped, got off my bike, walked the bike around the cattle grid and got back on again.

"You are going to lose valuable time if you do that next Sunday." Phil said, disapproving.

"I don't give a shit." I responded.

And I didn't, now was not the time to get over my cattle grid fear. It was enough that I was still even planning to compete after the knock my confidence had taken with the race pack email.

The next cattle grid was about a mile later, again I walked around. The last 5 miles of the route were the hardest. There were a few nasty inclines, although I'm glad to say I didn't need to go into my lowest gears, I always had something there. I do wonder what it will be like having already run 5.5k and knowing I'd have another 2.5k to go, but I got around the bike route in 1 hour 25 mins. I do suspect I will be slower on the actual race. However, what will be will be.

We arrived home from the cycle, had something to eat. I then had a bath and ended up falling asleep. I was totally wiped out. It didn't make sense, I'd frequently go on longer Sunday morning rides and would be fine? I didn't even make swim training in the afternoon.

That night I needed to get up to wee far more than usual, I had pain in my lower back. I struggled to get to work and whilst sat at my desk I phoned the GP. They asked for me to drop a urine sample in. Typically, 6 days until the race I had come down with a urinary tract infection, I felt ill, I was on antibiotics and suddenly the race was looking in the balance again. Would I even be able to compete in my first race of my second season?

The End

Photo: Phil and I at parkrun
The End

Part Four

A new season, a new hope

Dedication 4

I am dedicating this book to my club mates. Thanks for the training, the friendship and the laughs. I can honestly say that finding Celtic Tri has changed my life. You crazy nutters rock!

Prologue 4

Hello dear readers, the time has come for the fourth part of my tale and my second triathlon season. In book two I gave you an insight into triathlon distances. In this prologue I am going to share some triathlon terms.

Age group – one of the things I love about triathlon is that whilst all ages and genders compete in the same races, there are actually a multitude of races going on. When you get your final positions, you are told your overall position, your gender position and your age group position. I think this is such a lovely idea for the non-elite version of the sport. The bands will change on different races, but nice to know that I am competing against my peers, i.e. other forty-something women.

Transition – This is known as the fourth discipline of triathlon. Transition is where you go from one sport to the next. So, transition is where you get your bike and where you return your bike to.

In book one, I had to apologise about the number of Lauras in the book. For this one, it is the number of Sians. There are four of them, each of them gorgeous, lovely and unique and sharing the same name.

Now I've explained these few things, let's get started.

Chapter 54

Thankfully the antibiotics were working quickly. Only days before, it has seemed that all the odds were stacked against me to compete in the Vale of Glamorgan Duathlon, my first race of the season. Between panicked emails, discoveries of cattle grids and then my own body deciding to throw a spanner in the works, perhaps I should have just admitted defeat and decided that the universe was telling me to pass this race by.

However, I did not want to pass this race by, I didn't want to pass any race by. I had signed up to it. I had made a commitment and every fibre of my being (ok, maybe not my bladder) was screaming at me to compete.

It was the day before the race, I was feeling almost healthy again. I was glad the antibiotics had done their job. Whilst I wasn't 100%, I felt that I was well enough to register and compete.

I had spoken to Sian on Facebook. She had not had the chance to do a trial run of the cycle route, so we had made a plan for a road trip. I would pick her up, we would drive to the venue, I would drive her around the cycle route and then we would register.

As I arrived at her house, I felt excited and nervous and it wasn't even race day. We gossiped all the way to Cowbridge, chatting like the old friends we had become. Our conversation a mix of racing, training and life. When we arrived, I turned my attention initially to discussing the route… watch for those potholes, that incline doesn't feel as bad as it looks, watch for traffic here… however, we were soon back to a usual conversation and I'd had to quickly interrupt Sian mid flow when there was something race relevant. We arrived back at the car park as the staff were starting to set up transition. She said to me "It's not the best cycle route ever", and she was right, but it wasn't the worst either.

We made our way to the registration building and collected our race numbers, timing chips and t-shirts. I was given my number, number one. I laughed, knowing it would be the antithesis of where I would actually finish in the race. We chatted to the organisers for a while and they began to tell us about their concerns that the junior race would be unable to go ahead.

"Have you seen the weather forecast?" one said, "They have forecast 40mph gusts of winds."

I had seen the weather forecast, the day before, where the winds were only showing as 20mph. I began to worry about what was to be ahead of us.

Looking down the registration sheet, we could see Celtic Tri in the club section more than any other club. A Facebook post that morning had shown that we would be out in force as a club. Many of the crème de la crème of the club had decided that they were going to race. I didn't know whether to be happy about this or not. I didn't want to let the side down by coming last.

I had already baked some cupcakes before leaving to register. Knowing that there were going to be so many club members there, I thought it would be a nice thought to be able to provide any that stayed until the end (i.e. to see me finish) with a nice sweet treat.

After I dropped Sian back off, I nipped for a pizza. Phil was out that night and I was home alone. I'd planned a small pizza, with pineapple as Phil hates pineapple on a pizza, and then a very early night.

I was about to go to bed, when there in the bathroom was a spider, it was walking across the floor and was at risk of being eaten by a cat. I stopped and smiled at it, and relocated it to safety. It was at this moment that I remembered the spider falling on me whilst I was in the shower on my very first race day. I decided that this spider was a very good omen, a sign that I was meant to compete, and I went to bed, happy.

Chapter 55

I was in a bit of a temper when my alarm went off at 5am. I had not had the best night's sleep. What with Phil arriving home at 1am, whistling contently to himself. Then Sophie, the cat, deciding that she needed a fuss at 3am, I was not feeling refreshed.

I stomped to the shower and stepped under the water before it had heated up. As usual Sabrina was straight on top of the toilet, meowing, waiting for her post-shower fuss. This made me smile and forget that I was angry.

I dried myself off and headed downstairs in my dressing gown, accompanied by all three cats, to feed them first and then myself. I quickly checked Facebook, my news feed filled with club members excitedly posting about being up at 5am on a Sunday and it must be race day.

I quietly ate my granary toast with cashew nut butter, my banana and my latte and could hear Phil walking around upstairs. He was awake.

He shouted, "Good Morning!" down the stairs and asked when we needed to leave. I told him that we had to leave at 6.15 at the very latest.

Time moved incredibly quickly as I started to put my bags together. Before I knew it, it was 6.10am, Phil was not ready, I was not quite ready. We eventually got out of the front door at 6.20am. I was fairly chilled for the start of the drive. However, this was about to change. Firstly, I was travelling with a tired and therefore grumpy husband. If that wasn't bad enough, I began to realise that I was actually at risk of not getting my bike into transition before it closed. Because of this I started to get in a temper.

Phil and I rarely have cross words. In fact, our rare angry outbursts are usually over as soon as they started.

However, this particular morning, when I was running late for a race, he was pissing me off in a major fashion. He denied whistling when he arrived home at 1am, he scoffed cakes from the box for his on the move breakfast, but the final straw came when I asked him for the tablets I had put on top of the cake box which he categorically decided I had forgotten. I knew I hadn't forgotten them, I knew exactly where I had left them, on top of the cake box that he had taken several cakes out of. Although tired, grumpy, "man-looking" husband could not see them. I wanted to cheerfully strangle him.

When we arrived at the venue with literally moments to spare before I would have been too late to race, I hurled abuse at him as I angrily walked off with my bike to transition.

Sian caught up with me "You OK Deb?" she asked.

"No." I replied, in a temper, "he's doing my fucking head in!" He soon arrived at our sides asking me where he could pitch up and take photos. I snapped at him that I was racing and he needed to find out for himself. I was not in a good place, but hoped I could channel my anger into the race.

However, I began to relax and feel happy and proud when I looked around at other competitors. It was Celtic Tri club kit as far as the eye could see, like a sea of red and black. As we all gathered together for the race briefing at the start line, we crowded together. We were like a Celtic Tri army.

Chapter 56

The gun went off, the race was in motion. The first run was advertised as a 5.5 kilometre run. However, at the race briefing we were told that the previous route needed to be discarded after the death of a runner following an incident with a car, and so instead we were to do 5 laps of the traffic free racing track.

I began running, instantly falling behind the faster runners at the front. Only half a lap in and I was already last runner and a gap was opening up between myself and the lady ahead of me. As I finished the first lap, I looked at my watch. This wasn't 1.1 kilometres, this was not going to be the 5.5k run we had signed up for. I had only just started my second lap when I was passed by the fastest runners. Their speed and running skill was exceptional. As I continued to run I was being lapped by more and more people. As Celtic Tri runners would lap me they would say words of encouragement to me. I felt supported by my faster, more experienced and fitter team mates.

At every lap, at the same point, was Phil. There with his camera taking photos of everyone from the club. My anger at him had passed and I smiled at him every time I went past. As I started my fourth lap, Phil shouted "I'm off to take photos of the bike leg if that's OK." I nodded, I certainly didn't want him to miss anyone.

I was about half way through my fourth lap when Sian passed me on her final lap. She shouted as she ran past.

255

"Lying bastards, this isn't 5 and a half kilometres."

"I know." I replied.

I had already passed 5.5 kilometres and this was my fourth lap. In fact, even though I was very slow, I was quite sure that I had achieved a personal best at 5k and was feeling rather chuffed with myself (upon checking Strava later, I had. I had knocked over a minute of my previous personal best and now had a 5k PB of 36 minutes and 8 seconds).

I was on my last lap. I became aware that I was the only person I could see left on the track. Everyone else had already started their cycle, I was behind by minutes. As I was coming up to the final straight I could see someone running towards me. That someone was Lilian from the club. She was there supporting her super speedy husband and wasn't racing herself. However, she was going to join me for the last part of my run to give me moral support and to give words of motivation as I was to get onto the bike.

"I've been where you are Deb." she said to me, as she ran alongside me in her normal shoes, normal clothes and big coat. "Keep going though, as you are doing brilliantly."

I'd first met Lilian on my very first trip to the club, and whilst we had seen each other a couple of times in between and had chatted on the group Facebook page, I think she appreciated the hard work and effort that I was putting into my training having now seen me race.

I appreciated her wanting to help me, to encourage me.

I ran into transition with a spring in my step, even though I had run 1.5k further than I had expected. Running straight to my bike, the only bike left on the racks.

I joked to the marshals, "I'm going to have a problem finding my bike."

They laughed.

I ran up to my bike and instantly broke the first rule of triathlon and started to remove my bike, before I put my helmet on. This is a total no no and can incur time penalties if you are caught doing it. As one of the marshals started to run up to me, I instantly realised what I had done. I yelled "sorry, sorry" and re-racked my bike as I put my helmet and gloves on.

The marshal joked back at me "Yep" he said "the advantage of being last in is that you can find your bike. The downside is we are all watching you."

I laughed, he was good humoured, and could see I had made a genuine mistake.

With my helmet on, I unracked my bike again and headed out. As I cycled to the exit onto the main road, I could hear the safety motorcycle start their engine and leave behind me. I had my own safety bike, as I was in last place.

Photo: With Lilian keeping me company

Photo Credit: Phil Jones

Chapter 57

My bike felt alien underneath me as I came to a realisation. I had never cycled after running before. My triathlon training had given me "brick" sessions where I went from swimming to cycling and cycling to running, but I had never done a run to bike. I regretted this obvious lack of foresight. The first few minutes were a real struggle as I tried to get up to a decent speed on the first few kilometres, not helped by the appalling road surface.

I had cycled up the first major incline and was forced to take a quick break at the top, this was harder than it was when I had done a practice run. The safety bike overtook me and proceeded to the junction to wait for me. I quickly got going again, reached the junction and turned left onto the major road, the A48, along with my motorised support. At first this road is flat and a small incline, I was just getting to the top of the incline when I saw another competitor, dragging his bike at the side of the road. I stopped to offer assistance.

"Do I have any tools to help you?" I asked, not wanting him to give up if he had a puncture that I may have been able to give him what he needed.

"No." he replied "My race is over now." He waved me on, as I approached the descent.

On my first attempt at the descent, I had reached a speed of 32 miles an hour and terrified myself. However, there was something rather comforting about knowing that I had a safety bike behind me, there to give me protection, and so I continued to pedal hard and push myself. I was still terrified, don't get me wrong, but I was prepared to take an extra gamble. I wasn't entirely surprised when Strava was to tell me later that I had reached 37.6mph on that stretch! The turn point soon came, and a mix of brief climbs and quick descents were to follow. Then it was a left turn up a hill. I reached the top of the hill and I knew what was coming next. The downhill to cattle grid number one. I had decided, whilst speaking to Phil, that I would take an alternative approach. Rather than fully dismount my bike and walk around the gates to the side, instead I would come out of the saddle and walk myself and the bike over the grid. It did the job perfectly, although I was guessing the safety bike was wondering what I was doing. As he pulled up alongside me I felt the need to explain "I hate cattle grids" I told him. He nodded. I looked at the motorcyclist again and a realisation hit me. He was my friend's father, at least I thought he was. My friend's husband runs a safety motorcycle and media motorcycle company. His company did a lot of these events and I knew my friend's Dad often did safety bike duties. So I asked.

"Are you Lucie's Dad?"

"Yes." he replied "I'm Jeff. You must be Debs, Lucie told me to look out for you."

It was a wonderful moment. I had been struggling on the bike, I was tired after a 7 kilometre run when I'd only expected 5.5, my legs had struggled with the move from run to bike, but now here was someone I almost knew, and his job was to keep me safe. I felt positive and pushed myself a bit harder.

It was about a mile further along the road that the winds hit. We had discussed in the registration the day before about the potential of 40 mile an hour forecast winds, and now here they were, blowing in my face as I was trying to power up a hill. They were the kind of unsettling winds that any sane person would not have attempted to have cycled in. Gosh, if this had been a training ride, I would have stopped and waited for them to subside. However, I couldn't stop, I was racing. Appreciating the new danger in the conditions, Jeff pulled up alongside me and said.

"I'm going ahead to check on the competitors ahead, I'll be back behind you soon."

I nodded, appreciating the explanation before he passed me and left me alone.

I reached a long stretch and could see a competitor ahead of me. It surprised me if I'm honest, I was so far behind on the run that I really didn't expect that I would catch another competitor. It was a good motivation through the wind to have someone in my sights. My progress was slow but I was narrowing the gap.

I had reached another hill, I could see Jeff at the side of the road at the top. On this hill I experienced the worst winds I have ever cycled in, with the winds full force in my face as I tried desperately in a low gear to power myself, firstly against the elements and secondly, against the hill. I looked at my speedometer, I was going 4 miles per hour, a pathetic speed, I would have been faster walking up. The hill, whilst short, seemed to take forever. My lungs were exploding as I was panting desperate to try and get air. I reached the top and knew I had to catch my breath back for a minute and to stop and have a proper drink. I put my right foot down on the ground and the searing pain hit me. My calf had gone into spasm, it had cramped up like I have never experienced before. I let out a cry of pain, and had to get off my bike for a minute.

Jeff looked at me, the concern evident in his face "Are you OK?" he asked.

"My calf has gone.", I replied "I'll be OK in a minute."
I stood at the side of the road massaging my calf for a moment, knowing I needed to get back on the bike and on my way.

I got back on and started to turn the pedals. The agony was excruciating, however, at no point did I think I would give up. I actually screamed out loud at my calf "You stupid fucking calf" I yelled "You are going to finish this race if it kills me". My calf must have been feeling co-operative as about a mile further down the road the pain had subsided from tear inducing to just wince inducing.

I saw I was making up the gap on my next competitor again, and when we reached the next hill, I bit down on my lip, hard, diverting my pain to another part of my body as I pedalled hard on the next hill, determined to catch her and overtake her. As we pulled side by side, she turned to me and said "These winds and hills are killing me."

"Tell me about it!" I replied and I was off, the brow of the hill approached, I was heading back down the incline quickly. The cycle element was drawing to a close, the road had mostly flattened out. My calf continued to cry out in protest and I began to dread the final run that I knew was ahead of me. A bit of maths in my head had told me to anticipate a 3k run instead of the promised 2.5k, although how I was going to achieve that whilst my calf was in so much pain I didn't know. Just two laps of the track, that was all, just two laps.

I almost missed Phil at the side of the road with his camera, he took his photos of me and I told him that there was still one person behind me, but he didn't hear me. At this point she had fallen behind and was nowhere to be seen.

As I cycled back into the race track, competitors were leaving the car park. The bike racks were mostly empty as people had already moved their bikes. It was almost a scene from an apocalypse movie, a lone soldier, cycling back to a deserted place. The winds blowing over the large metal barriers that surrounded the transition area.

"Can you put your bike on the front rack." a marshal asked me. I nodded, and was grateful as the rack where I was originally situated was about to be hit by another windswept barrier. I racked my bike, took off my helmet and gloves and tentatively started to run.

Chapter 58

I couldn't run, the pain in my calf was too severe. However, I was going to do the last distance if I needed to crawl it. I walked briskly. At points, I tried to pick up the pace into a slow run, but after a few steps the pain would increase and make me walk again.

As I reached the home straight on the first lap I could see Phil running towards me.

"Are you OK?" he asked.

"No." I replied "My bloody calf has gone, I can't run."

He stayed with me, and looked like he was going to accompany me on the last lap.

"Please stay here." I asked him "I need to do this on my own."

I really didn't need the pressure. I could see that the lady behind me was now on the track, and whilst I didn't think she would catch me I needed to battle this on my own. I didn't need the distraction of my well-meaning husband. I continued, constantly looking for the other competitor. Whilst I didn't mind if I was last, being last but one was a slightly better result.

I managed a few short stretches of runs, just a few steps at the time, but as I approached the finishing straight again, I was joined by Lilian, who walked with me for my last stretch. She told me how much courage she thought I had. She had previously entered this race and had withdrawn during the race for calf pain like I was currently experiencing. I was not going to quit. With the last few metres, I forced a run and crossed the finish line. I was handed a medal, which I was not expecting, and I felt elated.

I instantly joined my club mates, all who congratulated me, as I did them. I got the cakes off Phil and handed them around, thanking people for hanging around when they really didn't need to.

I found a St Johns' Ambulance and managed to get a few ice packs for my calf. However, even though I was in pain, I was proud. It had been, without question, my hardest race to date. However, I had proved to myself that I could overcome difficulties, I could overcome unexpected changes, I could overcome mother nature and I could cross the finish line. I may have been the last Celtic Tri member to cross that line, but even through that I had achieved a 5k PB and my fastest ever speed on a bike. I had reason to be pleased with my performance.

Chapter 59

There is a new coaching kid on the block at Celtic Tri, his name is Rich. He had put up on the club page about a whole range of triathlon training sessions geared at the novice. For the first time, there was actually going to be formal cycling coaching aimed at adults. Phil and I had decided that we wanted to attend a number of sessions, so had printed off a schedule and stuck it on the fridge.

The first session we went to was a swim session, focussing on body positioning and breathing. It was a session I definitely needed. Whilst I was enjoying front crawl and now enjoyed my head being underwater, I needed help with honing my technique. After an hour in a cold pool, I had found the ideal head position for me, and was finally confident with how I would turn my head to breathe.

The second session was some bike skills. I had read on the schedule "Mount and Dismount", I was initially afraid that I would be encouraged to do the kind of flying dive on and off the bike that I had seen professional triathletes do, and was both delighted and relieved that it was, in fact, going to focus on the skills of "static" mounts and dismounts. Definitely less likely to end up with a visit to A&E.

Then it was a bike cornering session and skills on riding in a group. This relied on hand signals and proved my confidence that my previous bike skills I had done with Mike were firmly embedded.

We were back in the pool for the next session, focussing on "catch and pull", the technique on how to best use your hands and arms whilst swimming. Despite Rich's best efforts, these skills still elude me. I still need to focus and improve on this area.

Running was to focus on high heels and fast feet, I joked on the club Facebook page that I never wear high heels and I don't have fast feet. In reality, the session focussed on how slightly changing your technique can improve speed. I listened intently to the session and tried my best to achieve what Rich was asking of us.

The final running session was about stride length. Having short legs, I knew this would be beneficial to me, if I could increase my stride, I could go quicker without running faster.

I really enjoyed this new addition to the coaching calendar, and what every session had in common was Rich's relaxed and friendly style. Giving you confidence and making you truly believe that you could do it. I decided I liked Rich a lot.

Chapter 60

Having an alarm call at 5am on a Sunday is an interesting experience. This particular Sunday morning it was more interesting than usual, as I wasn't racing. It was the day of the Cardif Try a Tri and five of my friends from the triathlon club were going to be doing their first triathlons.

Mark. What can I say about Mark. I was in school with Mark and hadn't seen him for a quarter of a century when I banged into him at a coached swim session. His daughter is a very talented junior triathlete and I think Mark was hoping it was genetics she had from him, so was giving his first one a shot.

Karl. A genuinely awesome top guy who Phil and I both refer to as "a bit of a ringer", for someone who purported to have never swam, he was suddenly an instant fish. When he said he was having a gentle run to get around on a park run, he did a sub 25 minute. However, we were to discover that Karl was a former professional athlete, an ice hockey player. So in many respects it stood to reason that he would be talented.

Meinir. A lovely woman, young, dedicated and juggling the commitments of triathlon training with having a young family. I am always in awe of people who can balance this and do it so well. A truly genuine and friendly girl and had become a good friend in a short space of time. I was to discover afterwards that she had already signed up to a half ironman. And whilst I have been in the process of writing this book she succeeded in the half ironman. Whilst looking after a family with four children under ten years of age. Hardcore!

Karen. She had only recently joined the club but had already become a proud member, even borrowing some club kit from me to race in. Karen is one of those women that can always find the right thing to say. I always feel blessed knowing women that truly want to boost other women's confidence and be a supportive friend, and Karen is one of these ladies, she's gorgeous.

Sonia. Sonia featured in my last book. Her sense of humour always cracks me up. Although, it always amazes me how much she lets self doubt creep in. She's made some massive achievements, is improving week on week, yet she will frequently have crisis of confidence. She doesn't need to. Sonia, if you are reading this, you are amazing, don't you ever, ever forget that!

So the famous five were all set to race, Phil was set to take photographs, and I was armed with my best cheering voice and cupcakes!

We arrived at the venue and saw Meinir and Karen in the car park. They both looked fresh and strong and ready to undertake the challenge ahead of them.

Phil and I walked from the car park to the leisure centre and saw coach Rich there, also ready to provide support.

The leisure centre was small, and the only place to view the swim was from a glass window in the café area. I grabbed a table so we could observe our friends. When I say we, it was myself, Rich, Mike the coach who had also made the journey and Mark's wife Sara (who was later to be joined by pretty much the whole of Mark's family!). Phil was already out at his prime vantage point to photograph the bike and the run, and I was under strict instructions to text message him when each member left the pool.

Sonia was in the first swim wave. I knew she was more worried about her swimming than anything else. However, I also knew that she was very capable of the swim distance having seen her smash it at many a coached session. She waved from the far end of the pool as she was about to get in.

The race started and Sonia began her first length, her front crawl looking perfect. The other end of the pool was right by the window. As she reached the end, she waved again at me. This made me laugh, only Sonia would wave mid race. She swam amazingly and soon was out of the pool and on her way to transition for the bike leg.

Next in the pool, in the same wave, was Meinir and Karen. Both swam strongly. Then it was Karl and Mark. Both of them registered outstanding swim times, and on their last laps, Rich and I quickly headed out to transition.

As Karl mounted his bike, it was a textbook mount, so much so that Rich turned to me and said

"Is he taking the piss?" obviously thinking that Karl was exaggerating the technique that he had taught us.

However, that was not the case, this was just Karl, being Karl.

Whilst our five members were out on the course, I chatted to Mike and Rich. I had been tempted to sign up to the Llanelli Sprint Triathlon, both encouraged me that I should. I had originally planned that Blenheim Palace would be my first open water triathlon, but with one on the doorstep in a couple of weeks it was a tempting proposition.

Before we knew it, each club member returned safely from the bike leg and began their run. And a short time afterwards Celtic Tri had five new triathletes. Seeing the joy on every one of their faces made me glad I had gone up to support them.

Chapter 61

The club had decided that it was going to start back its Monday night cycling time trial. A twelve-and-a-half-mile course, with a few inclines, a few descents and not a massive amount of traffic.

Phil had become stupidly excited about this. He had been desperate to do a cycling time trial. He was like a small child about to do their favourite thing as he got more and more beside himself as the time came. Me, well I liked the idea of doing it, but I wasn't quite as enthusiastic as there was one particular incline that I wasn't a fan of.

However, I had agreed to do it, and so do it I would.

We arrived at the layby where we had agreed to set off from, we would be going in one-minute intervals. The race was you against the clock. Only competing against yourself.

Rob was to be time keeper on this first time trial, and I had asked if I could go first as I was sure that I would be the slowest. He'd agreed.

The countdown began...five, four, three, two, one... and I was off. Pedalling with all my might.

I was about two miles in when it happened. I had the weirdest feeling in my chest. It wasn't pain but it felt like my heart was fluttering, like palpitations but different. I shook my head and didn't know what to do. However, knowing I was in a race against the clock, I decided to press on for a mile or so and see what happened. After a little while the feeling went away, and I pushed up the pace again.

One by one, every other club member that was taking part passed me, all saying nice and supportive things. At the turnaround point, Sian was the last person to leave me for dust and I had the long cycle back.

I crossed the line slightly disappointed with my time, but grateful that I had made it back in one piece.

As Phil gloated at the fact that he had beaten me, I responded saying that times would need to be factored based on gender and he sulked a bit that I had taken the wind from his sails again.

Once we had left the other club members and were in the privacy of the van, I told Phil what had happened. I said that I would be interested to see what my heart rate was doing when I uploaded my data to Strava.

That is one great advantage of a heart rate monitor, you can see exactly what was happening. When I looked at the stats I could see that my heart rate had plummeted when I had the feelings, but had returned to normal cycling cardio territory when it passed. I decided I had better phone my GP for advice.

I rang from work the following day, she rang me back and said she would like to see me, we arranged a late afternoon appointment so I wouldn't need to leave work too early. When I showed her my strava report she found it very curious and decided to send me for an ECG and speak to the cardiologist in the hospital for some guidance and to see if they felt I warranted a referral.

I was given an appointment for an ECG at the hospital, which came back as normal. Phew! However, my doctor was to ring me to say that the cardiologist wanted to see me and that I shouldn't do any strenuous activity until after I had seen them.

Ok dear reader, I am going to be honest, I totally decided to disregard the last bit. I know, I know, I should have followed medical advice and taken my foot off the accelerator of triathlon training but that was not going to happen. I had signed up for Llanelli Triathlon, I had Blenheim Palace approaching, I had the half marathon coming up. Strenuous activity is part of my life, and so I made the personal judgement call that as my ECG was fine I was going to keep going. Who knows how long the cardiology appointment would take to come through.

I would like to say though that I know that this approach is foolish. I would not recommend that anyone found in my position should make the same decision. I am an idiot.

Chapter Nine

The time had come to use my wetsuit in open water. I was nervous, but also spirited about getting to swim in water that wasn't a pool. The venue where I would take these first intrepid steps would be Llanelli North Dock, a non-tidal body of water which would also be hosting my first open water triathlon just over a week later.

In the run up to this first open water swim, I had asked club members about how they managed to get dried and dressed outside of their cars, and it was then that Tracey shared her amazing idea of making a towel robe, supplying me with photo of it. Basically, it was two bath towels sewn together, leaving a hole for the head, and then a hand towel, cut in two, to make sleeves. Phil, being better at sewing than I, was then given the task to make me one. So, this first Friday night, only nine days before I'd have to race in open water, I headed to North Dock armed with my wetsuit and my new towel robe.

I had been warned that open water swimming was far colder than swimming in a pool, and advice was given as to how to best overcome this initial shock. I was also told that North Dock tasted disgusting. However, neither of these salient pieces of information were going to put me off. I was ready and excited to give it a shot.

I had chosen the right night to break my open water virginity, with the Llanelli triathlon quickly approaching I was joined by 30 other club members.

I'd asked Phil if he wanted to come in too, however, he declined saying he'd rather take photos from the sidelines, wuss! However, I had more than enough good friends to have a laugh with and not treat this event like a scary one. My aim was simple, get in and give it a go.

I had taken every cold-water precaution in the book... wetsuit boots, gloves, neoprene hat. Truth be told I didn't need any of them, but when you are inexperienced and fearful of the cold, you will make questionable purchases. I took my first steps into the water, as I was wearing boots, I couldn't really get an understanding of whether it was cold or not. Mike, the coach, was with us. He'd come along knowing that a few of us were going in for the first time and to give us moral support.

As I walked deeper into the water, I crouched down to submerge myself further into the water and allowed a small amount of water into my wetsuit. It wasn't as cold as I anticipated. I then popped my head under the water and blew some bubbles. It really wasn't that cold at all.

I was pleased, actually I was more than pleased, I was delighted. This wasn't the freezing cold nightmare scenario that I feared it could be.

I began my swim up the dock. I'd been told a length was around 275 metres. I was actually amazed how much easier swimming felt. The taste, whilst salty, wasn't anywhere near as bad as I had feared and certainly felt nicer on the skin than chlorine. My breathing was easier, I was officially loving every second.

As we got to the other end, Mike asked me.

"What are you wearing those gloves for?"

"To keep my hands warm, Mike." I replied.

"Give them here." he said, holding his hands out towards me.

I took off my gloves, handed them to him and he stuffed them down his wetsuit.

"That's better." he said "You'll swim even better going back down now."

And in fairness to Mike, he was right. In honesty, Mike always is! I swam down and decided I was a huge fan of open water swimming. I didn't want to see another swimming pool ever again. Ok, I knew that I would need to do pool swimming, but having this additional way to swim felt free, it felt liberating.

We got back to the other end, and Mike, being Mike, decided that he had a few exercises for us to do. Practising a triathlon mass start. With 30 of us there, it was fairly easy to get a simulation of a gun going off and everyone starting together. It was something I had previously feared, I needn't have worried. It is all about finding your space and not panicking.

As I got out of the water, I was grinning ear to ear as I was met by Phil.

"You enjoyed that didn't you?" he beamed at me.

"I bloody loved it." I replied.

We walked back to the van and I got changed under my robe. When I had posted a picture the day before a few people remarked that I looked like Joseph and his technicolour dreamcoat. As I was changing I heard voices in song.

"I closed my eyes, drew back the curtains.", I turned and looked to see Tash and Emma, two of my lunatic clubmates arm in arm singing and laughing. I burst out laughing. My first day as an open water swimmer was truly awesome.

Another body of water was soon added to my outdoor swim locations. Near to where we live are two manmade lakes. The lakes were dug out to get materials to build a dual carriageway, so people tell me. The fact that these lakes are next to a dual carriageway makes me think that this is a true story. Our club has an agreement with the landowner, we can use the lakes to swim.

A few friends had got into the lake a few days before I was able to go down. Tash had nicknamed the lake "Lake Placid" after the horror film and had said swimming there was a scary experience. We'd had a good giggle about it on Facebook and I knew I needed to experience this lake for myself.

The cycle time trial that the club hosts on a Monday night is only a short distance away from the lake, so one Monday a few of us decided we would swim to cool down after the time trial. This time, my coach Rob was in attendance to give motivation, advice and a few wise cracks about the potential inhabitants and dangers of the lake (which ranged from giant toe biting pike to a less believable wormhole to another universe). However, his witty repartee served to calm some nerves.

The one thing I instantly realised about swimming in the lake was that it was much colder than the dock, like significantly colder than the dock, like toe numbingly cold. The second observation was that it didn't really taste of anything. I had grown to quite like the salty taste of the dock (not that I try and drink it you understand), but the lake tasted of nothing. Bizarrely this quite disturbed me.

That said, I enjoyed swimming in the lake as much as the dock. Although I was slightly scared of the swans that live on the lake. When those chaps swim alongside you, you get an appreciation of how big swans actually are! I was feeling very blessed that I had so many beautiful places to train and so many lovely people to train with.

Photo: Swimming in the lake
Photo Credit: Phil Jones

Chapter 62

The day of the Llanelli Triathlon had arrived. Even though it was my first open water triathlon, I was surprisingly calm. The fact that I had swum in the dock a few times, the fact that I had practiced the cycle route once with Phil (thanks Phil) and the fact that I was doing this triathlon with so many club mates meant that I was a cool as a cucumber. (I am struck that is quite an odd saying, a cucumber is only cool if it's been in the fridge surely? Anyone who has touched a cucumber in a greenhouse on a summer's day would not say that saying, as it would not be cool, in fact it would be pretty warm. Anyhow, I digress)
So, we arrive at Llanelli, I racked my bike first to get this out of the way and then I walked around the car park and chatted to friends. I had purposefully arrived early as I didn't want to be panicking like I was in the Vale of Glamorgan duathlon.

I tried to find Mandy, one of my friends from the club who was also using this triathlon as her first open water and was incredibly nervous. Mandy is a lovely girl, very chatty and friendly and a selfie addict. I had expected her to be nervous following a few Facebook message exchanges in the days running up to the event. At first I couldn't find her, but when I did it was apparent that her nerves had escalated. Instead of her usual chirpy demeanour and phone snapping pictures, she looked quiet. We chatted for a few minutes and I tried to help her get her race tattoo on, however, it wasn't wanting to play. She had to rack her bike and a few other of her friends had arrived, so I left her to it and went in search of more clubmates.

I found Jayne. Jayne and her partner Richard had become good club mates of Phil and I. It was also Jayne's first open water triathlon, however, she was seeming laid back like me. When it was time to get in the water, Jayne and I stuck together with the same plan. Stay towards the back when the gun goes off to give you more space.

I have to admit to being slightly aggrieved when the race pack had come through. They were having four waves. So basically, the organisers would be setting off the swimming in groups, ten minutes apart. They had lumped all the women together for wave one, a women's only wave. I found this annoying. It seemed patronising to women. I think a much better way of organising waves would be on estimated swim times. That way, people would be swimming with people of similar abilities. However, this was done, women first wave, men alphabetically. I felt sorry for the fast ladies and I felt sorry for the slow men. I decided I was going to channel my sexism anger into my swim.

The klaxon went off and the swimming had started. My plan to stay at the back was a good one, as I missed the initial carnage and was able to relax into my stroke. I kept going up the familiar dock, I felt strong and quietly confident. I knew my time wasn't going to set the world alight, but I knew I was capable of the swim distance having already done it several times in the dock. I lifted my head to check my sighting and to look around me. I could see Mandy struggling behind me. The concerned friend in me wanted to stop and help her, however, I knew she was in safe hands with the support canoe, and so racing Debs took over and I continued my swim. As I reached the first buoy we were meant to swim around, we were to discover it had moved, meaning it was now in very shallow water and we needed to walk around. This put me off momentarily and I continued towards the next buoy. I heard the klaxon again, the next wave was off.

I was swimming in a different part of the dock by this point as they had done the route in an interesting M shaped formation. The dock is fairly clear, so you can see the bottom. We frequently see crabs walking along the bottom. What I wasn't expecting to see was a roasting tin and a pair of scissors. The mind really does boggle as to how things like that could end up in a dock.

I had only been swimming another 10 minutes when the fastest men from the next wave were starting to overtake me. I took a nasty whack to the head from one man, who apologised before continuing on his way. Another man basically swam over the top of me. It was something I had heard could happen but was a little disconcerting. As he swam over me, he dislodged my zip pull for my wetsuit, so this vulnerable strip of fabric began floating around me. I found this concerning, as all it would take would be someone to accidentally pull it and my wetsuit would come undone. I wouldn't allow any negative thoughts, I had to keep going. Before I knew it I was approaching the end of the swim. I began kicking my feet harder, a trick that both Rob and Mike had told me which gets blood circulating back in your legs to prevent dizziness when you first stand up.

As I did stand up, I started my run to transition and could hear my cheering friends. I turned to see Karl, Meinir and Karen who I had supported in Cardiff, along with Heledd who had recently joined the club. I smiled and waved at them, grateful for seeing friendly faces. I began to peel my wetsuit off whilst running and made my way to my bike.

Photo: Putting on a race tattoo

Photo Credit: Phil Jones

Chapter 63

As I reached the transition area, I could see Christine and Sue, they were also cheering. My wetsuit was quickly removed, revealing my Celtic Tri kit below. I felt so much pride at wearing my club colours again. I sat down to put my socks and shoes on, deciding being comfy was worth the few seconds delay it would give me. I took a long drink from my cycle water bottle.

"Good move." Christine shouted, grinning at me.

I put on my helmet, gloves and glasses and unracked my bike and I ran to the mount line.

Simon, from the club, was marshalling the mount and dismount line.

"Well done." he said "Have a good cycle."

I grinned at him "I will" I replied and I was off, pedalling up the road.

It's really interesting doing an event where there are so many levels of skill. I looked on in awe as some competitors, including some in GB kit, came flying past me at some incredible speeds, but equally, I was surprised at how many competitors I was also able to overtake.

The bike leg was passing quickly and I was enjoying every second of being at one with my bike.

I was a few minutes from the turnaround point when Mike passed me.

"Keep going Deb." he encouraged as he passed. Mike had been in a later wave than me, his strengths are the swim and the bike, and it was lovely to see my coach as he want past. "Make sure you keep drinking!" were his parting words as he sped past me, once a coach, always a coach. Even when racing himself, he could still find a brief moment to provide practical support.

I tried for a while to keep up with him, but I couldn't. The one thing I find most brilliant about racing in Club Kit is that other club competitors shout words of encouragement as they pass you. Just like I had received in the duathlon, I was getting words of encouragement, only this time, I was able to shout back encouragement too.

One of my favourite fellow competitors to race with is Anthony. He's a super speedy athlete, but doesn't take himself or racing too seriously. We swim together at the Sunday club swim and he always makes me laugh. "Get a move on!" he yelled as he passed me on the opposite side of the road. I giggled.

I was now past the halfway point and was feeling it in my legs, but felt I had the power to keep pushing. This was helped by a fellow competitor, he looked like he was starting to flag a little. Suddenly, I became a lioness in the Serengeti determined to pick off the prey. We were approaching an incline and I noticed his cadence drop, I threw my bike down a gear, stepped my cadence up a touch and powered past him on the climb. His face said it all, he didn't like being overtaken by a girl.

I flew down the hill the other side, a speed awareness sign at the side of the road told me that I was exceeding the speed limit at 34 miles an hour! Result! There are a lot of these signs on this particular route. I love them, as you get a great indication of how fast you are going (as my speedometer on the bike tends to only work on occasion). I get really frustrated when a car overtakes me as I approach one as it then logs their speed not mine.

As we were on the next flat, my prey overtook me, but I could see he was powering everything in his legs to gain his revenge on the girl who had passed him earlier. I grinned, I knew what was coming up, a big incline. I knew on that incline I would pass him again. As we approached, I could see he was dropping his speed again. I got out of the saddle (yeah I know I was showing off) and powered past him with ease, as I passed him, two other Celtic Tri racers passed me. One shouted

"Good effort there, Debs." I grinned, I knew I'd put in a little bit of a performance, but didn't realise that it would be witnessed by my club mates. My prey admitted defeat, I turned to see if he was catching me and his pace had slowed.

As I came back towards the end of the ride, I began shouting "Thank you Marshal" to all the marshals on the course. Without them, volunteers, super heroes, we wouldn't be able to race.

I pulled back into transition, jumped off my bike and began the run.

Chapter 64

My legs were knackered, totally knackered. I had given so much on the bike they really didn't want to run at all. After my initial pride of ensuring I stayed running whilst in view of the main body of spectators, as soon as I was out of sight I slowed to a walk. I was marching along when club mate Roy came up behind me.

"Pick it up Debs, and get a move on." he shouted to me, rightly criticising me for walking.

"I know, I know." I replied and started a slow run again. It didn't last!

I heard a familiar voice behind me again

"Come on Debs." I turned to see Anthony, he was running effortlessly.

"I'm bloody knackered." I replied, he laughed and sped past me.

Only a minute later, I heard "How are you doing honey?" it was Mandy. I checked to see she was OK after the swim. "I'm OK now." she confirmed, and being a much much faster runner than me, she was off.

I began to run again, and could see someone up ahead I was glad to see, Phil armed with his camera. I don't think I can put into words how much I motivates me seeing my husband on the course.

"You OK love?" I asked him.

He shouted an ironic "Come on Celtic Tri" and I grinned.

I wasn't long past Phil when I could see Mike up ahead. Due to Mike's disability, he struggles with running, not that this stops him. I caught up with him and was all ready for a quick break and a bit of a chat, but Mike was having none of it.

"Come on Debs, keep the running up, not far to go."

I smiled at him, said "See you at the finish" and continued my half run, half walk.

It was soon the turnaround point. I was feeling totally knackered. My legs felt heavy, but I knew I didn't have long to go. I'd passed Phil on the return leg, when two runners came up behind me

"Well done Deb, keep going." it was Nikki one of the club coaches, out on a social run with Emmaline also from the club.

They slowed their pace to mine, and Nikki offered words of encouragement on keeping my pace up, and how I could help my breathing on this last section. After a minute or so, they wished me good luck and sped off in the distance.

I ran up an incline and was to be greeted by Jo on her bike.

"Hiya mate." she said to me "How are you doing?"

"Bloody knackered." I replied.

She then proceeded to spend the next five minutes coming out with every cliché in the book.

"Dig deep."

"Nearly there now."

"You can do it."

And then my personal favourite "Go on, push the envelope."

"What does that even mean?" I laughed at her.

"I dunno." Jo replied "But it sounds good."

"I haven't got a bloody envelope to push." I responded, cheekily.

We both laughed. They say laughter is the best medicine, and I think in my case it was. Suddenly, I felt a final burst of energy. Jo cycled alongside me for a few minutes then said

"I'm off to tell your fan club that you are nearly at the finish." and off she cycled.

No sooner than Jo had left my side I was joined by Christine and Sue.

"Oh my God Deb, did you see him?" Christine said.

"Who?" I asked.

"Shane Williams." she replied.

"Who?" I repeated again, not having a clue who Shane Williams was.

"Shane Williams." Christine said a little louder "The rugby player."

"I haven't a clue who he is." I replied, genuinely, as I'm not really interested in rugby.

Sue pitched in "You should have seen her face when she saw him Deb."

They ran with me for a little while until the finish line was in sight.

"Off you go then." Christine said.

And I did, a full on, proper sprint finish to rapturous cheers.

The finish line crossed, I looked for my "race momento".

There was no medal (boo!) only a t-shirt.

"We only have small left." the woman said

"Oh no." I replied "Do I look like a small?"

She double checked the box.

"No only small left." I took it, despondently.

I went and saw my friends, had lots of hugs and waited for Phil to join me.

When I arrived home, I had a nice soak in the bath and we decided we would go out for lunch to celebrate. I tried on my t-shirt and it fitted!

"I can't believe I can fit in a small." I said to Phil.

My day would get even better when I was to see my results. My aim was to complete the race in under three hours, but I'd be chuffed with under two hours and forty-five minutes. I had to pinch myself as I looked at the stats:

Swim 750m open water - 27mins 49secs

Transition 1 - 4mins 13secs

Cycle 28km - 1hr 5mins 51 secs

Transition 2 - 1min 2secs

Run 5k - 40mins 38secs

Overall - 2hrs 19mins 35secs!!!

So not only did I smash my targets I got under not only 2hrs 30 but 2hrs 20!!!! I was totally chuffed to bits! I smashed it!

Chapter 65

The more you get involved in sport, the more you see what goes on behind the scenes to make it a success. Week after week, thousands of volunteers are working tirelessly up and down the country to support people participating in sport.

I had come to that point where I decided I needed to start giving back on occasion. I had benefitted from volunteer marshals at Parkrun events, running events and at triathlons and I felt this was something that I could contribute to on occasion.

The first event I marshalled was a Parkrun. So one Saturday morning, instead of pitching up in my running leggings and trainers, I turned up in a hoodie and jeans. I was assigned the marshalling point just after the halfway turn. There were two other marshalling positions in that area, and one of the marshals, an elderly gentleman who used to be a competitive runner said he'd take us down in his car. The car was old, and when I got into the backseat I was alarmed to discover there were no seatbelts.

Thankfully it was only a very brief car ride until we parked up and set up our areas and cones.

Both my elderly male companions had been competitive runners in their time. I found their stories of racing in the 1960s and 70s quite fascinating. They asked about my running, and seemed genuinely impressed that I was a triathlete.

I quite enjoyed marshalling. It was interesting to see the differences in abilities as people would run past you. I was in awe of the speed and skill of the front runners, but I was equally in awe of the people at the back. The people more like me, not natural athletes, but still giving it their best shot. The people in the middle were also pretty cool, including one rather handsome man who high fived me whilst running in his Celtic Tri running vest, ah yes, the lovely Phil was running whilst I marshalled. It felt strange to be supporting my husband and not the other way around.

The second event I marshalled was a junior aquathlon. The event was arranged by my club in honour of Steve one of our clubmates who had lost his life in a cycling accident. I had only met Steve a few times, however, he was a truly genuine man. He had been super encouraging to me and the club felt his loss greatly. I knew I had to volunteer my time to support this event, I had to do it for Steve.

You'd think for a junior event that it would be all about kids having fun and the parents helping and supporting their children. In the main, it was. There was, however, a sinister underbelly of pushy competitive parents.

I was marshalling in the pool, my job was to get the next lot of children ready once the group before were in the water. I can say, in all honesty, that every one of those children were a complete joy to support. Some were nervous, some were excited, some of the older children included me in their banter. Many of the children I knew from the club, and I high fived them before their swims. Most of the children I hadn't met before.

My heart went out to one disabled little girl. I have never seen so much determination in my life as I saw in her. Her performance in the pool was inspirational, and I was delighted to see photos of her later when she was on her run and when she had finished. I felt honoured that I had a glimpse into her determination and courage.

So as I said, whilst the children were totally awesome, and probably 95% of the parents were decent people, there were the dreadful parents. I swear this very vocal minority thought they were in the Olympics and not in Ystradgynlais leisure centre. I'd like to think I have fairly thick skin, but on too many occasions I had abuse hurled at me by these monstrosities. I paraphrase, but lines such as "Why is my talented super awesome child sports star in that swim wave with that child as they are crap?", "Why can't I stand next to the pool and check the laps are being counted correctly?", "Why hasn't my child got more room in transition, don't you know who they are?". Well the Brownlee brothers these kids weren't, however, that was not the parents' perceptions.

I didn't mind being abused by the parents, in many respects it amused me. However, what I did object to was when their behaviour was transferred to the children. Hearing one Dad shout to his nine-year-old daughter during her swim "Sort it out, your swimming is crap." made me feel genuinely heartbroken. The poor child!

The worst example was with one of the older children, a young girl who must have been around eleven or twelve. We had been advised that the water was incredibly shallow at the shallow end, and so any children thinking about doing tumble turns should be warned and advised against it for the shallow end. I had asked the children in the wave if they were planning tumble turns and a couple put their hands up. I explained the situation and the children nodded. With that, one pushy parent called over the daughter, and I honestly couldn't believe my ears when I heard what she said

"Don't listen to that woman, I bet she isn't telling people from her club that. If you don't do the tumble turns you will lose at least a second a length. You do them, ok?"

So, apparently, losing a second per length is worth risking giving yourself concussion or cutting your head open.

Good job parent, good job!

However, whilst there is often a minority who want to spoil things, the majority of people were awesome. I will continue to volunteer when I can. I take so much from this sport, I need to give back to it too.

Chapter 66

ROAD TRIP!!!!! It had sneaked up on us rather quickly. Several months earlier, Christine had said that she really wanted to do the Blenheim Palace triathlon and would I be interested in doing it and having a weekend away. I'd mentioned it to Phil, and he was supportive of the idea, so we had booked it. Two nights in the sleepy town of Woodstock, and Christine and I would both do the triathlon. As the race approached, we discovered that a new member, Sian, had also signed up for Blenheim. There would be the three of us racing from the club.

Phil and I would be travelling up in the van, and would be carrying the bikes for us competitors. Chris, her daughters Robyn and Kara, and her son in law Callum would be travelling in her car.

We'd set out later than we hoped, and as a result got caught in every traffic jam going. What should have been a three hour pleasant drive became a four and a half hour painful slog. Phil and I took it in turns to drive, and when I was passenger, I would text Chris updates.

Christine had the good sense to leave earlier than us, so on a later text saying that we had nearly arrived, she replied with.

"I'm in the hotel bar if you want to join me when you get here."

We were staying in different hotels, but both within the village. Phil and I arrived, checked into a gorgeous little boutique hotel, with beamed ceilings and proceeded to Christine's hotel and the bar.

We arrived to see Christine with a glass of wine in her hand. I have to admit, I don't usually entertain the idea of alcohol the day before a race, but after the journey from hell, I said to Phil, get me a glass of something dry and white. He returned with two glasses of Sauvignon Blanc, one for him, one for me.

The conversation flowed, we laughed and joked and before I knew it I was onto a second glass.

I have to say I love Christine and I love her whole family, they all feel like my family too. The six of us just had an amazing time, taking our evening into another pub restaurant eating al fresco in the beer garden with more wine.

At the end of the night we made our plans for the following morning. Phil and Callum were going to do the local park run and Christine and I would go and have a look around the palace grounds and get a feel for what we needed to do to get ready for the race.

The following morning, we were up bright and early. Whilst we were staying literally yards from the gates of Blenheim Palace, what we didn't realise was the scale of the place inside the grounds.

Myself, Christine and her younger daughter Kara looked in awe at the sheer scale of the grounds and the house which had been the birthplace of Winston Churchill. It took us nearly half an hour to walk to the transition area.

"I'm really glad we came in to check it out." Christine said. I agreed, knowing how much walking around was needed I was glad it didn't come as a surprise just before the race. I quickly sent Sian a text message to let her know to get to the palace in plenty of time.

The palace grounds were a hive of activity. There were 19 waves in total on the day, so many athletes were already racing. Sian was going to be in the wave after us. It was amazing to see so many bikes, so many athletes, so many families.

We walked down to see where the swim start was. It was then I had the text from Phil, he and Callum had finished park run. Callum was faster. I text him telling him he had brought shame on our family. Next thing Christine was laughing, Robyn had text her to say that Phil and Callum were in stitches at the text.

The day was passing quickly, we had met Phil, Robyn and Callum back in the village and had collected mine and Christine's bikes ready for racking. However, we had decided to leave the rest of our things (wetsuit, tri suit) until later. This was a decision I was to regret as it meant we didn't leave enough time for a proper lunch. Instead I was to be fuelling this triathlon on a lemon curd muffin from inside Blenheim Palace, and a Chelsea bun from a market stall in the village. Neither of which can be described as appropriate fuel for a race. However, it was a big rush to get back to the hotel, to change and to get back to the swim start with our wetsuits.

As we got to the waterside, Phil and Callum helped Christine and I into our wetsuits. I swear they take three times as long to get on as they do to get off! As Phil was pulling it up at the shoulder and I was half jumping to get it comfy, I looked like a baby in a baby bouncer. It was then we were joined by Sian. I was so pleased we'd seen each other before we started. It was her first triathlon and she was understandably nervous, however, a big hug can really help ease nerves. We wished her luck and said we'd find her at the finish. Phil took a photo of the three of us, the Celtic three!

Christine and I said our last farewells to our families and headed into the holding pen ready to start the race.

Photo: Getting in our wetsuits (left, Sian, middle, me, right, Chris)
Photo credit: Phil Jones

Chapter 67

The race pack had said that we would have 15 minutes acclimatisation time in the water. They lied! The announcer told us to walk to the end of the pontoon which was floating in the lake and jump in, then swim to the start line. Literally a minute or so to acclimatise. As I walked down the pontoon, Christine at my side, it wobbled with the water and I struggled to stay on my feet. We reached the end, there was no time to pause with others coming behind us, we just had to jump in and hope for the best.

We jumped, the freezing lake water hit us. It was even colder than the lake near home, we both gasped, not expecting to be hit with such cold water. We swam to the start, heads above the water, and I started splashing my face with water to get it used to the cold. Christine did the same. I stuck my face in the water and blew some bubbles, the freezing water stung my face as if it had been ice. This was going to be a mighty cold swim.

We had no time to think about it though, no sooner had we reached the start than the klaxon went off. And me and my very dear friend were actually competing in one of the most iconic triathlons in the country.

I began my swim, and managed to keep my head under fairly well, as I came up to sight, I could see Christine behind me. The distance between us was getting bigger, and as I knew we had roughly the same swimming ability I knew she must have been struggling. As I had done with Mandy in Llanelli, I needed to put my concern for my friend out of my mind, I needed to be concerned with my race. I stuck my head back under and powered away with my best front crawl.

I stayed under for ages, feeling strong in my stroke and then realised, I hadn't sighted for a while. I lifted my head from the water and was surprised to see a canoe next to me. It was then the realisation hit me. In my excitement with my swimming I had gone drastically off course! Instead of swimming in a nice straight line, I had deviated to the right with quite a dramatic fashion.

"Forgotten your SatNav love." the canoeist said to me with a grin.

"Oh my!" I replied.

"Get left, stick by the white buoys and for God sake look up more often." he continued, laughing as he said it and then he turned around and went back to the swimmer he was keeping a closer eye on. That swimmer was Christine. With the buoys on my left, and checking every 4th or 5th breath that I wasn't deviating off course, my swim became much better. I was in a rhythm and had totally forgotten I was cold.

I overtook another swimmer who was doing breast stroke, and then another, and before I knew it I was approaching the last buoy to swim into shore. I started kicking my legs a bit harder to get the blood back into them and my right calf cramped up. I did a kind of half kick, reached the pontoon to the shore and was helped out of the water by two volunteers. I began my run to the transition area, and felt I looked drunk as my stronger left leg sent me running to the left. (Incidentally, Blenheim Palace did videos of everyone on the swim exit, and the one of me trying to run in a straight line but heading left is hilarious. I think Phil must have laughed non stop for about quarter of an hour when he saw it.)

I was ripping my wetsuit off as I ran. The floor had been covered with hessian sacks to run to transition. The feel of the hessian really hurt my bare feet and it made me wonder why they had bothered.

I knew from watching the TV coverage from the year before that the run to transition was up a steep hill and then a 400 metre run around a part of the palace into the court yard. That steep run, up the hessian was horrendous. I turned the corner onto the flat and could see Phil, leaning over the supporters barriers, I gave him a high five as I passed. I turned the next corner and there were Robyn and Callum. Cal outstretched his hand and I could see a few jelly babies on it, I grinned and grabbed a few.

Then it was inside the majestic courtyard and over to my bike. One down, two to go.

Photo: Running to transition on the hessian sacks
Photo credit: Phil Jones

Chapter 68

I reached my bike and finished pulling my wetsuit off. I
quickly dried my legs and put on my socks and trainers. I
grabbed my helmet and put it on my head, it didn't feel
right. I tried doing it up and I couldn't. I lifted it off my head,
bemused, and realised I'd put it on back to front. I laughed
at myself, and carried on putting on my gloves and my
sunglasses. Then I took a long drink, I was surprisingly
thirsty after the swim and run to transition, then I lifted my
bike off the rack and began a half run to the mount line.
I reached the mount line at the same time as two other
competitors, the friendly marshal wished us all a good race
as we mounted. I quickly sped up the road for the start of a
three loop trip around the grounds.

With so many races in progress as there had been so many
waves, the bike course was very busy. It was an
interesting course, and my first lap was as much an
introduction to the terrain than anything else. The course
had it all, short steep climbs, longer gradual climbs, steep
descents, tight corners. Then I reached the cattle grid, and
breathed a huge sigh of relief that it had been boarded
over.

As I cycled, I found myself overtaking a lot of competitors, but also being overtaken a lot too. However, I have to say that some people were damn inconsiderate when overtaking. I know everyone is in race mode, but a few times I had my own progress inhibited due to some smart so and so not giving enough space and me needing to slam on my brakes to not get taken out.

It was on the second loop that I saw the most interesting thing. The bikes on display varied enormously from cheap and cheerful hybrids to top of the range road bikes and time trial bikes which wouldn't have looked out of place with the Brownlee brothers sat on them. So, this second lap, I was powering up a long slow climb and there at the side of the road was a man off his bike, pushing a Pinarello up the hill. I looked, there was no obvious fault with the bike, no puncture, chain seemed fine, but here was this other competitor unable to do this climb, on what was easily an eight grand bike! I smiled to myself as I powered my few hundred quid bike past him and the phrase "All the gear, no idea" sprung to mind. I know, I know, I'm mean!

As I cycled, I would pass Phil at the same point of the route, him armed with the camera taking photos. I'd wave and smile, and he'd get cross as he couldn't get "race face" shots. But I was having a blast. I was really soaking up the Blenheim atmosphere and was loving the race.

The last loop I found slightly harder, my gears dropped a little further as I powered up the climbs, but my cycle was nearly over. Time to turn back into transition and start my run.

The run was a two loop course. As is always the case, my legs protested as I started to run. Towards the end of the first loop, I could see Callum, hand outstretched with more jelly babies. I grabbed a few gratefully.

I had just started the second loop when someone ran up at the side of me. A woman I didn't know, wearing Celtic Tri kit. This surprised me, we introduced ourselves, wished each other luck and my new-found club mate Rhian continued on her way.

Just over half way through the second lap, Christine caught up with me. I knew she would being a much stronger runner than I. She complained about the swim being awful and ran into the distance. As I reached Phil taking photos he shouted "You've brought shame on the family." obviously deciding to seek his revenge knowing Christine was ahead of me. I laughed and replied "Knobhead!"

I was around half a kilometre from the finish when Sian caught me.

"You alright Debs?" she said, she was grinning from ear to ear and I knew she was loving her first triathlon.

Sian turned left for lap two and I carried straight on to the finish. As I ran towards the finish line, I could see Christine waiting for me. I crossed the line, got my medal, a pint of lager (alcohol free) and a bottle of sports drink. I gave the lager to Callum, seemed a fair exchange for jelly babies, and started my sports drink to replenish some of my lost energy.

We waited for Sian to finish and had a group photo on the podium. It was a truly awesome race.

Photo: The Blenheim Three at the Finish

Photo Credit: Phil Jones

Chapter 69

It needed to be done. My running distances had continued to improve so it was only a matter of time until the inevitable first half marathon. My first was to take place in late June, in Swansea. A flat half marathon literally a stones' throw away from home, in my nearest city.

I wasn't going to be alone on this run. Several of my club mates were doing it, including Meinir who was fresh back from having completed her half ironman! I also had another friend who wasn't a member of the club taking part. Vicki and I had become friends online through both keeping pet chickens. We had been friends for about 7 years but had never met in person. We talked regularly, Vicki is a keen runner who had run up to marathon distance and had been very supportive as I was starting out.

The morning of the half marathon arrived. I felt confident, my training had gone well. I had run 10 miles in training which was the distance Rob wanted me to do. I had stuck religiously to my training plan, one long run on the weekend which ramped up every week, two shorter runs in the week. We had agreed as a club to meet in the Castle Square, which was near to the start line. We would have a club photo before the race. I had arranged with Vicki to meet there too.

I had a race plan in mind, don't go off too fast, run the first 3 miles and then have two jelly babies every two kilometres and keep running for as long as possible. It was the approach I had taken in training and it had worked for me. I had a slight level of concern about running with Vicki, she had said it would be great to run together, and whilst I liked the sentiment, I was worried about keeping up with her. She assured me, however, that she would stick to my pace. This relaxed me, and made me glad of having company. So 13.1 miles were ahead of me. However, in my mind, due to the way I trained, in my head it was a 21 kilometre race. My pacing, my nutrition and my thinking had been in kilometres, so kilometres it would stay. This may sound odd, as ultimately the distance is the distance, but I had planned this race. If I had switched my watch and my thinking to miles, I genuinely think I would have been stuffed!

So I stood in Castle Square and greeted my friends as they arrived. My biggest welcome was reserved for Vicki, after so many years of friendship it was great to finally meet her and her husband Richard. We chatted like old friends. As we made our way to the start line we were organised into pens based on our predicted finish times. I said goodbye to my faster club mates who were heading to the pens in front and I stayed at the back. This didn't worry me one bit, Vicki and I chatted away until we were ready to start moving. I knew my timing chip would activate at the start line which was two streets away and I knew it would take a while to get there.

The first few miles were easy. The conversation flowed between Vicki and I as we ran, my pace was quicker than I needed, but I was OK with this as I knew it would buy me time later in the race. I had a secret dream of completing the race in under 3 hours. I knew it would be a tough call and I'd need to pull out the performance of my life, but I was hopeful.

We were around 4 miles in when I had a panic, at the side of the road I could see someone collapsed in a Bloodwise running vest. Meinir was running raising money for Bloodwise. I have to say I breathed a huge sigh of relief when I realised it wasn't Meinir, although I do hope the lady was OK.

A little further down the road was one of my club mates, Joe, he was there taking photos, no sooner than I passed him I passed Robyn ringing a cowbell and cheering. Then I saw Phil taking photos. The runners behind Vicki and I thought that he was a professional photographer, I was very proud saying he was of a professional standard but wasn't technically professional.

Before I knew it, we were hitting the half way point in the Mumbles, a beautiful seaside village. It was quite idyllic and we were serenaded by an elderly man playing a guitar on his porch. His contribution to supporting the athletes. I realised that my run was going well. I hadn't walked at all, I was eating my jelly babies every two kilometres, my race was going well.

I turned to Vicki, but she was struggling. The high pollen count in South Wales was playing havoc with her asthma. "You go ahead and I'll catch you up." she said.

However, that was the last I saw of her in the race.

I continued my running alone. However, I kept overtaking the same women and they kept overtaking me and we began to chat off and on.

It was about 5 miles to go when I saw Rachel from my club and gave her a high five. Seeing her gave me a much-needed boost. I was to have another boost shortly after when I caught Meinir. With the half ironman very much still in her legs she was struggling. We stayed together for a little while, but she was soon telling me to go ahead.

317

At the 10 mile mark I saw Phil again. This was the barrier I hadn't passed, but in my head I had told myself that I had 3.1 miles left to go, 5k, a park run. How many 5k runs had I done? Loads and loads and loads, and this was all I had left. By this point fatigue had set in and whilst I was still running of a fashion, Phil was able to keep alongside me at a fast walking pace.

He knew my ambition to come in under 3 hours, and he was timing.

"Debs." he said "You can totally do this, you keep going at that pace and you will get a sub three."

I nodded, I knew I was on track too, but now I was feeling tired. I told him to check on Meinir instead. I needed to continue alone, just like I had in the duathlon. This was a battle between my body and my mind and my mind was going to win.

At 11 and a half miles I was struggling. I'd hit a bit of a wall. I knew I didn't have far to go. At this point I saw Sian. I warned you there are lots of Sian's, I haven't written about this Sian before. I first became aware of Sian when she started following my Unlikely Triathlete Facebook page, I knew she was local and she was always saying encouraging things. Then I realised we had mutual friends. Then she joined Celtic Tri (although she is a total club tart, she's a member of loads, being a runner turned triathlete) and then we became proper real-life friends. She was marshalling, but it didn't stop her running towards me.

318

"Come here you gorgeous beauty." she said, her face beaming and we had a great big huge hug.

That hug meant the world. It was everything I needed to see me through the last little section of my first half marathon. That hug gave me energy, it gave me strength. I swear Sian has superpowers!

I left her, having covered her in my sweat (although she assures me that sweaty running hugs from friends are the best) and crossed over the bridge in Swansea marina. As I ran down the side of the road, I saw Sonia sat on a bench accompanied by her little dog, also there to cheer me on.

The end was getting closer. The hardest part was running uphill on the cobbled street towards the finish, but I knew I was close. As I turned to the last stretch, I saw my friend Mandy who was also marshalling, she pointed her phone in my direction taking a few photos and yelled "well done Debs."

I ran down the finish line, my eyes were welling up with tears as the realisation hit me on what I had accomplished, I looked down at my watch, it was under three hours. At the finish I was greeted by one of my oldest friends, Judith, who was marshalling and Sian who did the duathlon, and had big hugs off them both. My first half marathon was done. In 2hrs and 55 mins. I was proud of myself.

Photo: Before Swansea Half

Photo Credit: Phil Jones

Chapter 70

It was only a week after the half marathon when it was time
for my triathlon anniversary. The Pencoed Novice
Triathlon. This was a special race. It was going to be Phil's
first race and my opportunity to put a marker in the sand to
see if I had improved on the performance I had put in the
year before.

It was also the first triathlon of one of our new club
members called James. I quite often get people contacting
me through my Facebook page to say that they have read
my books. Most are women around my age, give or take a
decade or so. I was rather surprised to get a message from
this young man, James. He said how his friend and put him
onto my books and how he had laughed out loud and was
joining our club.

I remember clearly the first time that James came to a club
swim session, there was this rather handsome twenty-
something young man there with his swimming trunks,
muscular and tattooed and he was chatting to me! There
was quite some conversation in the ladies changing room
after that session as to who this new hottie was and how I
knew him. I think of all the people I have introduced to the
club, James is certainly one of the most popular amongst
us ladies. And on this July Sunday, I was pleased as
punch to be there to witness his first triathlon whilst
competing myself.

Phil was surprisingly relaxed, far more so than I had been a year before. It was going to be a first for us, racing together. Not that we were in the same wave. My speedier husband was in a later wave, as his swimming was faster. So he was there to watch me start and snap a few photos before he was to get racing himself. (My cover photo is one of those photos he took, and I think my favourite cycling photo to date).

I felt confident getting in the pool, with a few open water triathlons behind me, a shorter pool based triathlon felt almost easy. I had to mentally pinch myself about how my ability and mindset had changed in the twelve months that had past.

This time last year, I had done the swim doggy paddle, this year, the whole swim was done front crawl.

The bike leg was a route I knew well. Although in contrast to the year before, I found myself overtaking many people rather than being overtaken myself. I knew my cycling speeds had improved since the year before and as I powered past competitors, I had a physical reminder that this was true.

It was on the last section of the bike leg, not far away from transition, that I passed Phil as he was starting his cycle. We cheered at each other.

The run was as horrific as any triathlon run is. In fact, being a 3k run I think it was worse, as I didn't really have enough time to fully find my stride. It didn't help that I still had some soreness after the half marathon the week before.

However, I crossed the finish line, triumphant, and got my timings.

I had knocked nine minutes off my time from the year before. I should have been delighted, instead I was beating myself up, I had hoped for ten. My friends all were telling me that nine minutes was amazing. I felt annoyed with myself, if only I had pushed myself just a little harder on the run.

I stayed annoyed and upset with myself until Phil crossed the line. I watched as he made that final run to the finishing line, earning him the coveted title of "triathlete". He went to collect his timings and we compared.

I'd beaten him on the bike, a full 15 seconds faster than he was. And that simple salient fact (with the accompanying dance that I started doing) suddenly made me happy again. My minor victory. I no longer felt like a failure as every single time we had done that cycle route together, Phil had been faster (I should point out that Phil was faster overall, being a faster swimmer and runner. However, the bike victory was mine!). I was so very proud of Phil, as he had now become a triathlete too, we were a two-triathlete household, we were a triathlon power couple (Ok maybe that's taking it a bit too far).

Photo: The gorgeous Phil and I at the finish of Pencoed

Photo Credit: Karen Birdsall

Chapter 71

Our club has a championship. We are put into divisions, and certain races are classed as club championship races where you earn points based on where you finish the race, and the top three of each division get awards and get promoted into the next division up. I'd already completed two club championship races, The Vale of Glamorgan Duathlon and the Llanelli Sprint Triathlon. The next club championship race that I was able to take part in was the Tuska Sprint Triathlon. A sea swim triathlon set in the coastal town of Porthcawl.

Whilst I had swum in a dock and had swum in lakes, I hadn't swam in the sea. It was an idea that I was nervous about, suddenly there were waves, and tides, and currents. I had arranged my first practice sea swim with some experienced swimmers.

One of these swimmers was another Sian. This Sian, however, was the craziest yet. Whilst the rest of us had pitched up in wetsuits, she arrived wearing only a bather. Her perfect figure making her look more suited to an episode of Baywatch than a dip in Aberafon. She was on hand to give us some help and guidance whilst completing her own sea swim training, she swam around us in circles, pausing occasionally to help us with our strokes. She was about to embark on a monumental challenge. Swimming from Ilfracombe in Devon over to Swansea, a distance significantly further than swimming the channel. I'm pleased to report that she managed this swim, becoming the first ever woman to complete this challenge and becoming a world record holder in the progress, smashing by hours the times of the previous men who had done it. Anyhow, we were swimming in the sea. I found myself giggling as I was taken up and down by the waves. The taste was a different level of salty to the dock, and I had my first sight of jelly fish.

I was to get in the sea a few more times whilst the race was approaching, each time the conditions were different. One swim the jelly fish were the size of dinner plates, and I accidentally touched a few. Other times, it was calm and gentle and no sign of any life.

However, the day before the Tuska triathlon came a storm.

As I went to register in the scout hut next to the sea, I watched as the waves crashed on the pier. These waves were much higher than I had trained in. I felt a little scared. My friends Megan and Gareth were also registering, I chatted to them both and wondered if the swim would go ahead. The organisers told us of Plan B. If the sea was too rough in the morning, the race would become a duathlon. I requested my yellow swim cap just in case, a cap which would highlight me as a novice sea swimmer. I hoped I would be able to swim. My big race was approaching, the race I had trained all season for and that was a sea swim.

However, mother nature had planned to be unkind to me. The following morning, as we pitched up with our bikes and wetsuits, we were told that the race would be a duathlon. However, due to the high winds, they needed to change the run and cycle routes as well as stop the sea swim. It was certainly the most frantic pre-race briefing I had attended.

I watched as several other windswept would be competitors decided that today what not be their day. Some I understood, including my friend Tula who didn't want to jeopardise her ironman training, and some novice triathletes I knew. However, as I watched some very experienced competitors, some of whom I had raced against previously, load their bikes back onto the vehicles and drive away I did think that they were taking an easy option. I knew I would be in for a pasting, however, I wanted to earn those club championship points.

After I had racked my bike in transition and had locked my unnecessary wetsuit back in the van, I felt like a bit of a spare part. Phil was nowhere to be seen, and neither were any of my club mates. It was at this point a gentleman walked up to me and asked "Are you Deborah Longman?" "Yes" I replied. We chatted for a while, Nigel is a Welsh Triathlon official who had read my books. We laughed as I said that this race becoming a duathlon would make an interesting chapter. He thanked me for making triathlon more accessible to all through my honesty. That was one of the nicest things anyone had ever said to me.

The sport is in my blood now, whilst I acknowledge that I am never going to podium, or finish in the first half even, I still have that love of the sport and the sense of achievement I get when I cross a finish line.

After speaking to Nigel, I saw a work colleague, Andy, who is also an Ironman, we chatted for a while and before I knew it, it was nearly the start of the race.

I wasn't really looking forward to it, as I had decided that whilst I loved triathlons, I actually hated duathlons.

I went to the start and made my way to the back, joined by Sian who did Blenheim, and Lorna. I knew that whilst we may start together, it wouldn't be long before I would lose them as they are both far better runners than I am.

The gun went off, and as a group we made our best endeavours to battle the wind and attempt to run.

The amended route was four laps of a road that surrounded a car park, and as had happened in the Vale of Glamorgan, I started getting lapped on my second lap. However, just like happened in the Vale, as my club mates passed me they would provide supportive words and a pat on the back. One of these club mates was Awen, a beautiful teenager with an outstanding talent. She was racing in her Wales kit having the honour of representing her country as a junior. She gave me a half tap, half hug as she lapped me and told me well done. She's a sweet girl.

As with the Vale, I was the last competitor to finish the run. I was surprised as I ran into transition to see Awen cheering me. I looked concerned "Are you OK?" I shouted.

"Too windy for the bike." she shouted back, half rolling her eyes and tilting her head towards her coach. I nodded, and secretly thought it was a sensible move from the Welsh coach to not allow this talented young athlete to take the risks against the elements.

I reached the only bike left on the racks, mine, and proceeded to get ready for the next leg.

Chapter 72

I jumped on my bike and hadn't even cycled a hundred yards when my pesky left calf screamed out in protest. "Give me a break." I shouted at my leg, annoyed that my legs had decided to give me the same treatment as they had at the last duathlon. This sudden, but not entirely unexpected pain, coupled with the wind, served to make my cycling speed rather pathetic as I departed the seaside town.

I had cycled the route a few times so I knew what to expect. A few cheeky inclines, a few long open stretches (which I knew would be hell in this wind), one busy road with angry motorists and the infamous Three Step Hill, which does exactly what the name would suggest, make you climb in three steps.

I approached for my first right turn, the marshals had been forewarned on the walkie talkies that I was the last cyclist out. One of the marshals jumped on a bike, a normal bike not a motorbike and became my tail safety bike.

It was about two miles after I had company that we reached an open stretch by the golf course. The side winds were throwing me off balance, I had to slow down, as the road bended around, that sidewind became a brutal headwind. I turned to my companion who was just off my rear wheel and joked "Feel free to go ahead and let me draft you" he laughed, but rightly stayed behind me.

Throughout the first half of the cycle, my calf continued to remind me about its displeasure at cycling after running and I really didn't find my groove. I knew I was slower than I should have been. I kept saying in my head "I bloody hate duathlons" and I vowed on that first half of the cycle that I'd never do another duathlon again.

As I reached the long steady incline of Stormy Down, my calf finally decided to cut me a break and stop hurting, and my cycling groove returned. Suddenly I felt strong again. I felt a smile return to my face. At the top of the incline, my companion cycled alongside me and offered me a drink. He hadn't seen a drink bottle on my bike. What he hadn't noticed was my new handlebar mounted bottle with a long straw which I had been sipping on throughout.

"That's a bit nifty." he exclaimed.

I thanked him for the offer and we chatted for a few minutes about different races. He told me that he was more a cyclist than a triathlete these days and in fact, hadn't entered a triathlon all season. He asked if this was my first and I told him about how it was my second season and how I had developed a passion for the sport despite being rubbish.

I know I shouldn't have chatted really. However, I wasn't really racing for a time. The weather conditions had put pay to that. I was just going to salvage some enjoyment, get to the finish and earn my club championship points.

We approached Three Step Hill, and like with my previous climbs, step one was OK, step two was easy, step three was a total bitch. This time it was not helped by motorists who really wanted to overtake too closely. But once you are at the top then you have the long descent, back to the seaside town. I took the descent slower than usual, not trusting the wet surfaces following the storm and the still feisty winds.

I reached the end of the bike leg, re-racked my bike (as several other competitors were taking theirs to go home) and started my final two lap run.

As I was reaching the halfway point of the first lap, Anthony who was driving off in his van did an extended and excited beep of his horn and waved enthusiastically, and this support gave me all the fire I needed to finish the run and finish the race. I crossed the line, dead last, but with another successful event finished.

Photo: Totally loving the duathlon!!

Photo Credit: Phil Jones

Chapter 73

I had, against my better judgement, squeezed in another race. Phil was wanting to do his first 10k. We had looked at all the usual road ones but for one reason or another he couldn't make them. Then I saw the Llantwit Major 10k advertised on Facebook.

I sent Phil a link, and he instantly fell in love with the medal and decided he was going to do it. He signed up, I didn't. There was a reason why I wasn't keen to sign up. It was a cross country type 10k, lots of off-road running. I am very much a road runner. I like my terrain to be steady underfoot.

My previous dalliances with cross country had been in school. Probably one of my greatest school based faux pas! You see, I was rubbish at sport in school, I hated sport in school. I was one of those children that would get their Mum to write a note. I shudder to think how many supposed periods I had to avoid swimming!

Then there was hockey, I was banned from playing that after an aggressive confrontation on a field which resulted in a broken finger. I wasn't aggressive, but I was the finger breaker. I was just that rubbish at wielding a hockey stick around. Needless to say, the poor girl with the broken finger wasn't overly impressed with me.

But cross country was my greatest triumph at failing in sport. I hated cross country, however, the school route passed a field near my great Auntie's house. And so I hatched a plan. I would start running, make sure that I was nearly at the back, then I would hide in a secluded area of the swings in the park which I knew of from visiting my Auntie, and then I would re-join my classmates as they came back down.

I believed this to be a brilliant plan, I had foiled the system, I would only have to run about a mile instead of three. However, my plan had a flaw. I saw the fastest two girls go past and then I joined and ran back. Ahead of all my friends, ahead of all the girls like me. So when I arrived back at school my games teacher was delighted.

"Deborah, I think we have found your sport. I never knew you were such a good runner."

And so I was assigned a place in the school cross country team. A place I never took up on the grounds that I was actually a pretty crap runner and my fraudulence would have been discovered. Of course, it was discovered during athletics season as there was nowhere to hide on a running track.

So this was my experience of cross country, and due to that, I was happy to let Phil run on his own.

That was until Christine said "I'm running it Deb, you run it too."

Oh Christine, Christine, my gorgeous and lovely friend, why did you have to put that temptation in my way. My cross country days were behind me. However, the temptation to give it a go continued to gnaw on my mind.

"Phil's doing it, Christine is going it, Callum is doing it, Robyn is doing it." suddenly my head made me feel very left out.

However, it was the weekend before my A race, so I vowed to ask Rob and would go with whatever he said.

He said "Do it." Bugger!

So I signed up too. I don't know why, but I did.

We arrived at the venue and registered. However, they had messed up Phil's t-shirt order and so I should have decided then to go home.

We started the race, and the first kilometre was on the road and on the flat, and then we turned up the cobbled incline... ouch! It was steep, in was uneven. That then led to a very big stony field, many hills and so I messaged Rob.

"I bloody hate this." He messaged back "Get off your phone and run, run, run."

And so run I did, until we reached the sugar beet field. I don't know if you have ever run in a field of sugar beet before, if you haven't, I can tell you now, don't bother! Sugar beet look a lot like swede, only they stick out of the ground further than swede and they are harder than swede. And then it happened, I landed awkwardly on an overly protruding beet and my ankle went over.

Bloody great! The pain was instantaneous and I was forced to stop running. I was only 4k in, I was in the middle of nowhere and I had a twisted ankle.

I limped on, and with a bit of time the pain subsided, unless I tried to break into a run again. So that was that, I would have to walk the remaining six kilometres until I could return to civilisation.

However, the universe had chosen to be kind to me, as it sent me another person who was walking more than running. That person was Kimberley. And so we walked together, and we chatted and we became friends (we are Facebook friends now), and chatting to this lovely gorgeous lady got me to the finish.

I crossed the finish line in 1hr 40mins and instantly cursed my husband as I crossed the line. I wasn't the only one who cursed him. Callum had a fall too, and Robyn had vomited. Yep shall not be doing that race again. And when the club mentioned cross country season, I shuddered and am making my excuses! I'm sticking to the road, it's safer.

Chapter 74

It was the day of my big race, my final race of the season. My whole season had been geared at this point. My first Olympic Distance triathlon. A race where I would effectively double what I had done previously.

It would be a 1500m swim, a 40km bike ride and a 10k run. When my race pack had arrived I'd had a little bit of a wobble as it said that competitors would be expected to finish in 3 and a half hours. This was the first time a cut off had been mentioned. I was pissed off. I did my maths, 50 mins for the swim, 1 hour 40ish for the bike, an hour and a half easily for the run, add in transitions, I was going to be looking at nearer 4 hours. I emailed the organisers, nothing. I sent a Facebook message to the organisers, nothing. I found the name of one of the organisers, hunted him down on Facebook with a private message, nothing. So I made my decision. I was racing, I was going to keep racing and they'd need to wrestle me to the ground to get my timing chip off me. If they didn't have the courtesy to reply to me, then I wouldn't have the courtesy to stop at their arbitrary, no explanation given cutoffs.

I arrived, registered, racked my bike and stood looking at the sea. The waves were worse than Porthcawl where the swim had been called off. I had come to the conclusion that mother nature was having a laugh at my expense. Several competitors were asking if the sea swim would go ahead. Next to the sea is a harbour. The year before they had moved the swim from the sea to the harbour, but had complaints from competitors about the taste of diesel from the boats. I looked at the sea and decided I'd much prefer a diesel tasting harbour swim to battling the waves, which were around eight-foot-high with a big swell. It would have been a surfer's paradise, an unlikely triathlete's, not so much.

I waited anxiously for the decision. The start time for the race came and went, the organisers chatted with the lifeboats. What would the decision be?

Then a lifeboat was seen taking a buoy out to the sea, guess that was decision made. The sea swim was going ahead.

The waiting masses became a hive of activity "I can't believe they are letting us swim in that.", "Right that's it I'm out.", "Why don't they just use the harbour?" For every positive comment, I heard at least five negative comments, people shocked and bemused that we were being let in the sea.

I was chatting at this point to Tula and Lorna. Tula was now only a couple of weeks away from her ironman, she was focussed and determined, she was getting in that sea. Lorna, naturally, was a little more apprehensive. I on the other hand was totally shitting myself!

"What's the worse that could happen?" I asked nervously. Tula, without missing a beat, responded "You could drown Deb, you could drown, that would be the worst."

I laughed, she was right, but yet her macabre sense of humour gave me a slight moment of ease.

However, as I looked at the sea, I very much doubted that my swimming was strong enough. Whilst my swimming had improved, I was still very much a novice when it came to sea swimming.

I placed myself at the back of the pack ready to enter the water and kissed my husband goodbye. I felt physically sick.

As we headed into the water the waves were lapping and I saw a rescue canoe capsize. Bloody marvellous. A few of us at the back, instead of running full on into the water, walked gingerly towards the sea. Fear evident in all our faces.

Before I knew it, I was in and I started to swim the best I could towards the first buoy. The waves were relentless, they were high, the swell made breathing difficult. I began to realise I was out of my depth big time.

I watched as better faster swimmers were powering under the waves and making their approach to the buoy, I felt I was not moving at all. The waves hurt as they crashed over me. I was just getting a battering I was not swimming. The swim course was to be two laps, reach the first buoy to the left, swim straight to the buoy on the right and then swim into shore and start the triangle again.

I was still not even halfway to the first buoy; I knew in my heart I couldn't make it there and even if I could and could manage the easier horizontal section that I'd never be able to do it again after I'd finished the triangle.

As I tried a while longer on my assault against the sea, my arms began to ache and I was officially in trouble. In triathlon they tell you, if you get into trouble, roll onto your back and put your arm in the air and a rescue boat will come to you. I did just this, I rolled onto my back and put my arm in the air. However, with the eight foot relentless waves I couldn't see a rescue boat and more importantly a rescue boat couldn't see me.

As I was on my back a huge wave took me by surprise and crashed over my head, sending me hurtling under the water. At this point I thought that was it. I genuinely thought that the sea would take another victim, I was convinced I would die. However, I surfaced, I coughed and spluttered as I tried to rid my lungs of the water they had taken on.

I looked to my left and saw another competitor in trouble. I shouted to him.

"Are you OK?"

"No, I'm heading back." he replied.

And our decision was jointly made, we got close to each other and started to try and get back into shore.

We were about half way back when the lifeboat men spotted us. However, with the waves so aggressive they were unable to come to rescue us in a boat. They did, however, tether themselves together, and wait for us to become close enough to grab hold of us and drag us back in.

I felt beaten, I felt defeated. As the two men held onto me for dear life I sobbed and realised I'd had a very lucky escape.

As I looked at the shore, I could see Phil. It surprised me, usually when I'd say goodbye he'd be off like a whippet to his predetermined cycle photo spot. However, today something had made him stay. Call it a sixth sense, call it a premonition, however, he knew he needed to stay put.

I sobbed harder as I saw him, the relief really hitting me. I could see the love and concern in his face as he anxiously watched the scene unfold. As the lifeboat men handed me over to the ambulance crew, Phil was instantly at my side.

I couldn't tell you exactly what I said but I know it included the fact that I was a failure. He tried to assure me that I wasn't.

I apologised to the ambulance crew as I got the van soaking wet, but after them quickly checking me over I assured them that I was fine and was OK to go home. That was all I wanted to do, retrieve my bike, give them my chip back and go home.

I cried most of the way home. Part relief, part my sense of failure. If it had been any other race I don't think it would have mattered as much. However, this was my A race, my big race, my focus of my whole seasons training and it had defeated me.

As we reached home I said to Phil.

"I'm going swim training this afternoon."

I knew in myself I needed to get back in the water, even if it was in the safety of the pool.

I had messaged Rob, my coach, on my way home and he rang me to check I was OK.

As I lay in a hot bath, I made a decision. I was signing up for another race. I wasn't going to allow my season to end on a downer.

After I got out of the bath and whilst I was getting ready for swim training, I started to get some messages on Facebook.

Experienced ironman finishers and talented club mates had just finished the race and were posting to check I was OK. Several of the seasoned athletes who had been racing for years said how it was one of the worst swims they had ever done. As it happened, after the first lap, the organisers made all the competitors get out of the sea, deciding it was too dangerous to let the second lap go ahead.

At that discovery I began second guessing myself. If I had persevered could I have finished a lap? Being honest with myself I knew the answer, no I couldn't have.

I went swim training. As I walked into the pool I was hugged by my friends and coaches, them all relieved that I was OK.

Laura, God love her, punched my arm lightly and said "some people will do anything to get a good chapter." And I laughed. Although, dear reader, I can honestly say I would have preferred not having to write this traumatising tale!

I got in the pool, and I swam to the deep end. I got to the end, I turned and I swam back. As I hit the wall at the shallow end I started to cry again. The realisation hit me that I could have died. I spent much of the session chatting to Mike and Tracey, keen for tips on how to never let that happen again. And between chatting, I swam, I didn't do the set that was planned, I just swam a bit, talked a bit and counted my blessings to be alive.

Chapter 75

At the tail end of September there aren't that many races left. However, I was determined to do another. There was one that still had spaces. The Pontypridd Aquathlon, a nice easy 400 metre swim followed by a 5k run. It was held in the newly renovated Pontypridd Lido, a magnificent outdoor pool that had been much neglected until lottery funding restored it to it's former glory. Originally opened in the 1920s, the lido was a popular location, however a fire had resulted in it closing its doors in 1991. The listed building was now to be home to swimmers again, and I was excited at the prospect of swimming in an outdoor pool.

I was also excited as Phil was also racing, as were Karl and Helen from our club. What excited me slightly less was the weather. I used to live in Pontypridd, I went to university there, and in the two decades since I had I left I can say that the typical Pontypridd climate of pouring with rain was still very much in appearance.

I was a little nervous as to what the temperature of the water would be like. After Phil and I had got changed we dipped our toes in the water. It felt warm.

I was going off in the first wave along with Helen, Phil in the third wave, Karl in the fourth. Phil and Karl stood at different vantage points to cheer me for the swim.

There were to be four of us per lane. Each of us would wear a different coloured swim hat to help the lap counters. I jumped in, along with my lane buddies, however as one of them had chosen not to turn up our lane would only be three of us. The water was warm, like bath water warm. At the race briefing we were told we would be set off at 5 sec intervals, and if you caught the competitor in front of you, tap them on their toes and then they were to let you go first on the next length.

We were placed in order, the man first, then me, then the other lady. I had made a decision about the race. I was just getting over a cold so I was not going to push myself. I was just going to have fun and end my season. Phil waved to me from the other end of the pool in a spectator area, I shouted to him

"It's like a bath."

"What?" he shouted back, unable to hear me.

"IT'S LIKE A BATH!" I shouted again, louder this time, however, his shrug was to prove he couldn't understand what I was saying.

The whistle went and my lane buddy swam off, then my whistle went and I was off. As I reached the end, I shouted again to Phil who was now much closer.

"This water is lovely, it's like swimming in a bath."

However, what was different to it being like bath water was the heavy cold rain that was bucketing down on top of us as we swam.

I decided I really loved this Lido, and maybe this wouldn't be an isolated visit to my former home town.

I had done only two lengths when I realised I was going to catch my lane buddy, I was two thirds up the third length when I reached him and tapped him on his feet. We got to the end, but instead of letting me go first, he just pushed off. I shrugged to the watching Phil, pausing for a minute, and then started swimming back down. As I caught him, I hit his feet again. At the end, he pushed off again.

I played this game for a few lengths by which time my lane follower had caught me, she tapped my feet, we got to the end, I let her go. I watched as she reached the man. Did he let her pass? Did he hell!

On her next swim up, she waited until had I passed them in the opposite direction and then she overtook him. Good plan, I thought.

I didn't catch him at the next length, as I had paused at the end to check how many lengths I had done, having thought I'd lost count due to my frustrations. However, at the next length, I caught him as we were getting towards the end of the lane, I overtook him, I turned at the end, started back in the opposite direction and he kicked me. Hmmmph! I gasped at the surprise at being kicked and ended up swallowing a bit of water, so I turned to breast stroke whilst I was spluttering, as my breast stroke is significantly slower than my crawl he overtook me!

For the remaining lengths, every length I hit his feet, every length he'd push off the wall and wouldn't let me pass. With each passing length I hit his feet slightly harder. By the end of the 16 lengths I was quite sure I'd have bruised him. He got out of the pool, before me as of course the inconsiderate moron hadn't let me past, and I moaned to the lane counter.

"Did you see how many times I hit his feet."

He laughed and replied "and he wouldn't let you past would he."

However, I was doing this race for fun, to enjoy myself and to end my season on a high. So, I laughed with my lane counting friend and shrugged it off, quickly putting on my now very wet socks and shoes.

The rain poured down, I actually think that as I started my run in my tri suit I was actually wetter than I was when I got out of the pool. I was, however, smiling. This was a lovely race, the marshals were lovely as they stood in the weather getting soaked. I chatted and thanked each and every one of them.

On my second lap of the run, I saw Phil and gave him a high five.

I tried to really take in every minute of this 5k run, to really take the time to appreciate the beautiful park surroundings. To smile at my fellow competitors, to appreciate the people who had come out to support. And as I crossed the finish line and was handed a medal, my face beaming, I knew I had ended my second season as the Unlikely Triathlete a success.

Epilogue 4

So, I hadn't planned my season to be as dramatic as it had ended up being. It had some highs, it had some lows. I am pleased to report that I have since seen the cardiologist and all is well. Basically, the cardiologist believes my episode was caused by dehydration. She has, however, discovered I have a slight heart murmur. Although, she has confirmed that my training is the absolute best thing to keep it under control and so has actively encouraged me to keep going.

On reflection, I need to keep reminding myself how far I have come. When I started my journey into the world of triathlon, less than two years ago, I couldn't swim properly, I couldn't run and my cycling pace could be described "leisurely" at best.

However, in even this short space of time, I have grown and have reaped the rewards of my hard work in training. I can now swim front crawl and whilst I know my stroke needs some work (particularly in the sea), I have done far more than I thought possible. I regularly swim a mile in a training session and it keeps getting easier.

My cycling, yes there is room for improvement, but I have exceeded an average speed of over 15 miles per hour on two of my races, when I started I couldn't sustain 11 miles per hour.

And my running, I may be slow, but not only have I reached 5k and 10k, I have completed a half marathon.

So, with this in mind, I made a decision. I wasn't going to allow my failure at Olympic Distance to hold me back. I need to keep pushing forward, trying to be the best I can be. So, the register button was pressed, I have signed up for my first half iron distance.

In June, I shall be attempting to swim 1.2 miles, cycle 56 miles and then run a half marathon. I'm hoping that you will come along with me for my journey and hopefully read all about it in The Unlikely Triathlete Part Five!

The End - well for now!

Part Five

The Athlete Awakens

Dedication 5

I am dedicating this book to Olympic Gold Medallist, Joanna Rowsell-Shand. If you've read book one you will know that it was Jo who inspired me to get back on a bike. I honestly don't think I'd be where I am today if I hadn't met her. I wish her every luck in her retirement.

Prologue 5

Two triathlon seasons down. 2016 was certainly a dramatic year for me. What with needing to be rescued from the sea and a further heart scare. However, it also proved that I could blag it in the sport of triathlon. I still don't see myself as an athlete. Let's face it, I am still slow. I am never going to podium, but I am going to have fun. And if I have learned anything from the relatively short amount of time in this sport, I have learned it is important to challenge yourself, but it's equally important to enjoy every second. At the end of the last book I announced that I had signed up to do a Half Iron distance event. This event isn't Ironman branded, but it is Half Iron distance. I will swim 1.2 miles, I will cycle 56 miles and then I will run a half marathon of 13.1 miles. When I first pressed the submit button on the registration form these distances seemed scary. As my training progresses, I am no longer intimidated by them. Don't get me wrong, I understand and appreciate that these distances are long, very long, but they no longer hold an air of scary mystique. I am completing my training, I am working hard, and come the start of June I will be ready. However, a journey starts with a single step, so let's take a look at what I have been up to.

Chapter 76

My first half marathon was Swansea in the June of 2016. I had followed my training plan to the letter and I was ready. I executed the run of my life and achieved my goal of a sub three-hour half marathon. My second was to be less impressive.

Cardiff Half was another iconic half marathon, gosh even Mo Farrah had run it, so it must be good. However, in the October of 2016 I was not sufficiently prepared.

I had been working so hard on my swimming that my running distances had dropped, and in the run up to this half I had barely run over 10k, less than half the distance. It didn't matter though, I was still going to run, and I was going to enjoy the experience.

I had spoken to Rob, my coach, about it. He had been the one to have me concentrating on my swimming and cycling and so had said to me.

"Walk what you need to, just enjoy the day, go and have fun."

This was just what I needed to hear, and when Christine messaged me to say that Sarah was having a meltdown about the event, I knew what I needed to do.

Sarah hadn't long lost her Dad, her grief had thrown a spanner in the works of her training. However, she had signed up to run Cardiff Half to raise money for the Air Ambulance in tribute to her Dad.

I sent her a message to tell her not to panic. That I too was underprepared and we would stick together to get to the finish.

It came to the day of the event, Christine messaged us the night before to say that they were meeting in the pub for breakfast before the start.

So, the following morning on race day, Phil armed with his camera and a folding bike and I armed with my running kit and jelly babies headed to Cardiff.

I'm quite lucky that my sister lives in Cardiff, only a short walk from the city centre. We parked at her house and headed in to meet our friends.

It was honestly the most chilled out I had ever been about an event. I was going in without a plan, well unless you can class finishing and having fun along the way as a plan. I hadn't put any pressure on myself about achieving a time, and equally Rob didn't have any expectations for me.

As we sat in the pub with a coffee, chatting with our friends, it seemed that Callum was the only one feeling a bit of pressure. His running had become astonishing! He'd worked so hard at improving his pace and his times and he did have a goal, a sub 2 hr. Me? Well I was just happy if Sarah and I crossed the finish before the 4 and a half hour cut off!

Sarah was hyper, I was quite sure that she'd been at the jelly babies already as she appeared to be having a sugar rush! I knew I was going to be in for an entertaining time!

As we left the pub for the athletes' village, Sarah spied Phil's Brompton bike.

"Let me have a go, let me have a go." she squealed like an excited child.

Phil has learnt over the time we have been friends that it's best to give in to Sarah and her demands.

As she straddled the bike she was pleased. Phil on the other hand was slightly terrified about his beloved bike.

As we walked to the start area, I spoke to Sarah.

"Do you have a strategy you want us to follow?"

"I don't know," she replied, "what are you thinking".

I made an initial suggestion to run a kilometre, then walk a half kilometre and repeat for as long as we could.

"If we can also walk the hills, it sounds like a plan." Sarah approved.

The sheer number of athletes taking part amazed me. Also, the time expectations in the pens. It amazed me the number of people running that were in the early colour coded pens, people with sub 1 and a half hours aims, sub 1.45, sub 2 and then were the masses in the over 2 hrs. It shocked me that this was the last group. Gosh, in my mind I'd have expected a sub 2.5, maybe even a sub 3 divider. It seemed unfair that people who may come in at 2hrs 10 would be bunched with someone who may do a 4hr 10, but that was what the organisers had decided, so who was I to argue.

However, what this approach meant was that I could stay with Christine for a little longer. Sadly, we had lost Sue in a toilet queue, but she also had friends from her running club so we knew she wasn't alone.

"So, you know where we are meeting when we finished." Christine confirmed, having already given us directions to another pub. I saw a theme developing!

I nodded, Sarah tried to photobomb a selfie.

It was nearly time for the start. I looked to my side to see a man barefoot. Sarah also spotted him, and he would provide us with some conversation on the course.

"But what about stones, or glass, or dog poo?" We both agreed that barefoot running in Cardiff city centre was not a good plan.

When the klaxon went off, we slowly shuffled forward amongst the masses, until we had sufficient space to start to run.

The idea was to run at a pace where we could still just about have a conversation. We hadn't seen each other for ages, and this was going to be an ideal chance to catch up on what had been happening in each other's lives.

As we reached the first kilometre, we were both ready for a walking break. As we walked, Sarah came up with a plan. "When we see Phil, we need to pose for some really daft photos." she decided.

I giggled, she was right. If we were going to have fun, then we really wanted some silly photos to go with it. We decided the first one we would tango!

As we saw Phil we knew what we needed to do. We tangoed and he looked at us like we had gone insane. We laughed. This was certainly a different and entertaining race.

The approach of running a kilometre, walking half was working well for us. However, as we reached Penarth hill, we knew we'd have to walk up it and delay our run. It didn't matter. We were having a brilliant time. As we reached Penarth there was a woman who had on the back of her t-shirt "Please let there be someone slower than me who can read this." As we passed her, whilst grabbing some free sweets from an enthusiastic child, I said "I read it and there are plenty behind me." She looked at me quizzically, obviously forgetting what she was wearing.

It was then time for the Cardiff Bay Barrage. As I reached it, I rang my sister. A strange thing to do during a half marathon you may think. However, I wanted to provide her with an estimated time that we would be passing where she lived. I wanted my nephew and niece to come and see me run. I wanted to be a positive role model to them, so that they could see that doing things like triathlons or running races was a fun and good thing to do.

It was on the barrage that we first spotted the firemen. Several of them, all dressed in full protective gear. We admired them as we ran past. At around this point, I had noticed that our running pace was a little slower than it had been earlier in the race. We were, however, still very much enjoying putting the world to rights.

As we finished the barrage I turned to Sarah.

"I'm going to stop and give my niece and nephew a hug if you don't mind."

"Not at all." she replied.

As I approached Lloyd George Avenue, which was where I knew my family would be stood, I felt the need to run again. I didn't want to reach them and them see me walking.

As I saw my sister, I saw that only Martha my niece was with her.

"Where's Robert?" I asked.

"At home." she replied "He's not feeling very well"

However, little Martha was very excited at seeing her Auntie Deb and we had a big cuddle and a brief chat. Although I knew we had to get moving again.

As Sarah and I started running again, we almost missed Phil and his camera who was literally yards away from my sister but hadn't seen her.

We were now at around the half way mark, and we were slow! I could see that Sarah was struggling to run.

"We can walk if you want." I said to her.

She nodded and we were to pretty much walk the rest of the half marathon.

However, by walking, we did get to see the firemen again and I got a cheeky photo. We also saw Alfie and his angels. Alfie is a rugby player and was training people for the half. Sarah knew who he was and got very excited to have her photo taken with him.

We were still enjoying our conversation.

We were around mile nine when Sarah said .

"How are we doing for time?"

She knew I had been studying the mile splits on my watch.

"I reckon we will come in at about 3hrs 30." I said.

These last few miles were full of no expectation. We chatted to the supporters who were stood outside their houses, Sarah even asked one family for a glass of their Prosecco! We were just taking in the party atmosphere at the back of the race.

We were to see Phil another once, we pulled a few poses, giggled and proceeded to the finish, which we tangoed down, narrowly getting beaten by a man in an electric wheelchair.

3hrs 32mins, totally awesome race!

Photo: With Sarah at Cardiff Half Marathon

Chapter 77

Triathletes deserve some downtime, right? Well the perfect downtime would come in the shape of the Celtic Tri annual awards dinner. A night for dressing up and reflecting on people's achievements for the year.

I was excited about this event, as I had worked out, I would be receiving an award. I came third place in my division in our annual club championship. An achievement based not on athletic merit, but rather that I had done more races (albeit badly) than other people that shared the division.

In the run up there had been a lot of both excited and nervous posts about what people were going to wear. This had been from both men and women! My Phil was probably the worst offender. Whilst he loves the club, he hates getting dressed up. He wore a t-shirt and a pair of trousers when we got married. He did not want to wear a suit! The only suit he had was reserved for job interviews and funerals, but he decided to attend this event. He would need a new suit.

I also knew I needed a new dress. I am uncomfortable in smart clothes, and only own one pair of high heeled shoes, in black. I had no intention of buying another pair of heels, so knew I'd have to find a dress that would match the heels.

My mission was a simple one, it needed to be posh enough for a do, and it needed to be cheap! In the grand scheme of things, I don't think twice about paying £50 or more for a pair of cycle shorts, however, any money spent on normal clothes and I have a hissy fit if I am spending more than a tenner.

As luck would have it, my needing to buy a new dress also coincided with a clearance sale at John Lewis and I ended up getting a rather appropriate black lace dress reduced from £99 to the bargain price of £12. I didn't particularly like it, but I wasn't going to like any dress really. I did like the price and so that would be my dress!

Phil also was rather lucky, and he too managed to get a suit that didn't look "funerally" in the sale. Bargain, more of our hard-earned cash to spend on triathlon gear!

The event was taking place on a Friday night. We had chosen to book a room in the hotel where the event was taking place for a few reasons. Firstly, we wouldn't have far to go at the end of the night whilst hideously drunk. Secondly, by having our own room we could bring our own wine so we wouldn't have to pay inflated bar prices.

I was working in Swansea the day of the event, so went straight from work to the hotel only a matter of minutes away. I had decided that I would use the hotel pool and get a quick swim in (once a triathlete, always a triathlete hey!). Phil was working in Cardiff, so was getting the train back.

I returned to the hotel room after my swim to a few missed calls from Phil. The train had broken down. He was in Port Talbot, seemly stranded! My super hero, wonder woman vibe didn't kick in as it should have and I lamented to myself about having to fetch him with wet hair when all I wanted to do was chill out and get ready. Thankfully, luck was on my side, as he was already in a taxi to travel the last 15 miles to the hotel. Whilst I baulked at the potential huge waste of cash he was splurging, I was actually secretly relieved that I didn't have to come to his rescue. When he arrived at the hotel he came straight to the room with a cocktail for each of us and I knew we were in for a partying kind of night.

We met our friends at the bar, and I have to say we all scrub up pretty well. It was great to see all my friends dressed to the nines. Usually, we see each other in lycra and covered in sweat. Tonight, we were in our all dressed up and ready to party.

When we were allowed into the hall, we were given our tables. The way it had worked out, Phil was the only man on a table with seven women. This did not bother him one little bit, in fact, I think he secretly enjoyed having so many gorgeous ladies around him.

The meal was a fairly simple affair, but tasty and plentiful, even for people who burn enough calories to make themselves ravenous for 95% of the time.

It then came to the time of the evening when the awards were to be handed out. I enjoyed going up and collecting my award for coming third in the division.

Then Tracey started reading out some of the more unusual awards. Some were fun ones, like Phil was given an award for taking so many photos of club members and was rewarded with a selfie stick! Then Paul took over for the more serious awards for some of our athletes who had achieved some amazing things.

The next award, was the "uphill determination" award. This was traditionally given to an athlete that had overcome struggles and was determined to do their best in the sport. Paul began his speech "The person who is to receive this award would never think they deserve an award." I began looking around the room, seeing several of my club mates that could be worthy recipients of this award.

"However, we believe that she does." I thought to myself that the award was going to a woman. I had a few names in my mind as to who that should be. Several of my female friends had done some awesome things in the season. I couldn't wait to congratulate whoever it was.

Then Paul continued "This lady has struggled with her health, suffers with a long-term condition and still puts in 100% effort."

Hang on a minute.

"She never lets anything get in her way, even if that means getting rescued from the sea."

Oh no! Oh really? He's talking about me, I'm getting this award. Bloody hell.

I continue listening to the very kind words that Paul is saying about me. How I am inspirational! No, that's you mate! You are a multiple ironman and a former Welsh rugby international!!

I become acutely aware that all eyes in the room are looking at me, my ears start to burn in embarrassment and my eyes start to well with tears.

When he calls my name, I walk up with good grace becoming a self-fulfilling prophecy as I think to myself "I don't deserve this reward."

I can hear people cheer, people applaud. My friends and club mates obviously thinking I do deserve it. As Tracey, our club chair and my very dear friend, hands me my award I can barely hold in the tears.

Me! Getting recognition for my efforts. Being a multi award winning athlete in that night. The teenage me would never have believed it, having faked several "sicknotes" for PE claiming I had yet another period. But it was true. I was getting an award in sport. I don't think I have ever felt so proud of myself.

Chapter 78

With my two awards safely moved from the table to security of the hotel room I was getting drunk, really drunk! I still couldn't quite believe how the evening had unfolded.

As I sat in the corner, hugging Lisa, in that drunk way that people do, she whispered to me.

"You so deserve the award, you are bloody brillian.t"

We started to dance the night away, I had a few dances with Mark and it took me right back to school discos nearly two decades before. We were all having a totally awesome night. There was a scary moment when Phil was busted that we were smuggling our own wine in, but we just about got away with it.

We are there getting increasingly rat arsed when Phil announces. "I'm going to do parkrun tomorrow."

"Yeah right." We all respond. Mike the coach raises an eyebrow, "really Phil?"

"I'm doing parkrun." he replied indignantly.

At this point is was approaching 1am, parkrun would start at nine.

The DJ stopped the music at 1.30am.

"I don't want to stop yet, shall we go to town?" Sian asked.

Phil went to bed, I went out.

Sian, Meinir, Sonia, David and I continued to the nightclub, swapping wine for shots!

We were in one nightclub, dancing away when a rather gross old man comes up to me.

"You were in the Queen's earlier wasn't you."

"No." I replied.

"Yes, you were, I saw you in the Queen's."

"No, I wasn't." I replied, irritated.

He went to start speaking again when pocket rocket Sian butts in.

"Look she wasn't in the Queen's, now off you fuck."

This simple little saying "off you fuck" has now become a firm favourite of us all.

We carry on dancing, our heels now starting to cause us discomfort.

Sian and I take our heels off and continue dancing.

A bouncer comes up to us "You are going to have to put your shoes back on ladies."

Sian's response was the funniest things I have ever heard. Here was Sian, a smidgen over 5 foot, teeny tiny in comparison to this big burly 6 and a half foot tall and wide bouncer. She squares clean up to him, trying her hardest to look him in the eye, as she only came up to his chest, and she replied

"I am an ironman, I don't have to wear shoes."

At 3am we were kicked out of the club!

David was a total gentleman and ensured that I got back to the hotel safe and that the ladies got into a taxi.

The following morning, Phil did parkrun. I don't think I
sobered up until mid-afternoon.

Photo: with my two awards

Chapter 79

"I really think you need a new bike." Rob was on my case. He hated my flat bar road bike.

"Or at least put drops on your existing bike."

I was resisting, but deep down I knew he was right. With the half ironman I knew I'd be better off with the extra hand positioning of a traditional road bike, and knew that a carbon fibre frame would probably be better.

"I also think you need a turbo." Rob was pushing his luck! He was trying to bankrupt me.

However, sometimes fate hands you some weird curve balls. Earlier in the year, Phil had been made redundant. He had four months off work whilst trying to find a new job (and was the best househusband ever until he found work!). However, as we had been careful during his unemployment, we did have redundancy money left.

"Have the bike and the turbo." Phil said, adding "I'll get a new bike too."

I decided that an investment as big as that was something not to be rushed into. I went to the local bike shop and managed to get a demo bike for a week, so that I could see if I could get used to the more aerodynamic positioning. After a couple of rides, I decided it was something that I could get used to. It was time to take the plunge.

So here we were, splashing out more money than some people would spend on a second hand car on two new bikes and a rather swanky direct drive turbo.

A waste of money? Maybe. But we were lucky that we had the money at our disposal, and sometimes you just have to be a bit reckless.

We decided to go for bikes with identical specs and identical gearing so we could both use the turbo (as we needed to fit a cassette to the turbo), so became the proud owners of new carbon fibre bikes.

As soon as "she" arrived, I fell in love with her, naming my new bike "Katie". I wasn't one really for naming bikes, but we bonded.

I also enjoyed having the turbo too, with the direct drive being far smoother than the previous turbo I had borrowed from a work colleague.

I was in for a good winter of home training, and boy did Rob have some challenging indoor workouts for me.

Chapter 80

There is a generally accepted view in the world of triathlon that if you can do double the distance of each event, that you'll be OK on race day with the three combined. I don't know if that's true but I decided I needed to do a marathon. Knowing that I would need to do a half marathon at the end of a triathlon, I came out with a hair brained scheme that between Christmas and New Year I would complete a marathon.

I asked a few club mates if they fancied it, and whilst there was some initial interest, when the reality kicked in, I was to be left alone.

I asked Rob for his blessing, and he gave it, albeit reluctantly and under the promise that I was to walk it and not run it, spoil sport!

So, between Christmas and New Year, I decided I would be doing My Marathon, My Way.

The date was set, Wednesday 28th December, full of mince pies, I left the house to do my marathon.

As it was an event of my own making, there would be no feed stations. So instead, I wore my usual drink race belt I use for longer distance events, and packed a backpack with extra liquids, some sandwiches and a few bananas. I was set.

It was a surprisingly frosty morning as the weather had been quite good, so the first stretch getting out of the estate to the main road was quite slippery, slowing my pace before I even started. Ah well, it was about the distance not the time.

When I got to the main road, I had the two mile descent to town and picked my walking pace, stepping gingerly when I spotted patches of ice. December probably wasn't the wisest time to embark on this challenge. It was cold but I felt positive. I had plotted my route in my mind. I was going to head to the Mumbles and then walk back just past Swansea. Phil being his usual superhero self had agreed to meet me at the metaphorical finish line.

I was only four miles in when I had a bit of gastric distress, however, I was approaching an area with public toilets. They are the dodgiest public toilets I know, and on the rare occasions I have needed to use them I have kept my wits about me, fearing some kind of mugger... or worse! I did what I needed to do, washed my hands, and dried them in my leggings as there are no hand dryers. I celebrated being still in one piece and continued on my journey, deciding to eat a banana.

It was shortly after this that my hands started to swell. Like really swell. I could barely bend my fingers, I tried making fists and releasing it in the hope that this would improve them. It didn't and my hands were to give me grief for the remainder of my walk.

375

Between mile five and mile ten I was on cycle paths that are rarely frequented by walkers or runners. I said hello to the few cyclists that passed me, but I was mostly on my own. I quite enjoyed being alone with my thoughts, and I was surprisingly quite glad that my club mates had decided not to join me, as I came to the realisation that on race days I would be on my own, this was a mental battle I needed to do by myself.

As I reached the sea front at Swansea, I could feel my phone vibrating in my running belt. I didn't stop walking but I did get my phone out. I have a WhatsApp group with some of my old school friends. Some of us have known each other since we were babies and we are still all good friends. In the main, I don't think they really understand my sporting exploits, even though they are supportive. The one friend who did understand was Judith, as she had done the London Marathon.

The conversations were about what everyone was up to, I casually announced that I was part way around doing a marathon. Jud instantly reacted to provide me with motivation.

I hit the Mumbles at mile 16, and did what you have to do when you reach an iconic landmark. You take a selfie! I sent it to Phil, to my sister, to my friends on What's app and to a few club mates too. 16 miles and feeling strong.

The Mumbles is also home to the greatest ice cream parlour on the planet, and despite it being cold, I had promised myself that if I was feeling good at the Mumbles that I would treat myself to a Joe's ice cream; a coffee nut sundae. I would, of course, have to eat it whilst walking but it was worth the sacrifice as I had been on my feet for my longest distance to date and still had 10 miles to go. I had to join a short queue to get my frozen creamy treat, but it was worth it. I was rather warm due to the amount of exercise I had already done and the sweetness gave me a boost of energy. I continued with a renewed enthusiasm. I was doing a marathon.

At around mile 20 I reached my last set of public toilets, and whilst I didn't need to go, I made myself have a wee as I knew I'd have no chance in the last 6 miles. I sent another message to my friends on my Whats app group, getting the response from Jud to keep going and that I could do it. They say you hit a bit of a wall at mile 22, I don't know if knowing this salient fact actually made me hit a wall or if I would have done anyway, but I hurt. I was tired, I was struggling. I grabbed my last banana out of my backpack which was battered and bruised and I forced it down, along with about half a dozen jelly babies. I needed the energy.

From mile 23 it actually became easy again. Even though I knew that Phil had been tracking me online, I rang him to let him know where I was and to make sure he would be there to fetch me at our rendezvous point, a layby on a back road near the Amazon warehouse… glamorous finish line or what.

At mile 25, I started to cry a little, I'd left my house in the morning and I was going to achieve what I set out to do. I was going to do a marathon. As I walked down the Amazon back road I felt proud of myself. I saw Phil waiting in the car in the layby. I looked down at my watch 25.9 miles. I pointed at my watch, as if to say "not quite there" and continued past him as he looked a little bemused. With .3 of a mile to go to hit the magic 26.2, I continued down the road for another 0.15 miles, then turned back towards my waiting husband.

I reached him, threw my hands in the air in celebration. Marathon done. 7hrs 20mins. Not fast, not pretty, no t-shirt, no cheering crowds, no medal. But I had done My Marathon, My Way!

Photo: At the finish line of My Marathon, My Way

Chapter 81

I woke up excited. Today I was going to be trying something new. I was going to be doing something that made me fall in love with cycling as a spectator sport. I was going to the velodrome to ride!

Phil was going too and he was also crazy excited. We'd been trying to get a velodrome taster session for a long time, both of us eager to try our luck on the boards. The event had been organised by former GB paracyclist Simon Richardson in aid of the Air Ambulance. I was as keen to meet this sporting hero as I was to cycle.

We arrived at the velodrome and got our rental track bikes. Anyone not familiar with track cycling need to know a few salient points about track bikes. Firstly, there are no brakes! You have to slow down by pedalling slower and by grabbing the railings in the middle to stop. Secondly, they only have one fixed gear, so no changing up and down, you get the gear you are given and that's it. Finally, they are a fixed wheel. What this means is that you can't stop pedalling, there is no free wheel option. You stop turning your feet around and the back wheel stops, basically giving you a kick up the arse in the process.

Now, I like freewheeling, I like changing gears and I like brakes, so I knew this would be taking me way out of my comfort zone, but I was eager to try.

There was a decent number of us who had turned out. They split us into two groups, novices and those with experience. Phil and I would be in the novice group being track virgins.

The coach, Jason, was quite spectacular, friendly and supportive. He set us off around the blue band at the bottom of the track called the "côte d'azur". I had barely done my first lap when I forget that freewheeling was not an option and got a kick up the backside by the saddle. Ouch! I continued my laps, and already started to fear coming to a stop. I'm not the most co-ordinated person on a bike anyhow. My feet were strapped to the pedals, no way I could easily put my foot down. I'd have to "unstrap" once I'd come to a standstill. I was not liking this idea at all. As I continued going round and round in circles, I came to a realisation. I was totally hating it. I really wasn't enjoying it at all. The bike was in control of me, I was not in control of the bike. Bad bike, nasty bike, nasty riding, yuk, yuk, yuk. I slowed my pedalling and eyed the barrier ahead of me, I needed to grab it and pull myself to a stop. It wasn't a good stop, I nearly go over the handlebars, the bike starts sliding sideways. I plead to be let out of my pedals and decide, I've given it a go, never again!

I enjoyed watching the rest of the session, particularly watching Phil who seemed to be in his element, he was going further up the track. Navigating around cones for bike handling. You could see by his face he was loving every second.

I'm glad I went though, as I made a few new friends that day, not only Simon and Jason but also Jacqui, a woman who had completed several ironman events, including qualifying for and competing in the world championships in Kona, Hawaii.

Phil is now a regular at the velodrome. I am firmly in the spectator camp. What it gave me though was an even greater appreciation and respect for track cyclists.

Photo: At the Velodrome on a track bike

Chapter 82

Newport half marathon. I was past the scary edge that my first half marathon had. I was surprisingly relaxed about it all, like I was at Cardiff, even though I knew I wanted to put in a better effort. It was, however, Phil's first half marathon and he was bricking it. He needn't have been nervous, he had trained well and had put in the work, but a half marathon is a feat to be respected.

The day before we had travelled up to Newport, pausing en-route in Cardiff to see the family and to go for a family meal to celebrate my niece's birthday. The weather was awful, it was bucketing down with rain with a nasty wind. We pitched up in our cheap and cheerful Travelodge. Nothing fancy, just a bed for the night. With the weather being as bad as it was, and with a full belly after a family meal, also combined with the fact that Newport on a Saturday night is actually quite an intimidating place, we made the call to nip to the little Sainsbury's and just pick up a buffet of rolls and cheeses for our tea. We also came to the realisation that no coffee shops would be open for breakfast the following morning, so added some chilled coffee, some teacakes and yoghurts for our in-room breakfast.

I didn't have the best nights sleep, a combination of loud drunk people outside and the sound of rain lashing down made for an uneasy night. When the alarm went off, I was already awake, and I wasn't feeling refreshed.

I soon had a text message from Christine, whilst she wasn't running it, Callum was, and she, Robyn and Kara were coming to support us all. She'd had a challenging drive up due to the weather being so bad on the motorway. Phil and I looked out of the window with trepidation, it was looking like we were in for a soaking.

However, when we left the hotel half hour later to meet Christine in Weatherspoon's opposite the hotel the heavy rain had reduced to a light drizzle at best. We chatted and hydrated in the pub (water only) before heading to the start line. Callum was hoping for a PB, secretly, so was I.

I had set myself a strategy for the half marathon. The Run Mummy Run Facebook group that I am a member of frequently has conversations about jeffing. Jeffing comes from a man named Jeff Galloway, a running expert who has the theory that if you have a run/walk strategy it can often be faster than running alone as you can keep a faster pace when you run. I had mentioned it to Rob and was keen to trial it. Rob's reaction when I first suggested it was "run for 2hrs, walk for 2 mins, run the rest" I treated that with the contempt it deserved and developed my own strategy. I would run for a mile, walk .2 of a mile, then run the remaining .8 and repeat (but with keeping running at the 13 mile marker otherwise I'd be walking across the finish line!) I stood on the start line and I felt cold. I had a t shirt on, my club running vest over the top, long leggings and arm warmers but I was cold. I needed the race to start. I said goodbye to Phil, as he was heading further up the pack than me, with him being a faster runner.

I was relieved when it started and I was able to run to warm me up. I started at a comfortable pace, however, the start of a half marathon is always a challenge as there are so many people, it takes around a mile to get a bit more space. I looked around when I hit the first mile, I didn't need to stop running, but my strategy was telling me I had to walk. There was nobody close enough that my change of pace would affect, so I started my first 0.2 mile walk. I still tried to keep a fast walking pace, but it was amazing the recovery that I felt by walking not running. At 1.2 miles, I picked up the pace and started to run again.

It was just before the two-mile mark that I saw Christine at the side of the road. Whilst I had been freezing at the start line, I was now overheating. I quickly took off my arm warmers and threw them at her as I ran past. Before I knew it, time for my next walking break.

At around mile three I started my cat and mouse routine. There was a lady running in bright pink unicorn leggings and her friend running with her in a less colourful outfit. I would run past them, then on my walking break they would pass me, when I started running again, I would pass them. We continued this game until mile 8 when they finally said "we keep passing you and you keep passing us, but you are always walking when we pass you." I explained my strategy whilst running alongside them. However, at mile 10, my strategy was working so well that they didn't overtake me again on my walks.

Whilst the run was mostly uneventful, it was very well supported. People lined the street cheering, as we ran through some smaller terraced streets, people were stood on their doorsteps. It had a lovely community feel to the race, and somehow felt more intimate than Swansea or Cardiff.

I had been told that it was a flat route, this wasn't entirely true, as just when you least expected it you'd be faced with a hill. None that big, none that challenging.

It was mile five before I really looked at my watch to assess my pace. It wasn't long after a man had shouted to me "Hey, Celtic Tri, are you swimming home after?", I laughed and replied "Nah, I cycled up." It got a giggle from him, but it also got me thinking. When the Cotswolds half iron distance triathlon arrives, I'd need to do just that, cycle the equivalent distance from home to Newport (56 miles) and then run a half marathon. The enormity of my seasons challenge hit me. For the first time since I signed up my gut was whacked with an impending sense of doom!! What the hell had I put myself up for? However, I was in a race, no time to think of my stupidity now. So, I looked at my watch, I looked at my pace. It surprised me, it was faster than my PB pace at Swansea, result!

At mile seven, dead on, I was met with an abusive marshal. I had reached my next walking point and had started to walk.

"Oh come on Celtic Tri." he said with a level of anger in his voice. "Call yourself a triathlete and you are bloody walking."

I could have said so many things to him, how I was running to a schedule, how my club is inclusive, how he knows nothing about me. However, it pissed me off so much I simply said "just fuck off". I'm not proud, I try and be extra good when dressed in club kit, however, he had no right to criticise and I reacted.

This little interlude upset me a tad, however, when I hit 7.2 I started running again, and passed my new found buddies. It was also on this mile marker that I had a lovely chat to a lady doing her first half marathon, I ran with her for a while, but when we hit a hill I kept running and she decided to walk.

A little later on, as we ran under an underpass, there was a man with bagpipes. I did wonder if he had played them at all, as he was fiddling on his phone. I made a mental note to ask Phil.

It wasn't much further until we hit the biggest hill of the course leading to a road flyover. Even though I was not scheduled a walk, I was kind to myself and walked up the hill. I reached the flyover and as I ran over it, my legs became tangled in some tape which had blocked off the road, I had to stop to untangle myself before continuing on my way.

At mile 10, when I stopped for my walking break, I studied my watch again. It was definitely looking like I was headed for a PB. I felt chuffed with myself. It is just after this part of the race where you are running down the river bank. At the other side of the river bank you could see the finish and could hear the announcer call people's names as they crossed the line. I wondered if Phil had finished yet, I listened intently in case I heard his name. I didn't. A group of four people running near me were complaining about how awful it was that you could see the finish but still had a few miles to go. I had anticipated this, as my friend Mandy who had run the half the year before had warned me. I actually found seeing the finish and hearing the announcements strangely encouraging.

Mile 11 I admit I struggled. However, knowing that my PB was definitely in sight, I walked longer than my scheduled 0.2 miles. In fact, I mostly walked it. Mile 12 though I decided I was running to the finish, and that was what I did. As I turned the corner to head towards the finish I could see Phil, Callum and Christine and put on a bit of a sprint crossing the finish line in 2hrs 50min and 13secs, a 5 minute PB. Awesome!

When I met up with Phil his first question was odd "Did you see the pig?" he asked me.

"Pig?" I replied, confused "What pig?"

"There was a big pig next to one of the fences." he replied.

"I saw a bagpipe player, but I didn't see a pig."

"I saw the bagpipe player too, but I also saw a pig. Cal didn't see a pig either."

I convinced myself that my husband was hallucinating. The two other people on the course that he knew hadn't seen a pig, yet he had remained firm that he had. I thought he had lost the plot.

Later, however, on social media on the Run Mummy Run page someone wrote "Newport half, what a lovely race. Had everything from bagpipe players to pigs." the post accompanied by a picture of a pig.

I waved my iPad in front of Phil "Is this the pig you saw?" I asked.

"That's the pig!" he exclaimed in joy, "so you believe me now then do you."

Photo: With Phil at the end of Newport Half Marathon

Chapter 83

The next event was to be another run. The Cardiff Bay 10k. However, I was not looking forward to it. After my PB at Newport Half Marathon I had been struggling with shin pain. I had tried to keep running in my training, however, was forced to walk more than I could run. I had also kept the severity of the pain away from Rob, my coach, as I fully expected him to tell me not to do the 10k if I had let on. By rights, maybe I should have withdrawn from the race. However, I had decided to give it a go and walk it if I needed to.

The morning of the race, we parked outside my sister's and gave her an idea on where and when she could see Phil and I on the route, as my niece had decided she wanted to support us.

We met Christine and the gang in Weatherspoon's (I swear she must have shares in them!), headed to bag drop and to the start line. We were walking to the start when Callum said "Your calves are amazing Deb!"

Phil jokingly replied "Are you admiring my wife's legs?"

"I am, I really am." Cal replied.

I had become aware that my calves had become very defined. I'd been working so hard on the bike that they would have put some track cycling sprinters to shame, they had become huge! However, this had also come with a sting. I could no longer wear skinny jeans and I struggled with boots. I did, however, have some impressive definition.

Being a fairly local race, loads of my friends were running. Only a few of us from Celtic Tri, but loads of our friends from Run4All. We chatted to them before the start.

We lined up at the start line, Callum had gone further ahead now that he was super speedy. We knew though that even though we were further back, our times wouldn't start until our chips were registered when we crossed the start line. Within literally seconds of crossing the start line, all my friends had left me. I know I am slow, I deal with that. What I hadn't expected would be how soon the pain would hit me. Less than a kilometre in and my shins were killing me.

I had a choice, pull out now (and miss out on my medal) or keep going and hope for the best. I decided to keep going and walk instead. I made it a mission to find out how fast I could actually walk 10K.

It wasn't long until I saw my sister and my niece. As my race was already lost, I stopped longer than I should to have a quick chat and give her a big cuddle. Then I continued on my way, power walking.

I started to surprise myself. I was doing OK at this power walking and more to the point, I didn't have any pain.

I found that I was actually starting to overtake people who were running. For a while, I walked alongside a woman who was running.

"How can you walk so fast?" she asked me in surprised.

"I don't know." I replied "I'm running injured so I decided to walk it instead."

We chatted for a little while, then she found a spurt and started to up her running pace.

We were at the 5k mark when I reached a bunch of ladies doing the 10k as part of a hen do. All dressed up, the hen wearing a "bride to be" sash and all of them wearing matching hen party t-shirts. It was apparent that out of the five of them, four were runners and the poor fifth girl had been dragged along, obviously underprepared.

I felt so sorry for her, the bride and her three faster friends had obviously lost patience with her, as she stood at the side of the road, drinking some water and exclaiming that she was going to die.

"Will you just start fucking running already." one so called friend yelled at her.

"I can't, I just can't." she almost cried in reply "Go without me."

The bride chipped in "We had agreed to do this together." She was indignant in her tone and I didn't like it one bit, I couldn't help myself.

"If you had agreed to do it together, then you have to do it at the slowest person's pace, and if that means walking, then so be it." I didn't like these girls' attitudes at all.

The struggling girl smiled at me, and I was off.

I saw her later in the race when the two paths crossed over, she was trying to run, and was still getting yelled at by the others, poor dab.

It wasn't long after seeing these girls I saw Christine, Robyn and Sue. Their running was looking smooth and spectacular.

"Are you OK?" Chris shouted to me.

"Shin's fucked." I replied simply.

She nodded and carried on.

I have to say though, that whilst I was incapable of running, I was actually enjoying being outside, people watching and power walking. I had mentally made peace with myself that I was happy to walk and saw it as a good indicator for my half iron distance triathlon. I was quite sure that I wouldn't be able to run a full half marathon after swimming and cycling, so this would give me an indication as to how fast I could motor on without running.

At around the 8 and a half kilometre, possibly 9, we came back into the bay. There I saw Phil, he was long finished and tracking me to see where I was and told me that my sister and niece were waiting to see me again. It was so lovely to see my little niece's smiling face as she saw me again. I did try to run, to at least give the illusion that I was running this race, but the pain hit me instantly. I returned to my walk.

That meant I had a rather pathetic finish. There is a long stretch of pedestrianised path in the Bay. They had set up barriers for supporters to cheer, it seemed to go on for ever. Several friends, several strangers, even a couple of work colleagues, all lining the finishing straight, yelling at me to run.

I wasn't going to push it, I had bigger fish to fry. At the people I knew I yelled "I'm injured" but that was an embarrassing end to a race, I must have looked pathetic! However, I crossed the finish line in 1 hour 26 minutes, so amazingly was actually 2 minutes quicker than my first ever 10k which I had run. I took that as a good result.

The result of my pain was shin splints, and I had to take a few weeks off running. I don't do well being injured. I asked Rob "Can I power walk instead?" I felt his eye roll in his response to me via Facebook messenger "No!". Thankfully it didn't last long, and before I knew it, I was back running.

Chapter 84

I had never done an endurance swim.   Until the last couple
of years, I didn't even know that endurance swim events
existed. However, there was to be an endurance swim
event near to me. The Sospan Swim, held in Llanelli North
Dock, the location where I began my love affair with open
water swimming.

The word Sospan has been adopted by the local rugby
team in some way, which I don't really understand, I mean
why would you want to be called "saucepans" which is the
literal translation from Welsh to English. There is a song
that the rugby supporters sing called "Sospan fach" which
means "little saucepan", it's quite a rousing tune if you ever
get to hear it. Although the translation of the lyrics is a little
disturbing "A little saucepan is boiling on the fire, A big
saucepan is boiling on the floor, And the cat has scratched
little Johnny." Weird or what!

I did have to giggle though at this being called the "sospan
swim", having seen a roasting tin and kitchen scissors at
the bottom of the dock, it really wouldn't have surprised me
if there was actually a saucepan in there too.

The swim had 4 distances on offer; 750m (1 lap), 1500m (2 laps), 2250m (3 laps) and 3000m (4 laps). I looked at the prices, they were all the same, so I signed up for the big one!

When it came to the race day, Phil hadn't been feeling too well and he really wanted a night in. It was a Friday evening swim. I agreed he probably didn't need to come, as he hadn't entered, and so managed to get a lift with a friend from the club, also called Phil.

We arranged to meet, he was also giving another friend, Chris, a lift. These two men are lovely, great company too and I really enjoyed the trip in the car with them. I felt a little guilty as I knew I was a slower swimmer than them and they'd have to wait at the end.

As we arrived, we could see that the weather was deteriorating. We changed into our wetsuits in the car park.

As we walked over, there were loads of our club mates doing the race. In fact we must have made up a decent proportion of the entries. It started to rain, but that didn't matter, we were going to get wet anyway.

I decided I needed a pee.

"Can't you just wait and pee when you get in the water?" Mark asked me.

"No." I replied "I just can't pee in my wetsuit."

I had to use the portaloo and then struggle to get my wetsuit back on again.

Everyone had different swim hats, the colour was the distance you were swimming, several of the club had the rather delightful (not) pink swim hats indicating the big one.

We had been told that the event had an overall cut off of 2hrs, so that would allow me 30 mins per loop. I knew that I was capable of that.

It would be a mass start, but I positioned myself towards the back as I entered the water. After each lap, we'd been told that we needed to exit the water, run past the sensor where there would also be a water station if we wanted a drink, and then back in again.

When the klaxon went off, I started my stroke, and as is usually the case, I was at the back of the pack of swimmers. In fact, there weren't any other pink hat wearers near me. I didn't mind.

The first lap was pretty easy, and it was only 24 minutes until I was leaving the water and running through the sensor to get back in. I grabbed a plastic cup of water, drank it quickly and got back in the water.

During the second lap the wind started to pick up. It was also about half way through this lap that the faster swimmers started overtaking me, them a lap ahead. As I turned around the second buoy, I was aware how choppy the water was feeling due to the wind and I actually started to feel a little seasick.

I continued my swim, and the choppiness of the water started to get to me, I felt like I was going to be sick. Lo and behold, a minute later and I felt a small amount of vomit come up my throat. I spat it out, feeling a little disgusted in myself that I had thrown up a bit. However, I had a job to do. As I started to reach the shore the wind picked up again, this made the water even more choppy but the extra choppiness seemed to calm my sickness.

I got onto dry land, looked at my watch, 49 minutes, this was going ok.

Third lap, and the wind picked up even more. There were now gradually decreasing numbers of swimmers in the water. The shorter distances over, and speedy people doing the longer distances had also finished their swims. As I was sighting for the buoy, I could no longer see it. I lifted my head for longer than I should when Sian came up alongside me.

"You OK Deb?" she asked.

"Yeah" I replied "But where the hell is the buoy?"

We paused a moment and could see the kayaks trying desperately trying to grab the buoy that was floating away.

I was in a quandary. What was I supposed to do now? Did I swim towards the moving buoy? We'd been told we had to swim around them. I headed for it, the brutal wind making my progress through the water a challenge.

I swam around the buoy and started heading for the next one, which was also struggling to stay in position. Two kayaks were positioned next to it trying to keep it in place as the wind became worse and worse. I reached it, and it blew off its held course slightly, hitting me on the head. I kept going.

I was swimming towards the shore for the third time, I started to wonder how brutal the fourth lap would be. The rain had now joined the wind and it was hammering down on the water. Not that you really notice it when you are swimming.

I was conscious of another pink swim hat a few metres ahead of me, he got out of the water and went to run towards the swim exit for his fourth lap, I saw them stop him.

I got out of the water and follow suit, only to be told that the weather conditions were now too bad for the swim to continue. I was to stop at 3 laps. In a time of 1hr 15 minutes.

For a minute I was in a right temper. I had 45 minutes to do a final lap before cut off, something that I could easily have done. However, when I looked out to the water and saw that the kayaks were in trouble and the buoys were not staying where they should and I know the right decision was made. Safety must always come first.

I got my finisher's t-shirt and we headed back to Phil's car for the drive home. Whilst I was partly disappointed, I knew that I should also be pleased as it was my longest open water swim to date.

Chapter 85

It was about time for a triathlon. Running is one thing, but a triathlon is where the real excitement is.

We had decided that the first triathlon of the season would be Cheltenham, or rather the oddly named Mira Showers triathlon, named after the sponsors. The event was being held in the Sandford Lido, an amazing open air 50 metre pool. The triathlon was part of a variety of fundraising events, as the locals were desperately trying to keep the venue open. I really hope that they succeed as the venue is truly beautiful.

In the run up to the event, I had been a bit under the weather. Not really properly ill, rather a few snuffles and feeling a bit sub-par.

I was still looking forward, as we were going as a mini Celtic Tri team. Phil, Nev, Tash and I.

We had decided to make a bit of a weekend of it and had driven up on the Saturday. This gave us the opportunity to drive the bike route and get to know it. It had a few unexpected turns, so was good to get a flavour of what to expect. As we drove up a long hill, I looked at Phil and went "ooft", no further words were needed, he knew exactly what I meant. He nodded, that definitely looked to be the biggest challenge of the course.

With the bike route driven once, with Phil directing us through the instructions he had from the website, I decided I wanted to drive it a second time working from memory. If I could direct my way around it in the van, I could on the bike. I wanted to cement the route in my head. I looked for reassurance from my passenger husband as I said "It's left here isn't it" and surprised myself that I had learned it so quickly. The villages we passed through were rather quaint and lovely, with lots of thatched roof houses. I commented on how pretty they were, however, Phil, ever the pragmatist said "can you imagine the upkeep on those", he had a point.

With the route driven again we headed to our hotel. We realised we had the same issue as we had in Newport and got ourselves some breakfast to eat in the hotel room from the local garage.

405

Our hotel was next door to a TGI Friday's (other chain restaurants are available), so we knew we would have a good meal. Although I also knew that Phil wouldn't be able to pass up a Long Island iced tea!

The start of the triathlon was only around 2 miles from the hotel. When we had investigated the start we had noticed that there was a lack of parking.

As we sat in the restaurant Phil said to me. "Shall we Morse it tomorrow?"

I understand that this sentence will make no sense to any of you, so allow me to explain.

Morse relates to one of my club mates, Nigel Morse. I absolutely adore Nigel, he is a truly kind and genuine person. He is also a complete and utter nutter!

Nigel is the only triple brutal triathlete that I know.

What is a triple brutal? I hear you ask.

A triple brutal is three times the Ironman distance.... Three times.... Yes really, three times. So you swim 7.2 miles, cycle 336 miles and then run 72.6 miles!!! All without any proper sleep, a 60ish hour feat of human endurance. And Nigel has done it.

I think you will agree Nigel Morse is a nutter. However, the term "Morse it" is in reference to a few triathlons he has done where he has cycled to the start, done the triathlon, and cycled home after it. It has always made me giggle when I find out that he has. Only Nigel would be daft enough to do something so crazy as to commute to a triathlon on the bike he is racing on.

Phil had rightly suggested that as it was only a two-mile trek, it would be just as quick, and certainly easier to cycle to the start, do the triathlon and cycle home. We had back packs, so we could put our things for the triathlon in a backpack and it would be easier all around. It seemed a good plan. We would Morse it.

Since I started writing this book, Nigel has also done Triathlon X, widely agreed to be the hardest ironman distance triathlon in the world. You cycle up mountains, and run up mountains. I love him, the crazy lunatic!

Chapter 86

We woke up, ate our food, drank our chilled coffee and packed our bags for our cycle to the venue. As I had been unwell, Rob had told me not to push it. Take it easy, he had told me. This was a bit of transition practice and an easy start to the triathlon season.

The swim was 8 lengths (400m), the cycle about 20 kilometres and a 3k run to finish it off.

The cycle to the venue was short and easy. We arrived, and racked our bikes and set up our transition areas. The event was so laid back. They were racking us in number order, and as Phil and I registered together we were next to each other.

I took a quick selfie for Facebook professing, "I've been racked next to a right weirdo."

With that we saw Nev, he was also excited about the first triathlon of the season. Tash, bless her, despite being the most talented athlete out of our quartet was nervous. However, she had one aim. Her brother, who lives local to the venue, was also racing and she wanted to beat him.

Tash and I headed off the to the ladies changing rooms to leave our bags in the lockers, as we weren't allowed to leave bags in transition. At first, I wondered where I could leave the key for the locker, but thankfully it had a safety pin on it, so I pinned it to my tri top.

We met back with the boys and went to the briefing for our wave. We'd all gone into the same wave time, although we would be in separate lanes, well, Phil and I were in the same lane.

It was time to get in the water and we met our other lane buddies.

It always strikes me in these novice friendly events the wide range of people who take part. One of our lane buddies was a young man, probably early 20's who was competing in his first race. He looked like he'd be fast, but he was nervous. The fact that we had chosen wave times as opposed to being seeded on swim times meant that a person who could do the swim in 5 mins could be in the same lane as someone who could take 20mins. We tried to establish speeds and realised we were all roughly in the same ball park, or 11-12 mins give or take.

There were 5 of us in our lane, two men and three women. The marshal provided us with the usual instructions that if you catch the person in front, tap them on their toes and the person caught leaves them push off first. There would be a 5 second gap between each person.

The gun went off, off went the first person, the young man. Off again, and off goes Phil, and the third time and it's my turn. I started swimming up the lane. I don't know if any of you have ever swum in a 50m pool. A length seems to go on forever! I had trained in the National pool in Swansea so knew how long a length would seem. First length went well, but as I reached the turn, I realised that Phil had more than the 5 second lead on me, he was having a good swim.

On the third length the girl behind me caught me, however, her definition of a "tap" left a lot to be desired. She whacked my feet so hard it threw me under the water. I reached the end and let her pass. However, I was guessing her push to catch me had taken a fair bit of energy as no sooner than she had pushed off she suddenly switched to breast stroke which meant I was on her heels and couldn't pass her. As I wasn't properly racing I decided "sod it" and switched to breaststroke myself. However, this had the knock on effect of the girl behind catching us both. As we reached the end the girl behind obviously decided she wasn't going to attempt the toe tap and overtook us both in the other half of the lane and pushed off again. As myself and the girl reached the end, she had a resigned look about her and said "go on, you go first" and I was back to front crawl for the remaining four lengths, as she continued her breast stroke.

I did my final length, thanked the marshal and headed to my bike.

Photo: Being racked next to a right weirdo

Chapter 87

Phil was already in transition, so was Nev and Tash had already left and was on the bike course. Both the boys left before me, but I wasn't massively behind. Not that I was bothered as I just wanted to enjoy the experience.

It was my first race on my new bike! I loved her! I was probably pushing it a little faster than I should have been, as well, she's a bike that screams to be pushed!

The course has a truly shocking number of traffic lights, and during the race briefing we were told that in no uncertain terms were we to go through a red light as that would be instant disqualification. A marshal was posted at each set of traffic lights as was a timing mat to adjust for your waiting time.

I reached the first set of lights... red! I pulled up and stopped, and had a chat to the marshal.

"Lovely day for a triathlon." I said, making typically British conversation.

He responded in a suitably British way. "Yes, lovely weather today."

Our brief and cliched conversation came to a quick end as the lights changed and I thanked him for volunteering.

I looked out for all the road markings that I had learned on the drive of the course. This was proving quite easy to navigate, although there were plenty of signs that had been put out to guide the cyclists.

I approached the first right hand turn, and struggled to get out to the right-hand side of the lane due to the flow of traffic which had seemed to have come from nowhere at half eight on a Sunday morning. I slowed, stuck my arm out again to indicate I was turning, by which time I was almost sat on the junction. A kindly man in a van flashed me out, and I was able to make my turn without any further dramas.

Shortly after this turn there's a little incline. You couldn't call it a hill, but it was going upwards, barely. I was flying up and it surprised me how many people I overtook on this stretch. Then it was a left turn, a slight downhill and a roundabout to the villages. I took the downhill too fast and came dangerously close to colliding with the pavement as I overshot the roundabout. Oops! It actually scared me just a little bit, as with a big season planned and only a few weeks until my half iron distance triathlon, the last thing I needed was to come off!

I shook it off and returned to a more sensible pace. It was here I encountered the old woman and the speed bumps. For the record before I start with this tale, I have nothing against elderly people driving, honest! However, I do think that once you get to a certain age there should be some form of test to ensure that someone is still capable.

We were approaching some speed bumps, and I became aware of a car pulling up alongside me to overtake. It was a tiny little car, quite an old car but looked as immaculate as probably the day it was driven off the forecourt. Sat in the driver's seat was an elderly lady, she looked at least ninety, no word of a lie, this woman was ancient. I looked at her and smiled, but I was equally eyeing her with suspicion, the speed at which she was attempting to overtake me was only ever so marginally faster than I was cycling. She continued her painful delayed manoeuvre and we started to reach the speed bump. Obviously, her driving instincts were to cross the speed bump dead centre, and so she headed back to the left so she could attack it squarely. I had anticipated that this may happen and so thankfully had put my brakes on. Good job as she would have squashed me. I shook my head in a kind a resigned way. About another quarter of mile up the road, with me still rather close to her, without indicating, she pulled left against the curb and just stopped. She stopped quickly, you must have seen it with old people when they realise they are where they want to be and almost do an emergency stop! It took quite a skilled piece of cycling to swerve around her on the right and not go colliding into the back of her abruptly now stationary vehicle. She remained oblivious that nearly attempted manslaughter of a cyclist twice. I sped off down the road fearful that she would drive off again, thankfully she didn't.

As I continued through the village, I was able to admire the beauty of the houses even more, this was definitely the prettiest part of the cycle route, although it wasn't long until I reached the Lidl, a bit of a come down if I'm honest for the scenery and the less pretty part, this was also the part near the Cheltenham Racecourse and the biggest hill of the cycle route.

It was at the start of this hill that I could see Nev ahead and I knew I was going to overtake him.

"Alright Nev." I shouted as I cycled past. He replied something about struggling, but with fairly heavy traffic noise I didn't hear exactly what he said.

Further up the hill I passed another cyclist, a woman who looked a little younger than me.

"Please say this is the last hill." she almost pleaded.

"Yep and you are nearly at the top." I replied, trying to be both chipper and motivational.

With the hill conquered, and the iconic racecourse passed, it was time to head back to transition. However, one further obstacle awaited.

When we had driven the course the day before there was a set of temporary traffic lights on one section of the course less than a mile from transition. We'd been told in the race briefing that there would be marshals with iPads on this junction noting our numbers and times so that they could accurately record our times.

As I pulled up to the traffic lights I could see a Celtic Tri top, Phil was also waiting at the lights, along with about 15 other people.

"Hello gorgeous." I say, cheekily, as I pull up alongside him.

"I've got a problem with my bike." he replies, a hint of slight panic in his face

We chat for a minute or two, his handlebars were a little loose.

A few more cyclists pitch up, and there has become quite a crowd at the lights with no sign of oncoming traffic, and no sign of the lights changing to green.

The agitation becomes palpable as more and more competitors ask the marshals can they go through on red, normally an instant disqualification offence.

However, it becomes clear that these lights are not going to change and so the marshals look at each other and say "off you go".

Phil and I sped off, overtaking virtually every one of our traffic light companions. Phil, a little faster than me, took the last big corner before me, and I followed him into transition. Two down, one to go.

Chapter 88

I rack my bike, change from my bike shoes into my trainers, and move my race belt around so my number is visible from the front, and I am ready to follow my husband on the run. Knowing full well that as he is a faster runner than I, I knew the next time I would see him would be at the finish.

The bike course had been well signposted, sadly the run course didn't follow suit and I wasn't totally convinced I was running in the right direction.

I was, however, running surprisingly well for me. I had done quite a few "brick" sessions in the run up which were helping my legs that would normally at this point, feel like lead.

Brick sessions are so valuable, even running for just a mile after a cycle allows your legs to adapt to the sensation, my efforts had paid off and my running was as good as it would have been on a standalone run.

I was about a kilometre in when I reached a fellow female competitor, she was young, slim, looked very fetching in her lilac and purple tri suit, but it was apparent that she was struggling. I spoke.

"You OK?" I ask casually with a hint of concern.

"This is really hard." she replies, she looks defeated.

"First one?" I ask.

She nods.

"Then you are only two kilometres away from becoming a triathlete then." I try and sound upbeat "You've got this, you are going to do it."

Her eyes light up, and you can see her realise that she's nearly there.

She smiles at me, "Thanks I needed that." and she found a spring in her step, she was off.

I tried to keep up, but being around 20 years her senior and probably about three stone heavier I had no chance, although I smiled to myself. Good deed done.

Shortly afterwards I arrive at a junction, one runner crosses the road and goes straight on, another runner turns right. Now I had a quandary, which way was correct?

A runner just behind me was obviously having the same thoughts.

"Do you know which way is the right way?" he asked me.

"Not a clue." I replied.

We stood at the junction for a moment or two. Straight on there only appeared to be the one runner, looking down the road to the right there were lots.

Both, in a split second, having come to the same conclusion, we start turning right.

I shout to the straight on runner, "You are going the wrong way".

He turns and looks at me, I can see he's muttering some kind of expletive to himself and he shouts "thanks" as he turns on his heel and follows us down the road.

Another little way around the road I found myself in traffic. A woman with a pushchair was coming towards me, an old man with a walking stick was in front of me. No way to get through. I nip onto the road and return to the pavement when I'd passed. The situation, whilst fleeting, amused me. I'd never been caught in a traffic jam on a pavement before.

One last turn into a park where there was a marshal to guide and I look at my watch, around 400m to go. I decide to walk through the field so I could have a sprint finish. An old couple were sat at a bench, the lady says "Run, the finish is just through there." pointing to a gap in the fence.

"I want a sprint finish." I replied.

However, on going through the gap I realised when she said "just through there" she meant "just" as in 'immediately', like the finish straight was just through the fence. I giggled to myself and did my last teeny tiny sprint to the finish where Phil and Tash were waiting for me. I was handed my medal, my t-shirt and a voucher for a bacon sandwich and instantly decided I wanted to come back next year, as any race that gives you a bacon sandwich along with the usual race bling was worthy of repeating.

Chapter 89

It was only a week until it was time for my next triathlon. This time it was the turn of the Swansea triathlon, a closed road afternoon event. I'd only done one afternoon triathlon before at Blenheim Palace. Usually triathlons were something that you had to get up for at an unholy hour on a Sunday morning. Being able to get up at a sensible time was unusual. However, I did need to register for the event and decided to nip down in the morning to get my race pack.

This race is situated right next door to where I work, so I had already decided I was going to park in my works car park both to register and for the event itself. I wasn't the only one who thought this. Another work colleague who was racing had also come to the same conclusion.

Registration was busy and chaotic even heading out before the crowds, however, with my bag collected I headed home for a spot of lunch.

I had the same issue as I had in Blenheim. What on earth do I eat? A morning triathlon is easy, I train and race on a few firm favourites for breakfast, but when you aren't racing until 4pm what on earth do you do? Should I have a proper lunch at a normal lunchtime? Should I have a later lunch? Should I have two smallish snacks and no lunch at all? I decided on a small salad for lunch and an energy bar an hour or so before the race after I had racked my bike.

When we arrived back down at the car park that was transition there was a massive queue to rack the bikes. I mentally slapped myself for not getting down a bit earlier. As I was heading down the queue I saw Sian and her partner Rob, Sian shouted to me. She seemed so much happier and calmer than she had been at Blenheim Palace the previous year. She was also using the race as some transition practice having signed up for the Cotswolds middle distance triathlon the following week.

Transition was as chaotic as registration, and by the time I got in there wasn't much space left on the racks. I spotted a barely large enough space between two very expensive looking time trial bikes. I thought quickly, people riding these kind of expensive bikes would; a. not be interested in my comparatively cheap and modest bike and b. if they were riding something that expensive, chances are they would be much faster than me and I'd have more room in transition after the swim to get my wetsuit off. Decision made, I'd take this tiny slot.

As I started to lift up my bike and get my stuff arranged, a bloke heads in my direction. He doesn't say a word, but it becomes clear that he is the owner of one of the very expensive TT bikes. I grin to myself, as he watches me intently, protecting his pride and joy.

With my stuff arranged and time ticking on, it was time to go back to the work car park and start changing into my wetsuit.

Chapter 90

I put my wetsuit on as far as my hips only and headed to the general start area where we had agreed as a club that we would have a group photo.

There had been some recent terrorist attacks in the UK, so there were armed police everywhere. Two armed police officers even agreed to have a photo taken with us. I found the whole experience rather mentally complex to process. On the one hand, they were there with guns to protect us. On the other hand, they had big guns! To me, there is no place for guns. That said, there is also no place for terrorists. Did I feel safer due to this armed presence? On balance, probably not as I found it alarming that their presence was deemed necessary.

The whole area was teeming with activity, it was really hard to navigate through the crowds up to the swim start. I was in the first wave. When I first found this out I was amused no end. The reason was simple, the first wave was also the wave the pros were starting in. I found the whole concept of me being chucked in with the pros hilarious. I mean, I am the anthesis of a pro! Turns out a lot of the people in the first wave were people in local tri clubs, so most of my friends would be in that first wave too.

We were guided to the water and told to jump in. This is a body of water that I walk passed every day. In the run up to the event we had completed "jelly fish watch". Even though it is an enclosed dock, it is fed by the sea, and as such there were literally thousands of jelly fish in there. These fascinating little creatures though were all tiny, roughly the size of a shot glass. I jumped into the water, put my face in the water, and could see that our companions were lower down from the surface than usual. I don't know if jelly fish have emotions, but I can imagine that when you are used to having a nice big dock to yourselves, that the sudden arrival of hundreds of people in wetsuits comes as quite a culture shock.

I was bobbing around in the water, keeping myself towards the back as we waited for the start, and chatted to Karen and Joe from the club whilst we listened for the klaxon. Off it went, and it was time to swim. A 750m swim around the dock. Swimming is normally prohibited, which is probably a good thing otherwise I'd spend every lunch break in there, so I felt honoured to be swimming in this gorgeous body of water.

As the swimmers started to thin out, the jellyfish began floating back up near the surface. I forgot I was racing as I watched them up close and personal. I was in awe of their beauty and the way that their bodies moved. I swam and I admired, and I swam some more. In fact, I was so distracted by the jelly fish that I totally switched off from concentrating on my stroke, I was just swimming, no real thoughts, just moving forward and it felt strong.

I was well over half way through the swim when I heard the klaxon go again. I thought to myself that the second wave must have been delayed as I was expecting to be around half way when it went off.

The end was in sight and I kicked my legs a little harder to properly put some blood back in them and was helped out by a volunteer.

As I began my run to transition, Emma from the club was stood right by the swim exit she shouted "go on Debs, nice one, helluva swim", I looked down at my watch, realising I hadn't switched it to transition and she was right. Eighteen and a half minutes, I'd just had a swim PB.

I continued my run, high fiving all the kids along the way. Yes, I wanted to put in a good performance but as much as anything I wanted to enjoy the race and be grateful to the spectators. I began the run over the iconic Sail Bridge, Christine was at the bottom of the bridge. Giving her time to volunteer at this event for the second year running. She was my last high five before I turned into transition and my rather lovely spacious area to get out of my wetsuit and onto my bike. Yep, my idea to slot myself between two expensive bikes had paid off, they'd both already gone.

Chapter 91

The bike course had been described as "fast and flat", a three-loop course along Swansea seafront. It was flat, it had a huge potential to be fast. The first lap seemed just that as I hammered away, keeping my speed above 18mph. As faster club mates would pass me on their second or maybe even third loops they would cheer and encourage. During this first lap I saw some rather spectacular TT bikes.

I knew where Phil was going to be placed to take photos, so on the first pass I yelled "love you", after the first turn and the cycle back down I yelled "love you" again. By the third time he'd grown weary of this shout and just yelled "shut up". I did shout "love you" all six times I passed him, I'm consistent!

The second lap was also good, although the course was starting to get more congested as the faster people from the second wave had joined in the party. I was heading back to the turnaround point at when Jamo overtook me.

We have two people called Jamo in our club. With Jamo being short for James in both instances. You'd think when two people called the same thing you'd go to surnames to differentiate. This also doesn't help as they both have the same surname too. Both really lovely people. However, there was one thing that set these two men apart, the Jamo who had just overtaken me is a giant. He's stupidly tall, he towers above everyone I know and when he walks in a room you see his cheeky smile about a foot further in the air than other people's heads. So, I affectionately refer to these two men as "big Jamo" and "little Jamo", this is probably a disservice to "little Jamo" as he is quite a normal sized man. However, that is how it is.

So as big Jamo passed he shouted "Jump on board Debs!" Now people, drafting off another person in a triathlon is both wrong and illegal, but when my super tall chum gave me the opportunity, on a heavily packed course, I was not going to miss the opportunity and I sat on Jamo's wheel for as long as I could. Which was about a minute, as Jamo is not only tall, he's also very fast!

So, the turnaround point saw more cyclists being added into the fairly modest stretch of Swansea road. The second wave, however, had been the novice wave. Nothing wrong with that at all, we all start somewhere, however, novice comes with a variance of skills or none in some cases.

Don't get me wrong, I am very much a back of the pack triathlete. My bike skills are grim. However, this event saw people on mountain bikes, people on fat tyre bikes, even one girl with a basket on the front. These are all great things, and boy do I applaud them for coming into our wonderful sport. That said, we were reaching a point where two lanes went into one, fast people on TT bikes were hurtling past me, probably in the mid 20 mph range, I was hammering it some at around 17/18, and the congestion was about to make a scary bottle neck.

One man, on a mountain bike, very wobbly. I did the customary "On your right" to let him know I was passing, he veered towards the right, just as another TT bike came whizzing past. How the three of us didn't collide I do not know. But as I passed this poor guy he looked positively terrified! I doubt he'd ever been out on the road, let alone with hundreds of other cyclists.

I slowed my speed slightly after that. I had a more important race the following week, so my last half a lap was far more sedentary to allow the more nervous cyclists the space that they needed. The last thing I needed was a bike accident to potentially harm me or my bike.

I returned to transition, unscathed, and got ready for my run.

Chapter 92

The Swansea triathlon run was 5k, along the coast, an area where I frequently do a lunchtime run in work. When I run at lunchtime, I will see a few cyclists, a few dog walkers, a couple of runners. The triathlon, however, had brought people out in their droves.

One interesting little part was running through a beer garden, people packed in there with their drinks, cheering you as you ran past them in lycra! As we reached the sea front, I could see Vic from the club, she was supporting having just completed a middle-distance triathlon.

"You are looking really strong Deb." she said.

I looked at my watch and it was a good pace for me, faster than I'd normally run a standalone 5k at parkrun.

At this part there was now two-way traffic, and as club mates passed in the other direction we would high five each other.

We reached the part near County Hall and I saw Sally, she's Karen's wife and an absolute gem.

"Well done Deb." she called out to me.

I then saw a group of teenage lads, as our race numbers had our names on, they were shouting random things to triathletes using their names.

"Tt's Deborah big tits." one of them shouted to raucous laughter from his friends.

Was I supposed to be offended by this? I decided boys will be boys and took it as a compliment, even if they didn't mean it.

I reached the half way point shortly afterwards and turned to head back.

"It's Deborah big tits again." another lad shouted. Yeah yeah boys, I get it.

Shortly afterwards I saw Karen, she looked in pain and didn't high five, I could tell she was injured and suffering. I was glad that Sal was close by to support her.

Passed Vic again, and then over the bridge into town, where Angharad, my friend Sian's daughter was. She cheered for me and it made me pick up my pace a little, as I had started to flag, having gone out too fast.

There is one thing I can say about the company that run the Swansea triathlon, and that is that they know how to do a finish line. Barriers, red carpet, big stage with a DJ, it feels like a big event. I hear my name and my club being mentioned and I cross the finish line with a 5k PB and another triathlon in the bag. Good day at the office.

It was an eventful day for others in the club too. I was to discover after I finished that coach Mike had a DNF (did not finish). The reason why truly sets out why he is the awesome man he is. It was Steve's first triathlon. Steve is a fabulous man, has a lovely family too, his wife, son and daughter are all totally gorgeous people. This triathlon meant a lot to Steve and his family, as the children were really proud of Daddy doing a triathlon. However, on the bike course Steve had a crash which led to a terrible mechanical problem on his bike. Steve couldn't fix it roadside, he was about to withdraw from his first race, when Mike came to the rescue. Gave Steve his bike, he took the broken one and had a DNF, sacrificed his race so Steve could finish his first. What a legend!

The second eventful incident happened as I went to collect my bike from transition after the race. Phil was sat on his Brompton outside transition, just over the fence from me. He heard some women "Look at the arse on that", "That arse needs to be grabbed" and from nowhere, a group of pissed up women in their 50's grabbed my husband's arse!! It was a good job I was in transition as if I had been closer to him, these women wouldn't know what hit them. Phil was, quite understandably, traumatised. When our club mates found out, they generally found it hilarious. And I do have to admit it does sound quite amusing, however, if Phil had been a woman and the group of women had been men they'd have been banged up for sexual harassment. Poor Phil, there is only one person that is allowed to grab that lovely arse of his, and that's me.

Photo: On the bike leg of the Swansea Triathlon

Chapter 93

The time was quickly approaching, but I felt ready. Ready to tackle my first middle distance triathlon. The Cotswolds 113. It was a race that several of my clubmates had already done, several had done it multiple times which told me everything I needed to know. It must be a good race. Also several of my club mates were completing it at the same time, so it had rather turned into a Celtic tri party weekend!

In the run up to the event, we had several emails from the race organiser Graeme. I had already decided I loved the race as his emails were informative and witty. I had been glad that I had already had a go at the bike course (which Phil and I had done the afternoon after the Cheltenham triathlon, gosh we were gluttons for punishment that day!), as that took the fear of the course away.

So, the middle-distance triathlon, or half ironman consists of a 1.2 mile swim, a 56 mile bike ride and a 13.1 mile half marathon run to finish. I should have been terrified at these distances, I wasn't. I had trained hard, I felt so ready for it I could have burst.

We had decided to take the week off work following the event and have a little holiday. I didn't know how stiff I would feel after racing that kind of distance, so taking some time off seemed a wise move. Ok, what wasn't such a wise move was deciding to make our holiday a short break to London straight after the race to do all sightseeing and exploring things, but then I'm a bit of a sucker and I never learn.

The weather had been unseasonably warm in the run up, and a few days before the event Graeme had sent another one of his information emails. This one saying that the lake had warmed up dramatically with the nice weather and it was looking like the swim would not be wetsuit legal. There are strict rules in triathlon. Below a certain temperature and wetsuits are mandatory, above a certain temperature and you aren't allowed to wear a wetsuit, in between and the choice belongs to the athlete. The temperature of the lake was hovering just at the tipping point for no wetsuits with a few days of good weather to come. We were told that we would be informed for certain the day before the race when we registered.

Several of my clubmates panicked. Swimming in a wetsuit it easier than swimming without one. Swimming without would mean a harder swim. Whilst I secretly hoped that wetsuits would be allowed I wasn't in any way in a panic. I was swimming 1.2 miles several times a week in a pool, no wetsuit. It was a distance I was very comfortable with, with or without a wetsuit. When I spoke to Rob a few days before the race when he checked in to see how his athlete was feeling, I was like "mneh, what will be will be".

If I had a slightly longer swim time due to the lack a neoprene wrapped around me it wasn't the end of the world. It would maybe add 10 mins to my swim time. The overall cut off for the race was eight and a half hours. I knew I was capable of coming in within that, and so stressing about how I would be dressed in the swim was no big deal.

I was having a few stresses though about my kit overall. I knew I would be wearing my favourite tri bottoms and my club tri top. I had, however, tried a long cycle in just my tri bottoms. Whilst it felt good up to around 30 miles after that the tiny padding in the shorts was not enough. So I came up with the idea to put a pair of really good cycling shorts on over my tri shorts and see how that would work.

There is a general rule that you do nothing new on race today, so a few weeks before the race I had arranged to go on a ride with Tracey who was also doing Cotswolds. I turned up to meet her in soaking wet tri shorts that I had soaked in the sink and cycle shorts over the top. I think it amused her but equally she knew it was a sensible plan. I was also having minor concerns about my nutrition. When you do a race of that length you need to eat. I had a lovely new bag for my top tube of my bike that I could carry food in. I had tried a number of different things in training.... Peanut butter sandwiches, pork pies, lumps of cheese and nuts, cereal bars. However, I found two things that seemed to work well and were easy to eat. Slices of malt loaf, rolled into balls with little lumps of butter in the middle and caramel shortbread squares. The latter seemed particularly extravagant, as being diabetic, I would only need to look at something this high in carbs and sugar and my bloods would protest. However, whilst on a bike, my blood sugars would drop like a stone, making these naughty carby treats almost a necessity. Good grief I was loving my sport. The energy drink I was also consuming had been tried and tested as many people I knew had gastric distress from it. Not me, it seemed to work perfectly.

So I knew what I was doing with my kit, I knew what I was doing with my nutrition, all I needed to do was pack for the race, pack for the holiday and head to Cotswolds.

The hotel Phil and I had chosen was as a result of a recommendation from people in the club that had done the race before, and it didn't disappoint. Only a few miles away from the start and a bit more luxurious than the closer campsites. Phil and I don't do camping! Several of our clubmates did though and were all staying in the same campsite near the start.

We had travelled up on the Friday, registration was on the Saturday and then the race on the Sunday.

On the Friday night Tracey and Sonia came over to our hotel to have dinner, they were staying in the campsite. I had done so much training with Tracey, so she wasn't surprised that I wasn't feeling particularly nervous. Sonia, however, did seem more nervous probably as this was also her first middle distance triathlon, but was her usual chirpy self. We ate our food, chatted away like family and arranged to meet to register the following morning.

Registration was simple and straight forward and everyone there was so super friendly, we were also told that wetsuits were allowed which eased many a nervous competitor. Other friends from the tri club started to arrive and we chatted away. For several of us it was our first middle distance triathlon and we seemed to vary between dead calm and totally panic stricken. I was pleased that I felt so calm, even seeing faster friends panic did not shake me. It wouldn't be fast, it wouldn't be pretty but I knew I had what it took to get around the course.

After we registered, we went shopping to Tesco with Tracey and Sonia to pick up a last few supplies and we went to get some lunch. I was excited, I just wanted to get the job done and prove to myself that I had what it takes.

When Phil and I returned to the hotel, I finished getting my things together, made my overnight oats and made sure I was in bed by 7 as the alarm would be going off at 4am.

Chapter 94

The alarm went off, I had laid everything out so I wouldn't need to wake Phil. With the hotel being only a couple of miles from the start he had brought his Brompton folding bike and was going to cycle over later.

I nipped to the toilet, cleaned my teeth and got dressed. I knew that parking was potentially limited at the venue and I wanted to get there early to ensure I had a space. I needn't have worried as I was only the third vehicle to arrive.

I decided to rack my bike straight away as once that was done I would be able to relax.

I was on my way back from racking my bike when I saw my friend Dave. He's in a different local club but he's always been super supportive. He gave me a few last-minute words of wisdom, told me to enjoy myself and went to get himself ready. One of his clubmates wasn't too far behind, sadly they weren't quite so supportive saying "Don't worry if you fail" yeah cheers you scumbag!

I went and sat back in the van and decided to have a look on Facebook on my phone as I had plenty of time. I saw that the night before there had been terrorist attacks in central London. We would be heading there tomorrow. I felt sad for the people of London, but equally I knew that Phil and I would proceed with our plans as no bastard terrorist was going to make us feel fearful in our much-loved country.

I started to eat my overnight oats. Porridge oats, honey yoghurt, dried fruit, coconut flakes. All yummy delicious things, but at a little after 4.30am it was a struggle to get them down. I took teeny tiny mouthfuls and slowly chewed. I decided to stop at about three quarters of the way through. I couldn't stomach anymore. I thought I'd try and find a toilet, have a wander to see if any of my friends were around and then finish them closer to the start.

Even when you arrive at a race super early the time does fly at an astonishingly fast pace, and before I knew it there was a Celtic Tri army standing at the side of the lake. I was also on the lookout for someone else. I had spoken to the amazing author George Mahood on Facebook and knew that both he and his wife Rachel were racing and were in the same wave as me. Whilst George and I had never met each other we knew each other through our books and an online group of authors. It was only a minute or two later when I heard a voice say "Debs" and there he was. He introduced me to Rachel, I introduced him to my club mates and we had a little chat. I have to admit, I felt like a little bit of a fan girl. I can say, hand on heart, that George is my favourite author. His books are both entertaining and funny, if you haven't read any of them, check him out as he is totally awesome! As George and Rachel left he said "See you at the finish Debs" I assured him that he shouldn't do that, he'd be waiting a long time. From reading his books I knew that Rachel was a fast and talented runner. I knew that George would be pretty speedy too from his "Operation Ironman" book. George laughed and with Rachel headed in the direction on the portaloos, I turned to my friends all chuffed at having met him. This amused them with me also being an author and all, but as I prefer to get lost in books over getting lost in TV, to me authors are my film stars, and I'd just met an Oscar winner in my mind.

Wave 1 were ready to go, Sonia had opted to go in Wave 1 as she wanted the head start on the swim, the rest of the club were in Wave 2. After Wave 1 departed, we were allowed in the water. The variety of emotions surprised me, Lisa, who is one of my closest friends was very nervous. This surprised me, as she's a super-fast triathlete and an amazing Ironman. Her brother in law Mike was doing this race as his first ever triathlon, talk about throwing yourself in at the deep end. He was grinning like a Cheshire cat, obviously so chuffed to be about to start his first race. I got in the water and decided to stay towards the back. As I got in the water, I decided I was desperate for a pee. Until this time, I had never managed to pee in my wetsuit, however, I was so desperate, that for the first time I did. I started to pee just as the klaxon went off. I must have looked like a right knob, as I had to stay stood there until I had finished!

I started my swim, the water was so clear it was almost like swimming in a pool. It was also rather warm (not down to my bladder contents!) and so I could see how we almost weren't allowed to wear wetsuits. My stroke felt strong and I began to overtake some other swimmers. After the first turn, I noticed a man that was just a smidgen faster than me, so I tried to stay on his feet. My stroke felt comfortable and easy, much the same as it had in Swansea Tri the week before. It wasn't too long before the faster swimmers from wave three were catching up and overtaking and I lost my pacing friend. I was just happy to be in the water. Considering only two years before I was terrified to put my face in the water, now it felt as natural as breathing. I love the feeling of my face under the water, I loved the sense of escapism and calm that swimming gave me. As we were coming towards the last buoy, I reached Sonia. "Alight Son?" I asked, she nodded. I passed her and headed for the water exit. One down two to go and I had a good first triathlon leg.

Chapter 95

I made the run to transition and thought back to some words of wisdom that Dave had given me when I'd seen him earlier.

"Think of each sport as a separate event. Don't think about what is ahead or what you have done, just be in the moment of that event." He was right. On a longer distance event, you needed to be in the moment more than shorter triathlons.

I reached my bike, swim done, swim over, no more thinking about it I'm about to cycle.

My bike was racked in the first row, this meant that supporters were standing right at the fence cheering. I found this disconcerting, mostly because I knew I needed to take a big dollop of chamois cream and stick my hands down my tri shorts to lube myself up. I turned around so my back was facing the onlookers. Sonia, arrived into transition and was racked next to me, she was taking her time getting her wetsuit off, taking it relaxed. I thought it was a wise move having taken my time myself. I popped on my cycle shorts, my cycle top, socks and shoes. Helmet followed, and my bike was ready to be taken off the rack. I took a huge bite of a croissant, deciding to eat this on the run to the mount line and said "See you later Son" as I headed to the transition exit. Sara, Mark's wife, snapped some photos of me mid croissant scoff and cheered me on my way.

I knew what to expect with the bike course having done one loop of it already. I had no worries at all about the first loop. I was worried about having to repeat it all for a second time. The voice of Dave popped in my head again and I knew I couldn't worry about that, just be in the moment.

As I reached the first roundabout there was Phil armed with his camera as always. I felt happy seeing him there.

I reached the half hour point of cycling and it was time to eat my first malt loaf ball. I reached down the frame to my bag, and my bag swivelled around underneath the frame. I had to stop, turn the bag back around to the top and grab my snack.

"You OK?" a fellow cyclist asked as I was stopped. "Yes." I replied.

I shoved the ball into my mouth and started cycling. Instantly the bag shot around to the bottom of my frame again. I muttered "bloody brilliant" to myself in a sarcastic manner. This meant that every time I needed to eat, I'd need to stop. So I decided to eat every hour instead to limit my stopping time.

Out on the course, it was always a joy seeing a friend and a clubmate, to shout encouraging words or give them a little wave. It seems that everyone is in it together. When I had cycled the route with Phil it had seemed confusing, however, with the cheery and helpful marshals, navigating the course was easy. The only negative I could say is that some of the road surfaces left a little to desired, so I was constantly on the lookout for potholes.

I reached the hill for the first time. On my practice ride I'd needed to stop near the top (although I had already done a triathlon that day), I was hoping I'd get up without needing to stop, and I almost did. However, I ran out of gears and steam with metres to go. I paused for a few seconds and starting pedalling again to reach the top.

There was one drink station on the course, and I knew that when I reached it I would need another bottle of water. The idea is you approach them, discard your old bottle and grab a new one from one of the helpers who hold their hands out. Rob had talked me through what I should do. Take the bottle from my cage, empty it into my aero drinker, throw the bottle away and put a new bottle in my cage. As I started approaching the drink station, I slowed down a bit, grabbed the bottle from my frame, emptied it as instructed and threw it into the bottle drop area. I had purposefully brought my oldest and mankiest drink bottle knowing I would get a nice new bottle in its place.

I put out my hand to grab a bottle from a helper and totally failed, totally missed the grab! I was forced to stop and properly take it. We both had a laugh about it and I was back on my way, nearly at the turnaround point. I reached the roundabout where Phil has been earlier and he wasn't there. My heart sank as I was looking forward to seeing him again. I needn't have worried, he'd moved himself a bit further down the road. I spotted him and gave a big beaming smile at seeing my beloved, which I know he hates as he likes getting the "in the zone" photos.

I crossed the timing mat and it was time for the second loop. I began singing Bon Jovi's Living on a Prayer as "woah, we're half way there", it amused me. I often sing on the bike, thank goodness I don't have a tandem really as my singing is dreadful. Anyhow, I was over the half way point on the bike, my Garmin had also said that my pacing was right on schedule too. My aim was to maintain around 15mph on the bike and I was a smidgen more than that. The second loop I actually think I felt a little stronger than I had on the first lap. OK, I'd needed to adjust my nutrition plan due to my irritating tube bag, but I was still feeling strong. It wasn't long into the second lap where I was overtaken by Ceri-Ann a friend I had made online through a female triathlon group "Team Twinkle". The Twinks as we affectionately refer to ourselves are a group of crazy sporty ladies who don't take ourselves too seriously and believe whole heartedly in supporting each other.

"Debs Longman as I live and breathe." Ceri-Ann declared as she went whizzing past me on her fancy tri bike.

"Smash It Ceri-Ann." I yelled back.

She didn't have the best experience that day, she was hit by a car just after I'd seen her. But being the brave twink she is, she got back on her bike and finished her race. Before I knew it, I was back to the hill. Low gear, power up, that was my mindset. It lasted all of 10 seconds when a bloke who was struggling swerved in front on me. I had to brake. Game over. I stopped, I tried to start again but it was the steepest point and I just couldn't get a forward motion going. I quietly cursed the guy who swerved causing my abrupt stop, but it wasn't really his fault. I resigned myself to the fact that this time I was walking up. I moved myself out of the way of other cyclists and walked up on the wrong side of the road. Whilst the roads were open to cars, there weren't that many around.

At the top of the hill I got back on, and headed back to transition. When I reached the end of the cycle I had managed to maintain just over 15mph for the whole cycle, this pleased me.

Chapter 96

I racked my bike, took my helmet off, took my bike shoes off and put on my trainers. That was when I remembered I needed to take my cycle shorts off. I mumbled to myself about me being a tit, took my trainers off, took my cycle shorts off and put my trainers back on again.

I put on my running drink belt, opened the zip pocket on it and took out a half pork pie to eat. It made me feel queasy. So, two disciplines down, only a half marathon to go. I say only, but there really is no ONLY about running 13.1 miles. The course was a three-loop course. I had in my mind that I would follow a run walk strategy similar to what I had done in Newport half marathon, it had worked for me then, I was hoping it would work again.

I'd only just started the run when I was passed by Conrad. He's a member of our club, but he's also a member of another local club and today he was racing in their club kit. I find it truly strange that people can do this. To me, choosing a club is like choosing a football team. You wouldn't suddenly switch between the two, varying who you race for and what kit you wear. It's an oddity to me, but Conrad is obviously happy with this arrangement, and he gave very encouraging words to me as he ran past so I will forgive him.

My run walk strategy wasn't proving as successful as it had in Newport, probably down to the fact that I had already completed a swim and a cycle, and my running element became mostly a power walk. I wasn't beating myself up over this though, as my pace was actually OK. The only issue that I did have was that my arms were chaffing something dreadful. I wished I had some Vaseline.

I was about half way through the first lap when I realised I needed to go to the toilet. I reached the next feed station and was about to go into the portaloo when I heard a familiar voice behind me.

"I wouldn't go in there if I was you Deb." I turned to see Sian, she was already on the second lap of the run, with that I also saw Mike who was also on his second lap.

I opened the portaloo door and wish I had listened to Sian. I get that people need to use the toilet during races, exercise livens up your digestive system. What I don't get is how anyone could leave a toilet in such a state. There was literally poo everywhere, over the seat, over the floor, it was totally and utterly in a non-useable state.

"Oh my God." I exclaimed, shutting the door immediately.

"Told you." Sian said.

"Guess I'm waiting until the next ones then." I said with a grin, and I headed to the food and drink section to grab a flat coke and some food. I grabbed a fig roll.

Throughout the run, Phil kept popping up like the shop keeper from Mr Benn. As he had taken the Brompton, he could easily get to strategic parts of the course to photograph. It was like he'd been cloned, as no sooner than you'd pass him, ten minutes later he'd be popping up somewhere else.

I passed him about the third time in the first loop and he told me he'd been sending photos to my sister, so our nephew and niece could see me.

In many respects, this had begun to not feel like a race, as I would see families from tri club friends sat at the side of the road cheering, I'd pass clubmates. It felt more like a Celtic Tri street party.

I had been warned by Tracey about "the log", at one part of the run there is a fallen tree trunk blocking the path that you have to climb over. She also warned me that the log gets higher every lap. It had made me giggle. I climbed over 'the log' and it wasn't long until I was reaching the end of the first lap.

At the end of the lap there was a big line of portaloos, I tentatively opened the door and saw a beautiful clean toilet. By this point I really needed to answer the call of nature and this seemed like such a luxury, and such a relief.

So onto lap two. Lap two proceeded as well as lap one. Mostly power walking, some running. Same sense of joy at seeing Phil and my Celtic Tri family. However, it was lap two that I discovered the twiglets. I had struggled to eat the fig roll on the first lap, so decided to grab a handful of twiglets. These suddenly became the tastiest things I had ever eaten. The saltiness of them was a welcome taste. I also enjoyed every mouthful of flat coke. Being a diabetic I don't drink coke, but when you need to elevate your sugars during a race a flat coke does just the job. Over 'the log', which definitely felt higher, and to the end of lap two. As I reached the end of the lap, there was George and Rachel. They were cheering me on, both with their medals around their necks. I however, had another lap to do, but I knew I was going to do it.

I started on the third lap, and made it my mission to thank every marshal who had been on the course. They were all so encouraging. Just after the start of the lap was a man and woman who I was amazed still had voices, they were cheering really hard. I told them how amazing I thought they were.

All the marshals were amazing, and passing them for a third time they seemed like old friends. I high fived them, told them they rocked. It's a hell of a thing to volunteer for that long. I've volunteered at a few races and triathlons and it is more exhausting and a longer day than if you race yourself.

I then saw Phil.

"Do you want to make a film for the kids?" he asked.

It seemed like a really fun idea, so Phil ran alongside me as I made a little video for Robert and Martha.

And before I knew it the finish line was in sight. Me, Debs, The Unlikely Triathlete had completed a middle-distance triathlon. I had swum 1.2 miles, I had cycled 56 miles, and I had run 13.1 miles all in the time of 7hrs 43mins and 6secs, well within the 8 and a half hour cut off. And what was more, I felt fresh. I felt like I could have kept going.

Photo: With my middle distance triathlon medal

Epilogue 5

Shortly after the event, Rob messaged me "So Debs, which half of you feels like an Ironman?" I wasn't sure, but I knew I felt proud. But I knew one thing, I didn't want to feel like only half an Ironman.

So, what would be next for me? Well dear readers, I'm sure that it will come as no surprise that after completing a half iron distance triathlon there was only one place I could go. To the big one, to the triathlon holy grail. With every fibre of my being I wanted it, I wanted to be an Ironman. So next stop, Ironman Kalmar in Sweden. A 2.4 miles swim in the Baltic Sea, a 112 mile bike ride and then a 26.2 mile run. Watch this space and you can read all about it in the next instalment, The Unlikely Triathlete, Part Six: The Very Unlikely Ironman.

Part Six

The Very Unlikely Ironman

Dedication 6

In the spirit of triathlon, I am making three dedications.

Firstly, to Rob, my coach. Taking someone from nothing to Iron ready in a little over two years is a bit insane when you think about it. I wouldn't be where I am today without him.

Secondly, to my amazing boss Gill. I guess it's not often she has had weird working requests from people chasing athletic dreams. I wouldn't have been able to follow my training regime without her support and flexibility.

Finally, to my darling Phil again, who throughout my Ironman journey has been a total trooper. Without him picking up the slack at home there is no way I'd have been able to have done what I did.

You are three awesome individuals, thank you!

Chapter 97

"Have you got my passport?" Phil asked.

It wasn't the best timing, I'll be honest, as at this point we were already on a train to London, heading to the airport. I rolled my eyes, knowing full well that he had it. We'd checked and double checked as this was more than just a holiday. This was a voyage of discovery, this was my one big chance, this was me heading to Sweden to try my luck at an Ironman.

I had been tapering for a few weeks in the lead up to the big event, but this lack of training had made me a little fatigued and more than a bit cranky.

"It's in the front zip pocket of your flight bag." I replied wearily.

"Are you sure?" he replied, not wanting to get out of his seat to reach above him in the over seat racking where his flight bag was located.

"Yes." The weariness becoming more apparent.

"Ah, OK then."

Phil always gets stressed when we go abroad. From the moment we start packing until the moment we arrive, he is a bag of nerves. Ordinarily, I am the voice of reason, the calming influence. However, with the impending sense of doom I was feeling about the prospect of a 2.4 mile swim, a 112 mile bike ride, all polished off with a 26.2 mile marathon run, I wasn't my usual calm self.

We were travelling to London the day before, staying overnight in an airport hotel before our morning flight to Copenhagen. We'd been advised that the best way to get to Kalmar was to fly to Copenhagen and then get the train. It seemed straightforward enough, yet seemed a mammoth journey. I just wanted to get to Kalmar and get the race done.

We arrived at London Paddington, took the short trip over to Heathrow on the Heathrow Express, and then dragged our suitcases to the Hilton Hotel in Terminal 4. It was a hotel that we had stayed in on previous holidays. We had a sense of familiarity with the hotel, which eased both of our nerves.

We checked in, went to our room and I announced to Phil I was going for a swim as I knew the hotel had a pool. What I hadn't expected was what a teeny tiny pool it would be. A twelve and a half metre pool, which when you are doing front crawl means you are turning around ALL THE TIME.

I'd been in the pool about ten minutes, trying to de-stress and unwind from our journey, when a family got in. A mum, a dad, and three girls who I'd guess were between around the ages of nine and fifteen. It was clear the children wanted a splash around, the dad just wanted to chill out and the mum wanted a mix of breaststroke and chill out. I imagine I must have looked like quite an oddity to them. The family were great though, I stayed as close to the one wall as I could and they stayed out of my way.

I completed as many lengths as I could muster, and went to the changing room to shower and change. I was just getting dressed when the mum came in.

"You don't see many people swimming properly in a hotel pool." she said, smiling, sounding friendly.

"I'm a triathlete" I replied, "just needed to swim as best as I could."

"I'd love to be able to swim properly like that," she replied, sounding almost envious.

"Go and learn then," I encouraged. "I've only been able to swim properly for a couple of years."

She nodded. I decided to change the subject.

"Going anywhere nice?" I asked.

"Yeah, America." she replied "You?"

"Sweden" I reply.

"Oh, that's a strange holiday destination," she replied quizzically. "Why are you going there? Do you have family there?"

"No, I'm going to do an Ironman."

"Oh, what's one of those then?" a question that a few minutes later I was sure she was regretting asking.

Chapter 98

I stood in a lay-by with Rob, my coach. Our club time trial was going on, but today we had just met in the lay-by to chat.

"Do you really think I am capable of it Rob?" I asked.

"I'm not going to lie Deb," he replied. "It'll be the hardest thing you will ever do. You will hate me during your training, but I wouldn't have said I thought you could do it if I didn't think you could. I wouldn't set you up to fail."

Decision was made. I was signing up to the Ironman.

Dear readers, I do have to apologise maybe a smidgen for misleading you in Book 5. Even before I had started the sporting events in that book, this conversation between Rob and I had already occurred. I had signed up to Ironman Kalmar in Sweden almost a full year before I was to do it, and I had been researching Ironman events for longer than that.

Making that mental decision to complete an Ironman takes time. However, for many months after I had signed up there were only a few people who knew I was going to do it. I kept my intentions secret from the majority of people. My clubmates knew I had signed up to the half iron distance, but not the full.

I had asked a number of people for their input, including coach Mike, as he had already done Kalmar.

Researching what event to do was quite stressful, there were so many events to consider. Firstly, Ironman Wales was virtually on my doorstep. Only an hour or so away. I could have practised the bike course every weekend if I'd fancied it. However, I didn't. I knew what the bike course entailed. Lots and lots of climbing, lots of technical descents. Both Rob and I had agreed this was not the event for me. Being brutal and honest, my bike skills were not up to the course.

Ironman UK provided another option. Not as much climbing as Wales, and it would still be possible to practise the bike course. A lake swim, so could be an easier swim option. However, as I know my bike strengths lie on the flat, I wanted, dare I say, needed, a flatter course.

So, Ironman Vichy in France, another possibility. Flatter bike, another lake swim, could drive over in the van. However, I then looked at the weather. Traditionally very hot. I don't do hot.

The more I researched, the more I kept coming back to the same conclusion, Kalmar was the Ironman for me. The climate was almost identical to the UK. A sea swim in the Baltic sea maybe wasn't ideal, but I had time to work on my swim and it wasn't as tidal and wave prone as Wales. It was a fast and flat bike course, over the iconic Oland Bridge to the island of Oland. Then back on the mainland. A large island loop, followed by a smaller mainland loop. Then a flat three loop marathon around the city.

There were a few stings in the tail. As the bike course was deemed faster, the cut off was 16 hours instead of the usual 17. Also, due to the bridge and the island, it was viewed as one of the windiest bike courses in the world. A big advantage though, was that it was also one of the best supported Ironman events in the world. Everyone from the island and the mainland come out in force to support. I watched several videos about the course. Every video I watched, I cried. This insane level of emotion told me everything, it was the race I was going to do. It was going to be Kalmar. However, due to the cost involved, I had but one chance. I had to achieve it on the first try as I wouldn't be able to afford to go back in a hurry.

Chapter 99

I usually work in Swansea, and my boss usually works in Cardiff. However, there is a small office in between the two, in Bridgend, where we often meet up. This one particular Tuesday I had a big ask. I knew it was a big ask. We are a small NHS team, and so short staffed, but I wanted to explore utilising the flexible working arrangements that our trust had to offer.

After long conversations with Phil, and a few sums, I had come to the conclusion that I wanted to temporarily reduce my hours. If I could take time off during the week, I could complete my long cycles and long runs during the weekdays, which would impact less upon our weekends. It would also allow me more rest time.

I honestly didn't know how Gill would react to this. Don't get me wrong, we get on brilliantly and she is an amazing manager, but when as a team you are already working at full pelt, having one individual wanting to drop some time is a big ask.

We sat in the little meeting room. For some unknown reason I felt nervous about asking her. I think in part through my own sense of responsibility and thinking I'd be letting the side down.

"So what did you want to talk about Debs?" Gill had a slightly nervous look on her face. Which, in hindsight, was hardly surprising as she had witnessed my health scares previously.

"Well Gill," I tentatively started to pose what I had been practicing in my head.

"You know I am doing triathlons now, and how healthy I have been since doing them? Well I want to sign up for an Ironman and I want to go part time for a few months to support it."

Gill didn't look phased by this at all. We sat and discussed what part time meant. Basically, I wanted to drop one a day a week initially, rising to two days a week at the height of my training. This was obviously subject to business needs, and I'd be flexible over the days I'd take to fit in with work commitments.

After about 15 minutes of exploring, Gill replied, "We need to double check with HR, but, well, this is obviously important to you. Of course I will support you, although I think you are mad."

Quite simply, best boss ever!

Over the coming days, and a few discussions with HR as to how it could be managed, it was decided I could take individual days unpaid leave which would allow more flexibility around number of days and which days of the week, rather than formally changing my work pattern. However, I was to get time off to train. This was just the start of the money pit that became my Ironman dream.

Chapter 100

I don't like airports! There, I've said it! I used to love airports. As a little girl I used to ask my Dad to take me to the airport so I could watch the aeroplanes. When my grandparents went on holiday, I was always the first one to ask if I could go with my Dad to drop them off or pick them up. As a six or seven year old when other little girls wanted to be nurses or vets or teachers, I stood firm, I wanted to be either a pilot or an astronaut! I loved the idea of flying. I loved watching in awe at the huge vehicles that could get off the ground and fly you to wherever you wanted to go. It was a romantic and exciting feeling, and, as a small child who had never even been on a plane, I was obsessed. Jump forward thirty odd years, add in airport security and cheap flights. The romance of the airport was dead. It was a necessary evil to get you from A to B, and this particular visit to Heathrow wasn't proving particularly successful. Gone are the days of having proper tickets sent in the post. Now, you have a reference. You take this reference you take to a machine to get a boarding pass, then you join a long queue of people to get shot of your suitcase. And now, instead of going to a friendly person who does this for you, now it's a self-check in arrangement. An OK and routine experience for the frequent flyer maybe, but when you haven't been on a plane in three years, this confused the hell out of me.

Firstly, scan your boarding pass. Then scan your passport. Then pop your suitcase on the conveyor belt. I popped my suitcase on. It started to move and an alert went off. I'd put it on vertically and apparently it should be on horizontally. I stepped onto the conveyor belt to move my suitcase, yet another alarm, as now it thinks my suitcase is overweight! It shouldn't be this hard, surely! An assistant came over to assist and looked at me like I'm a total moron. With my case safely heading in the right direction (I hoped), Phil was able to benefit from my glaring errors to get rid of his suitcase.

We still had a decent amount of time until we needed to go through security so we went for a coffee and some breakfast.

Security was to be my next fun step. I set of the alarm on the scanner as I walked through. I had taken my belt off, I had taken my watch off, I had followed all the rules. However, as I obviously look incredibly suspicious, I was to have a proper search. I felt violated as the security woman stuck her fingers down the front and back of my trousers! I don't know what she was looking for.

Ordinarily, I would have a small alcoholic drink whilst airside. I mean, surely an airport is the only place where it is acceptable to drink alcohol at seven o'clock in the morning. However, I had given alcohol up to support my iron dream, and so I would have to make do with a glass of sparkling water.

With a less than positive airport experience, part of me had wished I had just done Bolton the month before.

We were called to the boarding gate. I spy a man with a Blue Seventy backpack, and nudge Phil. Blue Seventy is a popular wetsuit brand, I was guessing this man was going to do an Ironman. The question was which one. The day after Kalmar was Copenhagen. With the flight being to Copenhagen it was logical that it could have been either.

"I wonder what one he's doing?" I whisper to Phil.

"Ask him if you want to know." he replied.

I didn't, and we got on the aeroplane and took our seats. We both had aisle seats, so were opposite each other. Mr Blue Seventy was sat in the aisle seat behind Phil, and at that point I couldn't resist. As he put his rucksack under his seat I plucked up the courage.

"Copenhagen or Kalmar?" I asked, nonchalantly.

"Neither," he replied. The confusion must have been evident in my face, so he added "But I'm supporting my sister in law and she's doing Kalmar." He pointed at the lady sat in front of me.

"Ah cool, I'm doing Kalmar too!" I replied.

We talked for a few minutes on the flight, again at the airport and several times in Kalmar, but that story is still to develop. I had, however, made two new friends in John and Boo.

Chapter 101

People talk about the Ironman circus. Several lorries, numerous tents descend on locations across the world and pitch up. I needed to see this Ironman experience for myself, to know what one was all about having signed up to Kalmar.

"Fancy a weekend in Tenby?" I asked Phil.

We'd left it late to arrange a trip to spectate Ironman Wales, all the accommodation we would normally go for had sold out months beforehand. We were, however, able to get a caravan in the neighbouring Kiln Park. I was to spend the weekend in Tenby getting my first glimpse of an Ironman. This first time purely as an enthusiastic spectator.

Several of our club mates had signed up, so I knew it would be great to be able to offer them our support. It was going to be Sian's first Ironman, and the whole club were right behind her with enthusiastic support. Another friend, Tula, was also completing her first.

Christine and the family were also heading down to Tenby to support, so we knew it would be a good weekend with good friends.

We arrived at the caravan, and no word of a lie, it stank! It had a stale odour of BO and tobacco, a quite hideous combination.

"This caravan is gross," Phil announced in a temper.

He wasn't wrong, the bedrooms looked like they had seen better days. The mattresses looked tired and worn. But this was a three night stay, we had our own bedding and towels, and with a good airing it would do the job, just!

"I'm never, ever, going to stay in a caravan again!" Phil shrieked for about the hundredth time as we took the short walk into Tenby.

We were meeting Christine and the family for a pub tea. As we reached the town centre, I caught my first glimpse of the magnificent structure that was the ironman finish line. I was in awe!

I turned to Phil, "Oh wow!" I said. My stomach was in butterflies even though I had a full eleven months until my race. However, seeing the Ironman branding all over Tenby made it all become real. I'd signed up for an Ironman. Was I brave or was I stupid? Maybe a bit of both.

The weekend in Tenby was amazing, if we forget the caravan. I went to the expo and looked at what I could buy. I wasn't prepared to buy anything Ironman branded until I had become one, but in the children's section was something I wanted. A child's t-shirt with "Future Ironman" on the front. The largest size they had was a boy's age 12. I took it to the changing room and it just about fitted! That was to be my one purchase, much to the amusement of Phil.

Race day itself was electric, starting on the beach to the Welsh National anthem, which made me realise I would need to learn the Swedish National anthem!

I'd lost my voice by the end of the day, cheering everyone I knew, and I cried as I watch Sian and Tula cross the finish line and be announced as Ironman.

However, I then fully appreciated the enormity of what I had set out to do. I must train, train, and train some more. I must trust in Rob, completely and totally. I was handing almost the next year of my life over to him and I must do everything he tells me. He had faith in me, I needed believe that he would make me ready.

Chapter 102

Racing abroad brings some logistical problems. How do you get your kit across? Thankfully, I had booked my whole transport and accommodation package through Nirvana, a specialist sporting travel company. Who knew that such a thing existed, hey?

Part of the package was a "ship my tri bike" service. All I had to do was take my bike to my local bike shop at an agreed time. I could also take a rucksack containing other items such as my wetsuit, my helmet, my bike shoes etc, and then I would collect it all at my hotel at the other end. This was an amazing bit of customer service as far as I was concerned.

I took my time packing my rucksack, I wanted to maximise the use of space to limit what I would need to take in my suitcase. I had the insane notion that if I could fit everything I needed for the race in the rucksack, then when it became time to pack my suitcase a few days later, I'd be packing for a holiday.

My tri top went into a drinks bottle, my tri shorts went inside one trainer, my socks and sports bra into another trainer. My cycle jersey went into a cycling shoe, my cycle shorts into the other one. Everything was packed with military precision. Food was crammed into side pockets. The main part of the rucksack would only just close over my helmet, which had a wetsuit, and the tightly packed shoes under it. I placed the tags on my bike and on my rucksack.

The drop off was on the Thursday morning, nine days before my race. My drop off time was 8.30am which meant I also had to arrange a late start in work as I usually start at 8. I arrived super early, and sat in the van ready to hand over my beloved bike who I have affectionately named "Katie Kalmar". A man pulled up next to me, he had a bike and a rucksack too. We chatted briefly and I found out that he was doing Copenhagen. We'd barely had chance to wish each other luck when the van arrived to take our bikes and belongings. I watched as the man loaded Katie onto the van and took off the front wheel to join the bike to the side of the van. He placed the wheel in a bag and put that and my rucksack under the bike.

I stood, and watched. I then made a total tit of myself by saying, "Please take care of my baby!" and I left, getting back in the van and started driving to work. I sobbed the whole drive! I genuinely have no idea why, maybe it was the realisation that my big day was very, very, quickly approaching.

Chapter 103

The train station in Copenhagen airport is literally inside the airport itself. So getting to the platform couldn't have been an easier task. However, boarding a train in a foreign country is always a nervy experience. We had originally thought that our train took us directly to Kalmar, however, we had to change trains at Malmo after a sign appeared on the trains electronic notice boards. It said "Slutstation" which gave us both a few giggles. However, we were to discover that this meant "Final station" and we had to swap to another train.

We had a stressful few minutes until we figured out what we needed to do to get on the next train, but before we knew it, we had arrived at Kalmar.

The rep from Nirvana was scheduled to pick us up from the station. However, there was no sign of him. We knew though that it was only a five minute walk to the hotel so we decided to drag our cases through the cobbled streets of Kalmar and to the hotel.

I knew that the finish line was outside the hotel, and we could see that this was already being set up. I let the biggest grin cross my face. I was actually here! I was in Kalmar! In a few days time I would be doing the race of my life and hopefully earning the title of Ironman. I was so excited I could have burst.

We were checked into the hotel by a typical Swedish babe, long flowing blonde hair and a real beauty. Her English was perfect. She told us where to find our room. The room itself was very spacious, but I was disappointed to see that there was only a shower and not a bath. I had hoped that after the race I could have had a nice soak.

We had arrived too late for me to collect my bike that day, although the collection point was in our hotel, so I knew I wouldn't have far to go the following day. We set out to explore. The expo was closed, however, outside there was the "M-Dot" which contained all the names. I stopped to locate my name. As I saw my name there, I started to well up with tears again. There it was, no escaping the fact of what I had signed up to do. I located Mic and Dan's names too and knew I'd be able to meet with them the following day.

Michala used to be a member of Celtic Tri, but was living in London with her husband, Dan, who was also from South Wales. When the start list was published, I had looked through and had seen Mic's name with "Celtic Tri" written next to it. I had instantly messaged Tracey and asked her if she knew who this Michala was. She had told me that Mic had moved to London and that I should get in touch. We became friends on Facebook and we first met up at the Swansea triathlon a few months before. We had also managed to go open water swimming together when Mic was home visiting family. It was great to get to know her and Dan ahead of the race, and lovely to know that there would be friendly faces sharing the experience.

The next few days were all rather a blur. Boo from the airport was staying at my hotel so I had chatted to her a few times. I'd met the "voice of Ironman" Paul Kaye in the expo and had a photo taken with him. I also met up with Gemma, a fellow member of Team Twinkle who was racing and was living in Sweden. I'd registered, I'd signed the pledge to say I was a clean athlete.

I'd sat with Phil, Dan and Mic at the race briefing, trying to take in every word but barely hearing anything as my mind kept racing. I'd taken my bike out for a little ride, realised I had a problem with my brakes and the lovely on site mechanic fixed it. I had been on a minibus tour of the bike course, where I met another top person in Big Eric. I tried so very very hard to fully absorb each passing second, wanting to imprint it on my memory for life. Before I knew it, I was getting my transition bags ready and racking my bike ready for the race.

Photo: Meeting Paul Kaye

Chapter 104

I had joined a webinar a few months before the Ironman. The lovely Swedish guy taking the webinar had said that they had run a long distance triathlon in Kalmar for twenty years and it had only ever rained twice. When I woke up on race morning it was pouring down! Third time lucky, hey! I walked down to the transition area in my tracksuit to check on my bike, add a few snacks to my bag and returned to the hotel for breakfast.

I met with Boo, we sat and had breakfast together. She had told me that she always struggled with eating breakfast on race day, but together we managed to get some food inside us. She was also preparing some sandwiches for the race later. I wish I'd have thought of that, as I had bought some bread rolls and cheese from the shop the day before to make sandwiches for the race. However, these sandwiches were now safely deposited in my transition bags.

I still had my special needs bags. These are bags that you can collect if you want to whilst on the bike and run. I had put a few extra snacks in each incase I did want to stop for them. Although, I hoped that I wouldn't need them.

After breakfast, I tiptoed back into the room hoping that I wouldn't wake Phil up, as it was still only 5.30am, but he was wide awake. It was a good job he was as Rob had given him a mission. He was to write some motivational messages on my arms that I could look at during the day when I needed some extra inspiration.

I was given strict instructions to close my eyes as Phil took to my arms with a Sharpie! He wrote on my left, he wrote on my right. I was then told I could open my eyes.

I smiled as I looked down at my motivational messages telling me to move forward and what a tough cookie I was in Rob's unique language.

From that moment, I knew I had my coach with me all day, whether I wanted him there or not! I wanted him there. I wouldn't have got this far without him and his belief in me. Dull sod!

I changed into my tri top and bottoms, popped my tracksuit bottoms back on over the top, popped a hoody on, and grabbed my wetsuit, swim hat and googles and put them in my white "street clothes" bag.

It was now or never. Butterflies in my stomach had started, I was nervous and excited and a little terrified.

Chapter 105

It was only a very short walk to the swim start. The atmosphere was electric. You could sense the excitement and anticipation in the air.

I'd only just arrived when I saw Mic and Dan. Mic seemed a little quieter than usual, but both seemed ready for the monumental task ahead of us.

"Do you know where you leave your special needs bags?" I asked them.

It was then I discovered that I should have left them at transition when I went to check on my bike. Whilst it wasn't that far away from the swim start, with the crowds of people I knew it would take too long to get there and back. I started to panic!

"I'll drop them there for you Deb," Phil replied, ever my hero!

I needed to put my wetsuit on. There were two ladies sat on a bench, I asked them if I could share the bench with them to get my wetsuit on. They were friendly and obliged, wishing me luck.

Everyone was so ready for the race, be they participants or be they supporters.

The race start is a rolling start, so you seed yourself based on your predicted swim time. Myself, Mic and Dan had all decided on the 1 hour 30 minute time, which meant we were able to wait together.

As soon as we got into this line it was time to say goodbye to Phil. We kissed, he hugged me, rubbed my head and told me he'd see me later. It was quite an emotional moment, I felt ready to cry. I was just glad I had the support of my friends at my side.

I felt like my heart was racing as I stood in line. I, foolishly, decided to look at my Garmin. 135 beats per minute, zone 3 aerobic standing around nerves!! I told Mic, she laughed. If my heart rate was doing that just standing in line what the hell was going to happen when I started racing?

The national anthem started, broadcast out over loud hailers, the canon sounded. This was it. Holy shit, I was starting an Ironman!

Photo: With Mic and Dan before the swim

Chapter 106

I had reached one of the lowest points I have experienced in my triathlon journey to date. I had an email which reminded me how close my big event was, and whilst I was training hard and was on track, seeing something in black and white suddenly made me lose my confidence.

I was scheduled to do a two kilometre swim before work. However, I was not going to be working in my usual office as I had meetings, so I decided to go to another pool that was closer to the office I would be working in that day. This proved to be a big mistake.

I got poolside and tried to assess which lane I should choose. There was a large slow lane (populated by all ladies), then a "club lane" which had been booked out, a fast lane and a large medium lane (populated by all men).

I felt like Goldilocks looking at the porridge bowls as I assessed the lanes.

The slow was way, way, way too slow. The fast was too fast, the medium, probably too slow, but the closest to the desired "just right" that I could get.

I made the judgement call to get in the medium lane. As it was wider, I was thinking I could overtake when needed. I soon discovered, as I powered up the pool front crawl, that my presence was NOT welcome. Within a matter of minutes I was told, "You are too fast for this lane, you have no business being in here."

I explained to the stroppy elderly man that I was too slow for the fast lane and that as this lane was wider it was a better fit as I could hopefully overtake without affecting other people's swims. This was when the elderly collective decided to gang up on me!! They blocked me as I swam, they purposefully kicked and hit me. They crowded at the shallow end so that I couldn't push off the wall and access my water bottle.

I am a fairly passive soul, but this was too much. So I complained to the life guard only to be told "Don't piss off the regulars". Now, I don't mean to be rude, but I had paid my money to swim, I chose the best lane for me. The fact that the regulars turned into an angry mob against me was not my fault.

I continued regardless, getting increasingly battered and bruised, until I finished my set. I got out of the pool and tried to save my swim on my Garmin and it wouldn't save my heart rate. This minor irritation now became a big issue. I felt stressed, I got to the shower cubicle and it was disgustingly dirty. Grime, easily an inch thick, lined the cubicle walls, grey and thick with stray hairs. I felt defeated, as I showered, and I started to cry.

My crying became worse and worse, until I found myself sat wrapped in a towel, my arms hugging my knees in a pseudo foetal position, in the changing rooms, sobbing my heart out. I proceeded to be a blubbering wreck for a good 15 to 20 minutes.

Chapter 107

The mass of Ironman race entrants started to move slowly forward, much slower than I expected. I couldn't even see the water and time was ticking on. The elites would already be well into their swim by now.

It took eleven minutes to reach the water's edge and to activate my timing chip to start my 16 hour countdown to my destiny.

I got into the water and I was off, I was racing. Considering the Baltic is a sea, the water was not that salty to taste. This didn't come as a surprise to me as I had already tasted the water the day before. Maybe an odd thing to do, but I wanted as few surprises as possible during my swim.

I was making good progress, and managing to carve out a space for myself in the water without swimming over people or having people swim over me. It seemed to be starting well. However, as I started getting closer to the first buoy the water seemed more congested and it became a bit of a bunfight. A number of people collided with me. On a pep talk from Lisa a few weeks before, she had said to me, "Whatever happens in the swim, remember it's YOUR Ironman. Just push on." And so I said to myself "This is MY Ironman," and it was elbows out until I had a bit more space again.

The first buoy seemed to take forever to reach, and the closer it got, the choppier the water became. As the water was beasting me on my right hand side, I had to deviate from my usual breathe every three strokes and switched to breathing every four so I could breathe avoiding the waves. The 1km marker was in sight. I felt my heart sink. "Is that all!!" It had felt like I'd already been swimming for a decent amount of time and was only a quarter of the way through. The marker was passed and it was onto the next buoy for sighting. It was then he came up alongside me, doing breaststroke. He was close to me, I tried to move further to the right to avoid him. I failed. As he overtook me, he did his massive breaststroke kick, kicking me full on in the left shoulder. The pain was instant, and severe. I tried to move my left arm in the stroke but it was just too painful. I didn't panic. This was my day. I left my left arm at my side and continued forward using only my right arm.

Chapter 108

"Why on earth do we do these stupid drills?" I moaned to Mike for about the tenth time in that Sunday afternoon Celtic Tri pool session.

"Everything we do, we do for a reason." he replied, in a way that almost made him appear wise and all knowing. He was the swimming pool equivalent of the Karate Kid's Mr Miyagi with his wax on wax off of drills.

"I am never, ever going to need to do wide arm catch ups in real life," I replied. "And single arm drills are totally pointless, when am I ever going to need to swim with only one arm?"

"Just do the set Debs, and stop moaning." he replied. He smiled.

Chapter 109

So, I am swimming along in the Baltic Sea, on my Ironman swim. I'm doing single arm drills having taken the nasty kick to the left shoulder. I'm actually surprising myself with how well I am moving through the choppy water.

One of the safety boats can see I am only using one arm.

"Are you ok?" a kindly chap shouts from the boat.

"Yes, I'm fine," I reply, "Just took a kick to the shoulder, but I'll be OK."

The water seemed to be getting choppier and the buoys were getting increasingly hard to sight. The bobbing of the water made me feel slightly seasick. Something I had experienced before on a few training swims. I just had to keep moving.

It had probably been about twenty minutes since my shoulder kick, lots of people had overtaken me and I guessed my pace wasn't where it needed to be. I had to try and use my left arm again.

I lifted it out, I knew I didn't have the full range of movement. It hurt, but I needed to suck up the pain. I started swimming proper front crawl.

I was approaching another buoy and the water seemed congested with swimmers again. I switched to wide arm catch-ups to stop me getting kicked in the face.

I was getting closer to shore and the final stretch where you swim under two bridges. I was relieved to be closer to land as the choppiness reduced. It felt easier swimming in calmer waters.

For the first time in the swim I could actually see some sea life, a few small jelly fish and some little fish swimming in schools. There was also a rather shocking amount of seaweed.

As you swim under the first bridge, you are leaving the sea for more of a river type arrangement. The bridge was full of people cheering. It made me forget the pain for a moment. Under the next bridge, this bridge was wider and it was an unusual feeling as it seemed to go dark. As I came out the other side, I got my foot caught in some pond weed. I shook my foot free, the finish was in sight.

The relief at finishing the swim overwhelmed me, although I dreaded looking at my watch. My training swims I had been doing the distance in around an hour and a half. I knew the shoulder injury had slowed me down. As I exited the water I glanced at my Garmin as I switched it to Transition 1.

1 hour 52 minutes. 22 minutes behind schedule. Fuck!

Chapter 110

I knew I had to get through transition in the quickest amount of time possible as I was already significantly behind schedule.

I grabbed my bag off the rack and ran into the changing tent.

In my haste, I emptied the bag on the floor, not really thinking about the floor being soaking wet.

I started drying off my legs whilst eating a cheese sandwich.

As I started putting on my cycle shorts I remembered that I had extra power pain killers in my bike bag.

A few months before, I had met with some ladies from the club who had already done Ironman. One of these ladies is Jayne. She is a phenomenal athlete, I think she has done around twenty Iron distance events so had experience to share in spades. One of her top tips was to always have pain killers in your saddle bag as you never know when you may need them. I had heeded this piece of advice, and had Jayne been there I would have kissed her! I needed those pain killers. I wasn't sure I would be able to cycle 112 miles in the pain I was in, but I was hoping a cocktail of pain killers and adrenaline would be enough.

I tried to put on my cycle jersey. The combination of shoulder pain and the jersey now being very wet made this a very difficult task. However, I was now dressed for the cycle.

I threw my wetsuit, hat and goggles into the bag and dropped it in the bag drop. I ran to my bike. It was easy to find, there were only a handful of bikes left in transition. I reached my bike, put my helmet on and grabbed two tablets from my saddle bag and swallowed with a drop of energy drink.

I pulled my bike off the rack and headed to the "bike out". As I reached the mount line I saw Phil.

He was cheering, yelling, "Go on Debs!" at the top of his lungs. He must have realised I was way behind schedule. I yelled back, telling him that my swim was horrific and I was off.

Chapter 111

When I cycled as a child I had a bike with no gears. My first attempt at a bike with gears was a road bike that was way too big for me that belonged to my boyfriend when I was fourteen. I lasted all of two minutes before I had fallen off. After that, I wasn't to get on a bike again for twenty-four years. Learning to ride a bike with gears in my late 30s was a challenge, as was the switch from hybrid to road bike (which took a step back to flat handlebars before it took a step forward again).

However, it's not just the bike that needs to be considered. There are numerous other complexities for the modern cyclist. The first of these are the pedals and shoes. Gone are the days where the masses ride in flat pedals and trainers, it is widely accepted that everyone now cycles in cleats. For those of you that aren't cyclists, this is where you are physically attached to the bike. There is a certain contraption which joins the bottom of your shoe to the pedal, so your feet are physically linked with the bike. You need to clip in, and then twist your ankles to unclip when you need to stop. I knew I had to try cleats. I was nervous as hell. Thankfully, the lovely Jo had an old set of mountain bike cleats and shoes knocking around that she was prepared to lend me. A lot of people start out with mountain bike cleats on road bikes as they are viewed as easier to clip in and out of.

It took a number of weeks for me to pluck up the courage to put the pedals on my bike and give them a go. Rob had promised me that he would meet me in the infamous TT layby with a turbo trainer so I could practice on the turbo first and then go out on the road with them.

I tentatively did my first clip in. I found it stiff and difficult, but I persevered, clipping in, clipping out over and over again until Rob said it was time to try it on the road. We'd stop regularly so I could keep practising.

Initially, it went quite well. I was managing to unclip, stop and clip back in again once I was moving. We only cycled about four or five miles and returned to the layby. There was a big gang from the tri club there as it was time trial night. I slowed down, unclipped by left foot, leaned right! With my right foot still clipped in and attached to the pedal I ended up in a heap on the floor in front of an audience. How embarrassing. Everyone reassured me that this was a rite of passage and that everybody does it, but I didn't half feel like a tit.

I decided that I needed to practise away from the roads, and so chose a local cycle path to practise. My darling Phil came with me. I'd been over thinking things and was worried in case I'd need to unclip to do an emergency stop. Phil had been cycling in cleats for months, and was confident and reassured me that I'd be fine. Every half a mile or so he'd shout "STOP" and that was my cue to emergency stop and unclip. However, whilst there was no real emergency, I was struggling to unclip my foot.
We continued to cycle up the path and a dog was off the lead and running towards me. This was a cue for caution and I slowed down and tried to unclip. I couldn't. My foot was not budging. Thankfully the dog and I did not collide, but the experience shook me up. What if it had been a child? Or what if it had been on the road and it had been a car? I spent the rest of the cycle sobbing. Like properly crying. Phil was looking at me like I was a lunatic as I talked through the sobs.
"I don't like it Phil. I don't feel safe. This isn't for me."
I tried a couple more times, but I had become so scared about unclipping that my cycle speeds were getting slower and slower as I decided to over compensate. This made me realise that cleats were not for me.

Rob was annoyed at me. He told me that they would make me stronger and faster. However, I had discovered that the opposite was true. They had made me weaker and slower. He wanted to make me keep trying and that was when I had a mini melt down. I was not going to bow to peer pressure! Cycling is a joy, cleats were making me lose my joy. Cleats HAD to go. I thanked Jo and returned her pedals and shoes.

The peer pressure didn't stop. I was told nobody does Ironman without cleats. I was determined to find someone who had done it. It was then Tracey told me that Amanda from our club had done Ironman Wales TWICE on flat pedals and trainers and so I got in touch.

Amanda is a fabulous athlete, but like me, found that when she tried cleats she lost her cycling confidence. She told me to stick to my guns and I did.

I did, however, want to see if there was some kind of halfway house out there, and I eventually came across Maglock bike pedals. They are basically pedals with magnets in them, then you have a metal "cleat" attached to your shoe. You can get the advantages of cleats like pulling up on hills, but they are much easier to unclip. The downside was the company was based in America and I'd have to import them. It was an expensive gamble, but one I was willing to try. When they arrived, again, like the cleats, it took a few weeks of building up courage to put them on my bike. I also had to buy bike shoes but these could be easily returned if it didn't work out (as long as I had only tried them indoors of course!).

They did work out! Better that, they became a total game changer for me. They are so much easier to detach from, but still give you some of the cleat benefits. I totally and utterly love them. A lot of people have had negative views towards them initially, but when they see me "pull up" on them at traffic lights they are amazed. Top pedals, highly recommend them.

Chapter 112

The next cycling addition that many road cyclists have is tribars. If you haven't got a fancy time trial bike or triathlon bike then you can get clip on bars for your road bike. These bars allow you to get into a more aerodynamic position which can make you go faster.

Rob had a spare set that he put on my bike for me to try. Like with the cleats, he started slowly with me, getting down onto the bars and moving back to the main handlebars. Slowly, slowly, until I was getting used to it. He then sent me out into the big wide world to practise on my own.

It was Good Friday and the club had arranged a massive group ride. We met in a club mate's café for a cuppa and a bacon sandwich before we set off. We split into groups based on speed and off we went. I was in a group with a lovely bunch of people, one of the slower groups. We were around six miles into the ride. We'd just climbed a hill and there was a long quiet flat stretch of road. I decided this would be a great place to get onto the tribars. I started moving my hands and spectacularly lost my balance. I ended up in a heap in the gutter, my arm and hip both badly grazed and bleeding.

Kelli was the first to reach me and check I was OK.

"Oh my God Debs, are you OK?" she yelled as she came to a stop.

"Stupid tribars!" I replied as I got to my feet and got back on my bike.

And like the cleats, I decided that tribars were also not for me.

When I returned them to Rob, he made a joke about it. If I failed the Ironman it would be because I didn't use the Tribars. Bad swim? Tribars fault. Puncture? Tribars fault. Fall over on the run? Tribars!

What this did mean, was that I was going into the Ironman cycle as what would be classed as a poor cyclist. No cleats and no tribars. Just me and my road bike. I even attached a bottle to the front of my bike with a big straw so I wouldn't need to take a bottle out of the cage on the frame to drink, as I was still pretty rubbish at that too.

So whilst I was starting at a distinct disadvantage, as basically, I was attempting it as a rather crap cyclist in terms of skills. What I did have was a level of determination that I was going to prove all the doubters wrong, that you could cycle without these fancy additions and that I could and would become an Ironman.

Chapter 113

I sped off down the road. Amazingly my shoulder wasn't giving me too much discomfort. I had set off too fast really, but a mixture of adrenaline and knowing I needed to play catch up after my poor swim time was motoring me forward. I started overtaking a number of other competitors. This gave me some much needed confidence.

It was only a short cycle until Oland Bridge. It reminded me in many ways of the Severn Bridge which links Wales to England, only this was a longer, more impressive, albeit a narrower structure.

The only time when cycling is allowed on this bridge is during Ironman. They close one carriageway for the cyclists and set up a contraflow system in the other carriageway to allow motorists to still use the bridge. Most of the motorists didn't seem to be carrying out their day to day business, they were waving flags out of the windows and cheering the cyclists as they went past. They seemed to have taken to the roads with the purpose to encourage the athletes. It made me think that we wouldn't get the same reaction back home if we did this on the Severn Bridge, there would be hatred and anger thrown at the cyclists, not complete and utter support. Gosh I love Swedish people!

The bridge was windy, but that was OK, I had trained for that. I had purposefully gone out to cycle in exposed areas on windy days.

What I found both distracting and amazing were the numbers of little islands under the bridge in the Kalmar Strait. I knew as I was racing I shouldn't really be enjoying the scenery but I was soaking it all in. I wanted to savour every moment.

When I reached the other side it was time to start my trip around Oland. I had already been around it on a minibus, so I knew what to expect. Our guide had told us that people would line the streets and cheer, but I honestly hadn't expected to see so many supporters. Young and old lined the roads waving flags and cheering.

I hadn't long reached the island when I realised I needed to pee. The 19km aid station was coming up, the next one was at 31km. I decided to wait until the 31km mark. However, this was a decision I regretted when the need to pee started to cause me discomfort from around 21km. I had a painful 10k as I waited for the next aid station. When I reached it I decided that this was an ideal time to take on some nutrition. I had a peanut cereal bar with me, and I ate it whilst I was sat on the portaloo. I disgusted myself if I'm honest, but every second counted and I needed to combine the two. My pee seemed to take forever. However, I took this as a positive sign that I wasn't dehydrated.

Back on the bike I continued my journey. In fairness to the organisers they had done a magnificent job. The island had one lane open for the motorists, making the island a massive one way system and the cyclists had the other. So whilst my carriageway was closed to traffic, it did allow some movement for the locals too. Not that there were many vehicles moving, everyone seemed to be having a party.

Oland has a lot of farms, and one farm in particular amused me. There was a small child, wearing ear defenders, banging a drum kit for all he was worth at the side of the road. This drumming wasn't a proper rhythm rather just any old whacking to make a noise. A rock band drummer he would never be, but he seemed to be having fun. I imagined that on a normal day the family had probably sent him out to the furthest barn for him to pursue his hobby. I'd reached the first crossing point heading from the west of the island to the east. I knew this was where I would hit some wind again. As my speed seemed to pick up, I was guessing this meant I had a tailwind, which would mean a headwind later. I was part way up this section when I heard a whistle from a motorbike marshal. I panicked, I wasn't too close to the cyclist in front, I wasn't drafting. I turned, confused, and realised that this whistle was not aimed at me. Rather to the cheeky sod who I hadn't noticed was sat on my wheel, drafting me. I bet he wasn't impressed at his penalty. I breathed a smug sigh of relief and continued.

I overtook a number of people in this section. As I passed the next feed station I looked down on the frame of my bike. On it I had a small laminated piece of paper, which had been carefully calculated with the time of day I should be passing every feed station to be on track. I was gaining back a bit of time which made me relieved.

Chapter 114

I was glad we had spent the night in Cardiff. It would have been an early start if we hadn't. It was the day of the Carten cycle. An annual charity cycle where participants cycle from Cardiff to the seaside town of Tenby 107 miles away.

Phil had stayed with me, and was planning to drive down to Tenby, stopping along the route to take photos and be a mobile aid station.

I met Sian as she had also stayed in the hotel and we were cycling together. We hadn't even left the hotel car park when she had a puncture. The combination of her Boardman wheels and gatorskin tyres made the puncture repair a slow and arduous job, which meant we reached the start line later than we expected and missed the rest of our clubmates.

I didn't mind this at all. Sian is absolutely brilliant company. This is the Sian that is known first as a swimmer having swum from Ilfracombe to Swansea, she was also training for her first Ironman, she was doing Wales.

We had gone out with a tactic to enjoy the day and not worry too much about time. This was about covering virtually the Iron distance and following a nutrition plan. Although, the Carten route has lots of official feed stops, we wouldn't be stopping. Rob was coaching us both and we'd been told we needed our nutrition on the bike (with top ups from Phil in lay-bys) to simulate race day.

We started our cycle out of Cardiff, chatting away. I was amazed that Sian only had tri shorts on and not cycle shorts. However, like me, she was using this ride as a dress rehearsal for the big day, and she wanted to discover if she would be able to do the distance in tri shorts. I had already decided that I was going to put cycle shorts over my tri shorts in T1, so I had this combo good to go.

The cycle was going well until we reached just past Cowbridge. There is an exposed bridge and the crosswinds were horrendous. If Sian hadn't have been with me I think I would have cried. I felt like I was losing control of the bike. During the short stretch over the bridge I experienced numerous wobbles and thought I was going to come off more than once. I was relieved that Phil wasn't in a layby near here. I honestly think if he had been I'd have thrown my bike in the van and given up.

Cycling with a headwind is hard work, cycling with a tailwind is a pure speedy joy, cycling with a crosswind is bloody terrifying!

Thankfully it wasn't too long until we were in a sheltered area again and the joy of the cycle returned.

I made sure I was keeping drinking, and taking on nutrition regularly. Mainly malt loaf with butter.

We had reached Port Talbot and this was where we had our first scare of the day. Sian, being a better and faster cyclist, was slightly ahead of me. We were approaching a set of traffic lights, when a car passed me really closely and then pulled in straight ahead of me. I had to slam on my brakes, causing the cyclist behind me to nearly crash into the back of me.

The traffic lights changed to red and the close call car was stopped at the red. I cycled up to the side of the car and knocked, politely, on the passenger window.

The female passenger looked a little terrified as she opened the window an inch. I spoke directly to the driver.

"Do you realise how close you came to hitting me there?" I asked him, calmly, nicely.

"No I didn't." he replied.

With this the cyclist who was behind me pulled up.

"Mate," he said, "You were dangerously close and you pulled in too quickly."

I continued, "You need to give us cyclists as much space as you'd give a car."

"You shouldn't be on the fucking road anyway!" the driver replied.

"You've got 2000 people on bikes today who disagree with you there." my new chum responded.

Thankfully the lights changed, as I think it could have got ugly. The driver sped off, leaving me and my chum shaking our heads at the side of the road.

"Are you ok?" he asked me.

"Fine," I replied, "I've had worse close encounters."

Sian had waited for me the other side of the lights.

"What just happened?" she asked.

"Idiot tried to take me out." I replied.

Chapter 115

We'd only cycled another four or five miles when we had our next scare. We were on a cycle path, approaching a garage, when suddenly a man in front of us fell, hitting his head on some road barriers.

Sian is a doctor and was quickly springing into action. Another cyclist, Simon, who we discovered is a nurse was also straight off his bike to assist. Before I knew it, my hero friends were in medical mode and an ambulance was called.

I felt about as much use as a chocolate teapot until I found my niche. I could go further back up the path and warn cyclists to slow down and warn of the danger ahead. So that was what I did. Off my bike, still in my helmet, frantically waving my arms.

A few people stopped and offered assistance which reaffirmed my faith in humanity. However, as soon as they knew that a doctor and a nurse were on the scene they seemed satisfied and carried on their way.

The paramedics took around 45 minutes to arrive, and once Sian had successfully done the handover and once Simon had arranged with the garage to store the bike, we were able to get back on the move again.

We were less than a mile up the road when we saw Phil in a layby. He'd been getting concerned as he had obviously expected us to be passing sooner. We explained what happened and he seemed genuinely relieved that we were OK.

It gave Sian and I the opportunity to top up our water bottles before heading off again.

If anyone fancies the Carten cycle, it is a lovely ride. However, the challenges come later in the ride. Up until Carmarthen the ride is pretty flat, then for the last 30 miles, when you are already fatigued, comes the onslaught of hills! Big hills!

Cycling up hills requires more energy, and as I had been training on flatter terrain this was where my nutrition messed up royally.

We had been cycling through some country lanes, and Sian was paying closer attention to me than usual.

"Deb when did you last eat?"

The honest answer was it had been a while. I had been struggling to get up the hills and trying to keep up with her and had neglected my nutrition as a result.

"I dunno," I replied, my voice slightly slurring.

Sian had spotted that my blood sugars were too low before I did.

For the second time in the day she sprang into doctor mode, forcing sugar down my throat.

We weren't that far away from a feed station and when we arrived there, breaking the rules or not, she made me stop for more energy drink and another cereal bar.

"How could you be so stupid Deb?" the doctor now mixed with my gorgeous friend. "You know you need to keep eating. Even more so as a diabetic!"

I felt fine, we didn't have far to go, only another 15 miles or so.

"Come on," I said, "We've lost enough time, let's get to Tenby"

The biggest hills were behind us, we just had one long really slow drag to get up, a slightly bothersome incline but not a hill. The incline seemed to go on for ever and ever. However, we were soon to get our reward. The "Welcome to Tenby" sign. When we reached there, Phil was already there, armed ready with his camera.

Only a couple more miles until the finish line in the town centre. We crossed the finish line together after a rather epic nine hours in the saddle. Slow, yes, but considering the adventures we had on route hardly surprising either. However, I had achieved something I needed to do, my first century ride.

Chapter 116

I was loving the Kalmar cycle and amazing myself by still passing people. One person I passed I recognised. My friend Gemma from Team Twinkle. It was also her first Ironman.

"Go Gem!" I yelled as I overtook her.

We weren't too much further up the road when Gemma overtook me again. We were both grinning like Cheshire cats.

My grinning was to be fairly short lived, as I needed to turn to cross from the East to the West and this was where I knew the cycle was going to get tough again. I knew I was going to hit the headwinds.

It was like cycling into a brick wall. I was pedalling with all my might, yet when I looked at my speed sensor I was only doing a little over nine miles an hour. A truly pathetic show. I knew I had probably around five or six miles until I reached the point where I would be turning to head south. I just needed to keep my head down and keep plugging away.

I looked at the writing on my arms. I needed to feel Rob's presence at that time. Everyone reaches dark moments during an Ironman (or so I'm told) and this was one of mine. I'd amazingly got through the kick to my shoulder and after taking the tablets it wasn't giving me too much discomfort. I'd guessed this was to be my bike dark moment.

When I had been on the bike tour, I had been told that this was the toughest section, but as soon as you saw the church bells it would be over. I prayed for those church bells to come.

The relief when I saw them was incredible, it was a point to turn. A female marshal was stood at the other side of the road with her arm extended telling me to go left. In my complete relief at reaching the church I forgot I was in Sweden and went down the left hand side of the road. Cue frantic waving from the woman, yep, I wasn't in the UK now.

Chapter 117

Interestingly, Sweden hadn't always driven on the right-hand side of the road. Originally, like us in Great Britain, they had driven on the left.

Driving on the left isn't really a problem for us in Britain. Being an island, we have no borders to get in our way with other driving rules from other lands.

Sadly, Sweden didn't have that luxury. All of Sweden's neighbouring countries, including Finland and Norway where Sweden has land borders, were driving on the right. It had become a logistical nightmare.

So in the mid 1950's the Swedish Government put it to the vote. Should they change to the right hand side? The Swedish people voted unanimously to stay on the left. However, over the next decade, the number of cars on Sweden's road tripled. The number of border crossing also increased, causing mayhem. In 1963, the Swedish Government decided to ignore the people, and begin the planning to move to driving on the right hand side of the road.

The switch, known as "Dagen H", took place on 3rd September 1967. From that point on, Sweden would fall in with it's Baltic neighbours and drive on the right.

Chapter 118

I knew this salient piece of Swedish history thanks to our cycle tour guide. Even though I knew they drove on the right, and therefore, I was also to cycle on the right, a combination of tiredness and euphoria at leaving the head wind made me make a total tit of myself.

I apologised profusely at the marshal, hoping that she would accept my pathetic feeble British faux pas and wouldn't disqualify me for breaking the rules of the road.

I continued, on the right hand side, and came to a slight downhill with a turn at the bottom. I went to brake to take the corner and my hands totally cramped up. All that time of gripping the bars as I fought the wind had made my hands uncooperative to say the least. I flew around the corner like a lunatic, barely able to stay upright.

I knew I needed to stop at the next aid station, even if for just a minute to try and get my hands working again. I also felt I could benefit from another toilet stop.

I reached the stop and popped a malt loaf ball in my mouth. It turned my stomach. The same had happened when I had put one in my mouth thirty minutes before. My nutrition plan was starting to fall apart. My best tried and tested endurance foods were making me feel queasy.

I chewed and swallowed the ball and went to the toilet. I wasn't prepared for what I saw.

I have endometriosis, a problem which causes a thick womb lining to grow outside of my womb. Due to issues which I won't bore you with, I get a quarterly injection which pretty much stops my periods so this lining doesn't cause me issues. I only have a period on very rare occasions. So you can imagine my surprise that my bastard body had decided that half way through an Ironman triathlon was the ideal time and place to give me a period. I looked in my shorts and it could have been a scene from CSI Kalmar, if such a thing existed. There was blood everywhere. And of course, being unaccustomed to periods, I didn't have anything feminine hygiene wise with me. Thankfully, there were wet wipes in the portaloo and I was able to clean myself up a bit. However, no point stressing about it, I had to get back to the mainland, do the mainland cycle loop and then run a marathon. I just hoped the blood wouldn't be too obvious through my shorts, I was just glad that my favourite cycle shorts were a bit wrecked anyway.

Chapter 119

I was loving my days off work. Getting up early on a non-working day and going out for a long cycle was a joy. My company varied, as did my routes. I tried my best to get a Friday off where I could. Most Fridays I would ride with Tracey as she doesn't work on a Friday. Sometimes it would be just the two of us, sometimes others from the club would join us too.

We used these long rides as an opportunity to test nutrition, test clothing and most importantly put the world to rights. Tracey was great company to cycle with, full of experience, enthusiasm and a great sense of humour. Also, as someone who had done Ironman already she gave me insight, encouragement and confidence.

In the school holidays, Lisa would join us. Lisa is a little pocket rocket. She's an absolutely tiny person, but a fearsome athlete (although I know she will blush when she reads this). Both of these ladies were amazing to cycle with, and as they were both better than me were also great to keep pushing me.

Lisa would joke when I slowed down to imagine she was poking me with a stick to make me go faster again. The reality is she wouldn't have a stick long enough!

Lisa is also an Ironman, she did a lot of mental preparation to help me. She was the one who got me to envisage the finish line.

"Now Deb" she said to me once in her car as we were heading for an open water swim session. "I want you to really imagine that finish line, what you will do, what it will feel like. I want you to run this in your head every day so you will know you have to get there."

I don't think Lisa really appreciates how much this resonated with me. Every single day after that conversation I played out in my mind what I wanted that finish line to be. I felt it, I could almost smell it, and I knew I needed to achieve it.

Anyhow, this one particular Friday, I wasn't accompanied by either Tracey or Lisa. I was accompanied by Vic, who is a most amazing cyclist; Kelli, who was starting her iron journey and was already a better cyclist than me; Ian, who I'd put on a par with me when it came down to cycling speeds; and Lisa's brother in law Mike.

We had decided we were going to do around fifty miles from Neath to Llanelli and back. It was a favourite route of mine. A mix of cycle tracks and roads.

We were on a dual carriageway a few miles away from Llanelli and I could feel myself lagging behind. Ian was flying, sticking closely to the wheels in front, and the other three were motoring on like usual, although I knew Vic was treating this as an easy going and social ride. I was getting disheartened. I was the only one with an Ironman booked and I was the weakest cyclist. I started doubting if I could really do it.

We reached North Dock in Llanelli and turned around to head back, again I felt myself lag behind.

We turned onto the Clyne cycle path, and as it is used by dog walkers and runners we all allowed ourselves to slow down slightly. This suited me, as I now stood a chance of keeping up.

We were about a third of the way down the path when Mike, somehow, lost concentration for a moment. He swerved, losing his balance, and came crashing down right in front of me. I reacted quickly, slammed on my brakes, but sadly I was too close and the inevitable happened. I found myself off my bike, landing in a ditch of brambles. Mike came running over "Are you OK Deb?". He was clearly very worried and knew it was only a matter of weeks until my Ironman.

Thankfully, we were both pretty much OK. Mike had picked up a rather nasty cut to his leg. I had managed to escape with only scratches to my arms and legs from landing in the brambles. Whilst they looked pretty bad as there were large areas of my body bleeding, they were only superficial. I had, however, managed to get a rather nasty hole in my brand new £100 cycle shorts, the ones I was planning to wear in Kalmar.

After I had arrived home from this eventful cycle, I had drawn myself a warm Epsom salt bath to clean my scratches. This hurt more than the fall did. Whilst in this bath I had a panicked phone call from Lisa.

"Has he broken you? If he has I'm going to bloody kill him!"

Chapter 120

It was the last section of the island of Oland. I could see the bridge in sight. I approached the roundabout and turned. I shouldn't have turned, I should have gone straight on. As I started down the road I could see a marshal running towards me waving his arms in the air. I'd taken a wrong turn, my second one of the day.

I thanked the marshal, and continued towards the bridge, my course corrected.

The winds on the bridge were brutal again, but I didn't care. I was two thirds of the way through the cycle, and I knew that as the cycle on the mainland took me near the start again, I stood a good chance of seeing Phil.

Lo and behold, there he was sat on a grass verge, camera in hand.

"Rob says keep going, you're doing OK!" he yelled to me. I stuck my thumb up to acknowledge that I had heard him.

My pace was on track, or thereabouts, and I was still feeling strong and comfortable.

As we were close to the centre of Kalmar I watched in awe at the number of competitors already on the run. When I still had a third of the cycle left.

The scenery on the mainland is very different to the island. The island is full of fields and farmland. The mainland is either normal city streets or tree lined suburbs.

I was heading up one of the city streets and some people in high vis jackets were standing on an intersection. They were chatting away to each other. I carried straight on, when one of them shouted. They were there to show people to turn right, although were so engrossed in their conversation that they missed me. For the third time, I was forced to retrace my steps and head in the right direction. As we reached the wooded area, the weather took a turn for the worse. Like it had done first thing in the morning, the heavens opened and it poured down. When I say poured down, I don't mean heavy rain drops, I mean rain so intense it appeared to be coming down in sheets. Within seconds I was soaked though. This area was also near to the turn around point and competitors were coming in the opposite direction. People were shouting words of encouragement to each other across the carriageway. It was on this stretch I saw Mic. I was delighted to see her, we shouted to each other and I continued on my way, knowing I wasn't that far behind her.

Despite being soaking wet, I was really enjoying this part of the mainland. I thought it was very pretty.

I was a touch concerned though, as all my food was making me feel sick. I had switched to bananas from the feed stations and hoped that this would help. They seemed to be sitting with me fairly well.

I was actually surprised how comfortable I was feeling on the bike, although at 97 miles I did start getting pain again from my shoulder and also a bit of discomfort in the saddle. I was still able to keep my speed up and was achieving the golden 15 miles per hour average I had set myself.

At 105 miles in the saddle discomfort came quickly and was suddenly unbearable. I started shouting at myself, "Come on Deb, 7 miles to go, that's less than a commute to work." I also saw people coming the other way, I felt sad for them knowing they wouldn't make bike cut off. I was pleased for myself as I knew I would.

Just get me to transition and GET ME OFF THIS BIKE!!

Photo: On the bike course

Chapter 121

In my short triathlon career, I don't think I have ever been so pleased to see a dismount line! My mind was one track only, rack my bike, take more tablets and do a marathon. I knew my bike time was on target. I'd made up some lost time for the swim. A bit of quick maths in my head told me I had about 6hrs 25 minutes to do the marathon.

My bike racked, I grabbed my bag and headed for the tent. I was so glad that I had a second pair of socks and a towel. It was blazing sunshine in Kalmar now, but my socks were still totally sodden from the torrential downpour.

I dried my feet, put my trainers on, and then remembered I hadn't taken off the cycle shorts again. I felt annoyed with myself having already made this error at Cotswolds.

I took my trainers off, took my cycle shorts off, and inspected my tri shorts for blood. They seemed to be managing well, the padded lining acting like a makeshift sanitary towel. I put my trainers back on, put my running water belt around my waist and headed out. Two down, one to go.

I started the run with a cheese roll in one hand and a bag of twiglets in the other. No time to stop and eat that, I needed to be on the move. A bit more maths in my head told me I needed to keep the run pace to around a 14 min 10 second mile. However, I decided to keep it at under 14 for safety's sake.

Whilst simple math calculations are a strong point of mine, I didn't entirely trust it after racing for 9 and a half hours and I wasn't totally sure what time exactly I had crossed the start line.

Fourteen minute miles were doable. I just needed to keep that up for twenty six miles. The longest I had run in one go was just over thirteen. I needed to trust in my training.

Chapter 122

It was the Swansea half marathon, and as it was only a couple of weeks after my half Iron distance in Cotswolds, I had volunteered to marshal instead of run it. I also didn't trust myself to run it. My training plan with Rob for the Ironman marathon was to keep my pace in check, a mixture of running and power walking, all about time on my feet. If I had done the Swansea half marathon I would have pushed the pace, and that would have risked injury. I needed to think of my A game and play it sensibly.

I was pleased to be marshalling though, as I was in good company, volunteering with Meinir and Joy from the club. The weather wasn't great and as we waited to be assigned our station we were getting wet.

The point we were assigned was fairly near the end. Good in one respect as we could cheer on people on the final stretch, but bad in another as it was next to a hotel and a normally busy closed road. If people were in the hotel car park, they were trapped.

There were closed road signs up everywhere, but that didn't stop some right idiots trying to mow us and the traffic cones down. We are three feisty ladies though and stood our ground. No injury to runners or volunteers and only a few altercations with disgruntled motorists.

It amazed me how quickly the first runners reached us. We were around mile from the finish and the fastest people reached us in under an hour.

Bizarrely, (I thought), was that they had a drink station only just before us. This meant I suddenly had a new job. Picking up all the discarded bottles from the gutter and putting them in recycling bags. Thousands of them, a steady stream of water bottles being hurled in my general direction, several of them nearly full resulting in an extra soaking.

I made my peace with this amendment to my job description and decided that all the bending and stretching was probably good strength and conditioning training. I would stop to cheer anyone from Celtic Tri though, although I almost missed Phil, who was running.

Volunteers usually get a t-shirt for their efforts. Usually similar to the finishers t-shirt. However, this year they gave us all the left over t-shirts from the year before. Meinir protested this. She was told to wait until the end and if there were any finishers t-shirts left we could have one.

I was chuffed to get a finishers t-shirt, but I also knew I couldn't wear it until I had run the route. That Wednesday I had a day off from work so ran the half marathon route at my Ironman pace. Now I felt I could legitimately wear it. Even more so when I did the route again only three days later.

Chapter 123

I tried to take a bite from my cheese roll but it turned my stomach. I decided to hold onto it for longer even though I must have looked a very odd sight as I powerwalked down the road with a cheese roll in one hand and a bag of twiglets in the other.

There was no sign of rain in the centre of Kalmar, the sun was glorious. I watched as other athletes passed me and could see bands on their arms. I had been warned by Lisa of band envy! On each lap of the run you receive a band, you needed all three bands to cross the finish. Some of these people had two bands, I didn't have a band yet. They were near the finish, I wasn't.

It was only about two kilometres into the run where I passed the finish line for the first time. You'd have to pass it on three separate occasions before taking my turn down the red carpet. As I passed it on this first occasion, there were people being announced as an Ironman. Whilst I know that there are people who are that quick, my head can not get around it. The speeds you need to maintain and achieve to complete a sub ten hour Ironman are just insane. Yet people had done just that. Me, I was just hoping on a wing and a prayer that I had it in me to cross that finish line before cut off.

Ironman is an equal but cruel sport. Each of the disciplines have a cut off, and there are intermediate cut offs on the individual disciplines themselves. At the end of the race, when there is no possibility of crossing that finish line within the time limit they put a barrier across the finish chute. Harsh, but them are the rules and that is why it is one of the most sought after titles in sport. I knew about the barrier as I had been told by people who had witnessed it. People were found to be sobbing at it, so near but yet so far. I couldn't be one of those people, I just couldn't.

I couldn't allow any negative thoughts to enter my head. I just had to keep moving forward. I knew the feed stations were roughly every mile or so and that needed to be my focus.

I reached the first feed station and had a flat coke and a banana. I tried another bite of my sandwich, but that continued to turn my stomach and so I threw it in the bin. I certainly wasn't going to hold onto it for the whole 26.2 miles. The twiglets, however, I kept.

Phil had been on a one loop run of the course on the day I went on the bike tour, so he knew some of the best places to camp out and photograph. This also meant that he kept popping up, which was truly a joy to see his smiling face. When we saw each other he passed on messages from well wishers.

"I swear Deb, there must be thousands of people tracking you right now," he told me.

He had taken over my Unlikely Triathlete Facebook page for the day and had posted a few photos, and he said he was astounded by the quantity of comments he had received. People were also sending in messages, which sadly Phil could not keep up with. Then there was the club page, several posts about where I was on the course, people asking Phil how I was doing. Then, most importantly, it was Phil's job to keep my sister up to date. She was excited for me, but obviously concerned and terrified about what I was putting my body through. She needed to know, at regular intervals, that her big sister was OK.

Before I knew it, I had reached the second feed station. I took an energy drink and a pickle. I was hoping the sourness of the pickle would counteract the sweetness of the drink.

When I reached the next feed station I thought to myself, "What am I supposed to be having now?"

Photo: Running with a cheese sandwich and twiglets

Chapter 124

I genuinely like most of my club mates. There are some that I totally adore. There are some that I am in awe of. One person who ticks both of these boxes is Jon.

Jon is a breathtakingly spectacular athlete. Even making the GB squad at age group and qualifying for the half Ironman world championships. He even gets into the London Marathon without the ballot due to his insane speed. However, despite these amazing accomplishments, he's one of the most thoughtful, down to earth and lovely people I know. He treats everyone in the club with respect and encourages everyone. Jon had been super supportive to me.

A few weeks before Kalmar we had been for an open water swim session down the seaside. Jon had a great idea to go for a quick run along the promenade afterwards and go for a coffee in one of the seaside cafes.

I'd partially protested, "Jon, that's a fab idea, but I can't run with you."

"Why not?" he'd replied.

I looked at him like he'd grown two heads, the answer to that question was obvious. Knowing me, like he does, he smiled and said, "I'll go at your pace."

So three of us did a run. Jon, Vic the speedy cyclist (who is also not too shabby a runner), and me.

I felt like I was sprinting, and looking at my watch I was certainly doing a much quicker pace than I usually would. Jon was chatting away like he was doing a casual walk in the park. In hindsight, seeing as he is twice as fast as me, he probably was! Vic was also chatting away. Any questions aimed in my direction were given monosyllabic answers. I was blowing smoke out of my arse, I was wrecked.

We finished our run, I did my best not to either throw up or die, and saved my near death inducing activity to my Garmin. It flashed up a new achievement. "Fastest ever mile.", I was chuffed with that.

As we sat in the café, Jon decided to have breakfast too. Whilst I was happy with a skinny latte, I did want to take that opportunity to pick his brains. I knew that Vic would certainly be doing an Iron distance in the not too distant future too, as you could see the hunger in her for it. Seeing as we had such a fabulous athlete as a captive audience, it would be rude not to ply him for tips.

A lot of Jon's tips had been echoed by other experienced athletes, nothing new on race day, don't be afraid to test things out, keep focussed, know there will be dark moments. However, one tip I hadn't been told before.

"At each feed station, alternate between a flat coke and an energy drink." he said.

"Is there any particular reason for that Jon?" I enquired. "Is it due to maximising electrolytes and sugar?" I continued, trying to look intelligent.

"Yeah, that makes sense, but mostly it gives your brain something else to think about as you pass the time, and gives you something to look forward to at the next stop."

So, that was another string to my bow. Another strategy for race day.

Chapter 125

I thought, "is it flat coke time? I think it's flat coke time?" I took a flat coke and another banana. No time to stop and eat it, just take, consume, move on.

I was overwhelmed by the support from the people of Kalmar. There were street parties the likes of which I have never seen before. Music, dancing and lots of encouragement for athletes. This level of support took my mind off the pain. Despite taking more tablets in T2, my shoulder was hurting and my left hip has decided to give me a world of agony. I was only 5 miles into the run. However, despite the pain I kept moving forward. The shouts of "heja, heja" (go, go) from the crowds were brilliant.

I tried to open my bag of twiglets, but my hands had swollen up. There was no way that I was going to get them open. When I saw Phil I threw them at him.

"I can't bloody open them, take them." I frustratedly shouted.

All athletes had a flag on their race numbers, so you could see the different nationalities. Whilst well meaning, I was regularly getting cheers of "Come on England!", I didn't have the energy to say "Wales, actually", but it came from a kind and supportive place. There had been one such cheer when I was overtaken by someone wearing a Cardiff Triathletes top. He winked and said "Come on Wales", recognising my Celtic Tri kit.

It must have been about mile six or seven when Mic came up behind me. It surprised me, if I'm honest, as she had been in front of me on the bike. I looked at her quizzically as I doubted she could be on lap two already.

"Had to stop for the loo," she said. "Slowed me down." We stuck together for a little while, but my power walking speed was faster than her walking speed, yet slower than her running speed and we could tell we couldn't stick together. She ran off saying "See you later".

Before I knew it, I was going through the sports stadium just outside the city centre. I had to run around the running track in order to receive my first band. My first lap was nearly over.

Chapter 126

I'm not a big fan of running tracks. I find the surface a bit dodgy to run on. However, Rob wanted me to attend the weekly track session that the club put on to do some speed work. I was happy with this, as I knew Mike always coached it and it would allow for weekly Kalmar chats.

I'd always arrive early and would chat to Mark. He's an interesting character is our Mark, he has a wicked sense of humour but sometimes you don't know if what he says is him being sarcastic, funny or serious. I like him though. The juniors in the club, however, adore him. The hours upon hours of coaching that he provides for the juniors in the club is proof that he adores them as much as they adore him.

Once Mike would arrive though, I would leave my bizarre conversations with Mark and try and get my Kalmar tip of the week before the session started.

I am always dead last at track, even all the juniors are faster than me.

One particular week springs to mind, we were doing a cool down after the session and were running slowly in the opposite direction. For some unknown reason, you always warm up and cool down clockwise, but race anti clockwise. So, I was running and a new member of the club decided to provide some words of encouragement to me. About how if I kept coming, I'd get faster. My friend Jodie was there too and could see my slight annoyance, as the newcomer didn't know me.

Jodie laughed and said, "Debs is a half Ironman, and she's doing Ironman soon." The conversation suddenly changed. Never judge a book by it's cover, I say. Yes, running is my weakest discipline, but I keep going.

Chapter 127

The finish line was in sight again, I'd pass the finishers chute and head out on lap two. As I passed the finish line Paul Kaye made eye contact with me and mouthed "I'm watching you", backing this up by pointing to his eyes and me. It made me laugh.

My pace was on target, every time it went over the fourteen minute mile I would run for a few minutes. Every time I ran the pain in my shoulder and hip got worse.

I felt really guilty, as children were lining the streets and I was unable to high five them. My pain was too much. This second lap was where I had my run dark moments.

However, thanks to Jon, I was able to think flat coke next, energy drink next, and this quite amazingly distracted me from the pain.

I passed Phil, he could see I was struggling, and he said the most perfect thing he could have said at that time. He reminded me of the determination award I had been given by the club.

"You got that stubbornness award for a reason, Deb, now finish this thing."

He was right, I wasn't going to allow the pain to stop me. I kept moving forward, like a terminator, nothing would stop me.

In my head I was repeating to myself "Pain is temporary, pride lasts forever."

Photo: Later in the run

Chapter 128

When you are getting closer to an Ironman, your mind starts playing tricks on you. You become paranoid about every germ, about every ache and pain.

You constantly obsess over your stats, is my bike time on target? That brick run was too slow? I only did 2 kilometres in the pool not the 2.2 that was on my plan. Have I eaten enough protein today? Shall I set the alarm for five to do a turbo session before work or shall I do it after?

The whole of your life is taken over. I could think about nothing else. Virtually every minute of every day I was obsessing over something Ironman related. It became like a drug to me.

On my serious wobbles I would phone Rob, and he would calmly tell me that my feelings were normal, I wasn't cracking up and it showed what it meant to me.

I was on a fairly short six-mile training run and my hip was in pain, I was about four miles in.

I stopped on a bench and tried to phone Rob, should I continue through the pain or should I stop. He didn't answer.

I started to run again, my hip still hurt.

I phoned Phil.

"Darling, I need you to come and get me, I'm injured."

He gallantly jumped to my rescue like the knight in shining armour he is.

We were on the drive home when Rob phoned me back. "You are too close now Deb. If you are in pain you stop. The only time you carry on through the pain is on the day."

Chapter 129

I wasn't long into my second lap and the pain in my hip was getting worse and worse. As a result, I had slipped beyond the magic fourteen minute mile average pace.

I saw Phil. "Rob says to put a bit more pace in." he said.

"Tell Rob to go fuck himself!" I replied

I continued, angrily, although my pace picked up. Thanks Rob for pissing me off.

I was later told by Phil that when he relayed my rather candid message to Rob, he replied to Phil that he was delighted as it proved I still had fight in me.

It was on this lap that some really bizarre things happened to me. Whilst there were other athletes on the course, and occasionally they would talk to you. In the most part I was alone with my thoughts.

My thoughts turned to my parents, both of whom had died many years before.

I thought about my Mum, about how her diabetes had taken her, way too soon, in fact only a few years older than I am now. As I was thinking about my Mum, a song came blaring out of one of the pubs, a Barry Manilow song. My Mum loved Barry Manilow. I took this as a sign from her that she was watching over me.

A little while later, following a quiet section, I was thinking about how my Dad had learned to swim in his forties only a year or two before he died. I turned into a residential street to be greeted by Queen and 'A kind of Magic'. A favourite of my Dad's, I continued and the next song made me know my parents were with me. Tina Turner and 'Simply the Best'. The last concert my Dad and I went to together was Tina Turner.

I asked them could they help me, I knew they were with me, I knew they were watching out for me.

I entered a quiet part of the course and approached the next feed station. I was officially over half way through the marathon. Although now, I couldn't face any food, only drink.

However, a few miles later my parents' help kicked in. My hip went completely numb. The pain left me. I could feel nothing. I had no clue how my legs were continuing to move forward but they were, and they were on pace. I had a renewed spring in my step as I ran around the stadium track and collected my second band.

Chapter 130

Just before the town centre is this rather odd section when you go through a kind of medieval structure and over a bridge. I was on this section when someone cycled up beside me. That person was Paul Kaye.

He told me how much he loved Celtic Tri, about how I was his favourite athlete (although in fairness he probably said that to lots of people), that I was still looking strong, my pace was good and that I only had one lap to go and he would make me an Ironman.

I only realised afterwards why he was probably on the course on his bike after I was about to start the third loop, which was a kilometre after I saw Paul.

The rules stated that all athletes needed to start the third loop of the run by 9pm. Any who missed this were missing a cut off and would be pulled from the course. I started that last loop at 8.57pm, three minutes to spare. Paul was probably there to console people who wouldn't make it. Thankfully Rob didn't know of this intermediate cut off. I think if he had, he would have been having kittens.

I was on the final lap, my last final push. My hip was still completely numb, however, the strange sensation of my legs moving despite me having a numb section from my stomach to my thighs had become strangely familiar.

The sky had gone dark which made for some difficult visibility in places. Although some lovely people had lined some of the darker areas with tea lights, which looked so incredibly pretty.

I wasn't that far into the third loop when I saw Phil. Most of the time he had snapped a few photos and had passed on some words of encouragement from people we knew. This time I needed him, I needed my husband.

"Can you stay with me Phil?" I asked.

He started with me, well slightly behind me, as he was completely paranoid that I would get disqualified if he was next to me as it may have been viewed as outside assistance.

The lighting had become too bad to take photos, so he packed away his camera and stayed behind me.

I needed a distraction.

"Talk to me Phil." I asked.

"What do you want to talk about?" he asked.

"I dunno," I replied "Just talk shit to me."

Now my husband is a gorgeous, caring and loving man. However, making pointless small talk is not his forte.

"I could really murder a Pepsi right now," he said.

I took this as a cue that he was thirsty. I looked around, couldn't see anyone, and threw a water bottle from my belt at him.

"Here you go darling," I said, happy that I would ease his thirst.

"What the hell did you do that for?" he snapped angrily. "I have water, I just fancy a pepsi. Now I'm stuck with your bottle!"

He wouldn't give it back. His paranoia about outside assistance still evident.

Chapter 131

I was to discover later why he had become so paranoid. Earlier in the day when I was out cycling around Oland, he had seen a few people had written in chalk on the street. He had called into a shop and had bought some chalk, and proceeded to walk through the streets of Kalmar writing messages of encouragement to myself, Mic and Dan.

Things like "Go Celtic Tri" "Go Debs, Dan and Mic" and worst of all our names and numbers.

He had posted this onto the Celtic Tri page, and had been warned that this could have got us disqualified.

The poor chap had spent the whole day panicking. In reality he needn't have worried, as hundreds of supporters had done exactly the same thing. Also, being chalk it would easily wash off.

I am embarrassed to say I didn't see any of his floor notes. My eyes were forward, focussed firmly on the prize.

Photo: The chalk writing I didn't see!

Chapter 132

Phil stayed with me as long as he could, and then headed back to the town centre. He wanted to get a good spot to see me finish.

By this point it was pitch black. I reached one point and couldn't see a thing. It was around the back of a residential area but there were no lights on in the houses. Probably as they were all out the front enjoying the street party.

I realised that I couldn't feel a hard surface under my feet, I could feel grass. I knew I had accidentally wandered into a garden.

I moved back towards the harder surface and tried my hardest to focus on following a glimmer of light. I could see some street lights in the distance where I needed to be heading towards and focussed on that.

There are some parts of the run course which cross over, and I was on my final stretch back to Kalmar when I could see people heading in the other direction. They had officials with them, telling them they needed to run, that they weren't going to make cut off. My heart was breaking for them. I smiled at them, willing them on, willing them to find the strength in themselves for a final hard push.

As I entered the stadium for the final time, one of the helpers ran towards me as I was coming towards him.

"Do you know what time you got in the water?" he asked me.

"Eleven minutes past I think." I replied.

"In that case, you have thirty minutes to do the last 2k. Keep going, lovely lady, you are going to do this."

He gave me a little hug and my final band. The end was in sight.

Chapter 133

I had nearly reached the medieval section again, and I saw
Mic. I yelled to her and she turned back to me grinning.
"We are going to do this!" I yelled.

The was not a doubt in my body that I was going to
complete my mission.

It surprised me that I didn't feel overwhelmed or emotional.
It amazed me that as I realised it was going to happen that
tears didn't come. What I felt was a mixture of calm and
relief.

This was a journey that was years in the making. It had its
ups and downs. I'd achieved that first triathlon in Pencoed,
I had learned to swim front crawl, I had made the switch to
a road bike, I had seen myself graduate from couch to 5k in
running to completing a marathon.

I had also had some scares along the way. I'd had falls off
my bike, I had been rescued from the sea, I had injuries
that prevented me from running.

However, I had just kept going. I was made for this finish
line. Every second of my training from my first steps out of
the house was building to the ultimate crescendo, not that I
knew it at the time. It had built to this, this moment that I
had rehearsed in my head every single day for the past few
months.

I turned the last corner and there it was. Lit up in all its
glory. The Ironman finish line. My finish line.

I slowed my power walk to a more sedate pace. Even though it was gone 11pm, I knew I had time left. And I was going to enjoy every single section of the red carpet.

I stepped on it. Put my hands into a heart shape which I placed in front of the Celtic Tri logo on my top just like I had practiced and then I threw my arms in the air.

The other announcer went to speak. Paul stopped him and said, "I've got this one. Get under the clock, Debs, I need you under the clock."

I took that last step, my time flashed up 15 hours 49 minutes 49 seconds.

Paul's voice spoke the words that I needed to hear.

"Deborah Longman. You Are An Ironman"

Photo: My Ironman Finish

Epilogue 6

"I told you you would do it." Paul said, he looked genuinely delighted for me.

I saw Mic she had waited to watch me cross the line. She hugged me, both of us there having succeeded in our dreams. She pointed at Phil in the crowd, he had forced his way to the front. I didn't realise that the cameras broadcasting live to the world were still on me.

In South Wales, I am sure there were a few emotional reactions as mine and Phil's embrace was broadcast. The tears of pride were streaming down his face. I stayed there with my husband for a moment or two. However, I needed to get my medal.

One of the volunteers wrapped me in a foil blanket and led me outside. There was a doctor there waiting to check the finishers over. I assured the friendly fellow that I was fine. The next stop was collecting my finishers t-shirt. I held my t-shirt and my medal and felt an immense feeling of pride. Dan had come back to see us in the athletes only area and told us that we needed to eat. They had a tent set up where they were providing hot food. I grabbed a burger, but I wanted to get out of the restricted area and find Phil.

You'd think after completing such a feat that you could allow yourself an hour or so to chill out. Sadly not, my bike needed to be collected from transition by midnight. Phil and I walked down there, my earlier cheese sandwich was now replaced by a burger and I still had no appetite.

"Do you want some?" I asked Phil.

"You need to eat it!" he replied.

With my bike collected, we were able to return to the hotel. The first thing I did was get Phil to pour me a glass of wine. I'd earned it!

That night I couldn't sleep. Luckily Lisa was in LA on holiday and a club mate, Chris, had emigrated to Australia. Their time zones meant they were able to keep me company through the night.

One person I did contact, despite the unearthly hour, was Tracey's sister, Kaz. Her husband is a tattoo artist. I needed to book my Ironman tattoo.

The following day was like a party in Kalmar, people hobbling to breakfast with their finishers t-shirts on. We'd become a community of Ironman finishers.

The first place I needed to go was back to the expo. Now I was an Ironman, I was ready to spend!! Kalmar t-shirts and tops, Ironman mugs and most importantly a finishers jacket. I was going to dress in Ironman related clothes for the rest of my days and milk my title for all it was worth.

John had come over to our hotel with Boo, and he had managed to film my finish on his phone as he had a backstage pass due to him running a triathlon magazine. I could have kissed him. I watched the video and that was when I cried. The realisation that I had actually done it. Boo had returned from the awards ceremony. I had forgotten that it was on. As a "heroes hour" finisher there was no point me being there. Boo, however, was a different matter. She had qualified for the Ironman World Championships in Kona, Hawaii! I was so proud of her. As athletes from totally different ends of the talent spectrum, we had become good friends.

Later, we saw big Eric, he had been tracking me after his finish, and he had also filmed my finish for me. I was overwhelmed by the kindness that my new friends had shown me. They had all been first timers once and they knew what it meant to me. Eric joined us for dinner that night, you could tell he wanted to stay up and party. Ordinarily I'd have been up for doing it. However, my lack of sleep was catching up with me. I needed to go to bed.

The following day we were heading to Copenhagen. Tracey had done Ironman Copenhagen the day after I did Kalmar. Sadly she missed the bike cut off. She was gutted, she was so close, under two minutes over the cut off time. However, when we arrived at Copenhagen train station, she was there smiling and ready to hug me as an Ironman. Tracey had achieved Ironman previously, and thankfully the title doesn't have a time limit so we were planning to sightsee and party as two Ironman finishers. The sightseeing became mostly partying! Hans Christian Andersen's house had scaffolding outside and seemed to be closed, but we did go and see the Little Mermaid. However, mostly we sat in pubs and restaurants and ate and drank too much!

Tracey agreed that she would come with me to get my tattoo done as she was also planning a new tattoo. I am now permanently imprinted with the "M dot" logo. People have asked me did it hurt and my response is always the same "Not as much as the Ironman did".

They say it takes a village to raise a child. I hope that as you have followed me on my rather insane journey that you can see that it took a community to make me an Ironman. Without doubt, if I hadn't have found Celtic Tri, I would probably still be pootling about on my bike, swimming doggy paddle and maybe doing the occasional pool based sprint.

I have also had an additional support community through my army of followers on my Facebook page. Every message and comment I receive I appreciate and makes me feel a part of something bigger than just this podgy middle aged diabetic playing at triathlon.

So, after going from pool based sprint triathlon to Ironman in 25 months, was I going to return to be a couch potato? I think the answer to that is no. Since the Ironman, I have got personal bests at 5k, 10k and half marathon (being paced by Phil). I have completed more triathlons, including another half Ironman. And I have tried to give myself a new challenge on my weakest discipline by signing up to an Ultra Marathon. You can keep track of what I'm up to on my Facebook page.

I am also going to continue my writing. I have a few other book ideas up my sleeve.

Thanks for staying with my triathlon journey through my books. This instalment would have been rather a let down if I had failed.

A few more photos:

Photo: The Ironman finish line

Photo: The big M Dot made out of participants names

Photo: Finding my name

Photo: There it is!

Photo: Posing by the M Dot

Photo: Racking my bike the day before

Here is a sneak peak at the next book.

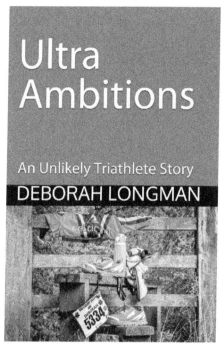

Link to book 7: mybook.to/tut7

Prologue

Achieving an Ironman was the biggest success of my life. Crossing the finish line and hearing those words "Deborah Longman. You are an Ironman" were the sweetest words I had ever heard. It made all the hundreds of hours of hard work and training worth it.

If you were to see me in the street, you wouldn't think I look athletic. I still have a belly that is way too big for the amount of sport that I do. I am but an average woman. However, I am an average woman that has grown to love a challenge and has grown to love exercise.

I knew after Ironman that I would need to set myself a new challenge. I enjoy having a goal to focus on. The question was, what should it be? I knew I wouldn't be able to do another Ironman, it had taken its toll on my body and I needed a rest from training 15 hours a week.

However, I needed something that would feel substantial enough that it would feel like a real achievement. As most great challenges start, my decision for my next challenge came from being in the pub!

Chapter One

Buy one, get one free on cocktails is a dangerous thing. Particularly when you want an espresso martini and your husband wants a long island iced tea. However, what are you meant to do? You obviously have to have two each when the bar decides you can't "pick and mix".

We sat at a table large enough to allow for our drinking companions to join us whilst sipping our respective alcoholic goodies. Before too long we were joined by Christine, Callum, Robyn and Kara. We had enough time for a drink (or two) before going to the Italian restaurant for dinner.

As always, the conversation flowed as smoothly as the drinks we were consuming, and being a bunch of rather crazy sport obsessed people it didn't take very long for the conversation to turn to race entries.

"I think I want to do an Ultra Marathon" says Cal

We look at him, the other three with the sense that he had lost the plot, me with great interest.

"Oh" I reply, my interest well and truly piqued "Tell me more"

"Well there is one in Salisbury that it meant to be good. Its 50k, so not massive either and it's meant to be fairly flat" Cal continued, not realising he was mentally ticking all the boxes I was interested in... nice place, not a crazy distance, flat.

"When is it Cal?" I enquired, tentatively, looking to Phil to see if there was any kind of reaction.

"August" he replied.

It was October, that gave me 10 months.

"I'm in" I replied. I had decided to do an Ultra Marathon.

Chapter Two

I love analysing stats. Call me a geek, but analysing pace, heart rate, distance all excite me. I had been studying my stats in detail. My VO2 max had risen to 41, this meant my body was doing a marvellous job of taking oxygen into my body and making my muscles work effectively. Whilst my running would still be deemed as being slow, I was in the shape of my life.

My first marathon took me over seven hours. OK, I did it on my own, with a backpack full of drinks and nutrition on a cold December day, between Christmas and New Year, the festive season before my Ironman. An investment in my legs and a way to avoid the endless mince pies and glasses of Baileys. It wasn't a good time, it was walked, but it was an indication that my feet could take me 26.2 miles. My second marathon was at the end of the Ironman, a far more impressive time of just under six and a quarter hours. No mean feat after the 2.4 miles swim and 112 mile cycle before it.

I was delighted with how my fitness was going. People said that after Ironman I should take at least a month off to allow my body to recover, but after the first week of drinking vast quantities of wine and eating all the food I was feeling fantastic. It was two weeks after the Ironman, and I had set myself a target. I felt I could beat my 10k personal best. I should have allowed a greater recovery time by rights, but I had already signed up for the Cardiff 10k before I did Ironman Kalmar and I hated the thought of wasting a race entry.

"For goodness sake take it easy!" Phil said to me.

But I was on top of the world! I was an Ironman! I was invincible!

"I'm going for it Phil, I'm going for it"

And go for it I did, I smashed my personal best by nine minutes and came in in a time of 1hr 13 minutes. OK, slow to many people, but an outstanding time for me.

The next thing in my sights was improving my 5k speed. My previous 5k best had taken place at the end of Swansea Triathlon at 34mins and 3 secs, I was confident I could beat this. This took place at Grangemoor parkrun in a time of 33mins and 56 secs.

This left the half marathon. I also wanted to beat my time in that too, so I approached my faster husband with an unusual request.

"Darling?" I asked, one evening whilst sat at the dinner table tucking into a home cooked meal

"Yes?" he replied in a suspicious tone, the tone that is reserved only for me

"How would you fancy sacrificing your own time and pacing me to a PB in Cardiff Half?"

He looked at me for a moment, I could almost see his brain working as he thought about how to respond. Knowing my husband I knew he'd be thinking the following:

1. He likes running for himself, he likes improving his own times

2. He'd get frustrated with me if I wasn't running as I should

3. He'd worry that we'd end up having a massive argument

4. He'd need to plan it to the tiniest of details if he did.

His response proved to me that I knew him very well indeed.

"Right, let me think about this. If, and I'm not saying I am going to, but if I do this, we need to establish some ground rules, I need to work it out and you need to listen to me"

"OK darling" I replied

"I'm not saying I will yet, I wanted a PB myself this time too" he replied "Let me think"

He's a good man though and within a few hours, he asked what time I wanted so he could work out the pace and had decided that if we didn't kill each other somewhere around the streets of Cardiff, he'd give it a shot.

I should add that the only time that Phil had ever paced anyone before was when he paced Cal to a 5k PB of under 30 minutes at Oxford parkrun the day before Chris and I did Blenheim Palace triathlon. That was a good friend, it wasn't family and it certainly wasn't his missus!

We were both apprehensive, but I craved that half marathon PB. I wanted 2017 to be the year I PB'd at each of the distances… 5k, 10k, half and full marathon.

Link to book 7: **mybook.to/tut7**

Also like other styles of books?

You can read my quick reads thrillers. Here is a link to the first in the series.

If you had an abusive partner, would you take revenge?

When Jennifer met the charming Oliver Knight, he seemed like the perfect man.
Loving, generous, attentive.
That changed when they got married and he revealed his darker side to control her every move.

When his control turned violent, could Oliver be subjected to the ultimate payback?

mybook.to/ProjectPayback

Or even a sci-fi comedy

Chuck always thought being an astronaut would be cool. But he never believed in aliens.

His terror quickly turns to love in this hilarious short novel about space, friendships, and the unexpected.
When Earthlings meet aliens we discover that Earth really is the most stupid planet in the universe.

mybook.to/EarthTMSPITU

Follow my author page on Amazon for information on new releases.

You can sign up to my newsletter too.

Or you can visit my website.

If you enjoyed reading, it would mean a lot to me if you would leave a review on Amazon. As an Indie author I rely on good reviews and recommendations to help me share my experiences. It'll only take you two minutes, and will mean the world to me.
If you message me on Facebook or email me through my website I always reply, so feel free to say Hi.

Printed in Great Britain
by Amazon